User Generated Law

User Generated Law

Re-Constructing Intellectual Property Law in a Knowledge Society

Edited by

Thomas Riis

Professor, University of Copenhagen, Denmark

Edward Elgar
PUBLISHING

Cheltenham, UK • Northampton, MA, USA

Published by
Edward Elgar Publishing Limited
The Lypiatts
15 Lansdown Road
Cheltenham
Glos GL50 2JA
UK

Edward Elgar Publishing, Inc.
William Pratt House
9 Dewey Court
Northampton
Massachusetts 01060
USA

A catalogue record for this book
is available from the British Library

Library of Congress Control Number: 2016931760

This book is available electronically in the **Elgar**online
Law subject collection
DOI 10.4337/9781783479566

MIX
Paper from
responsible sources
FSC
www.fsc.org
FSC® C013056

ISBN 978 1 78347 955 9 (cased)
ISBN 978 1 78347 956 6 (eBook)

Typeset by Columns Design XML Ltd, Reading
Printed and bound in Great Britain by TJ International Ltd, Padstow

Contents

Contributors

Olga Kokoulina, Ph.D. student, LL.M., Centre for Information and Innovation Law, University of Copenhagen, Denmark

Björn Lundqvist, Associate Professor, LL.M., LL.D., Law Department, Copenhagen Business School, Denmark

Michael J. Madison, Professor of Law and Faculty Director, Innovation Practice Institute, University of Pittsburgh, USA

Timo Minssen, Associate Professor, Jur. Dr., LL.M., Centre for Information and Innovation Law, University of Copenhagen, Denmark

Clement Salung Petersen, Associate Professor, Ph.D., Centre for Enterprise Liability, University of Copenhagen, Denmark

Thomas Riis, Professor, dr.jur., Ph.D., Centre for Information and Innovation Law, University of Copenhagen, Denmark

Ole-Andreas Rognstad, Professor, dr.jur., Department of Private Law, University of Oslo, Norway

Jens Schovsbo, Professor, dr.jur., Ph.D., Centre for Information and Innovation Law, University of Copenhagen, Denmark

Sebastian Felix Schwemer, Ph.D. student, Dipl.-Jur., M.Sc., Centre for Information and Innovation Law, University of Copenhagen, Denmark

Henrik Udsen, Professor, dr.jur., Ph.D., Centre for Information and Innovation Law, University of Copenhagen, Denmark

Esther van Zimmeren, Research Professor Multi-Level Governance, Globalization and Federalism, Research Group Government and Law, Faculty of Law, University of Antwerp, Belgium

Preface

The purpose of this book is to study intellectual property law from a new perspective. The book is part of a research project that shifts intellectual property law research away from the study of statutory law and other forms of authoritatively determined regulation and towards an examination of how intellectual property law actually works and changes.

Much of the on-going debates on intellectual property law are aimed at the substantive rights and respond to questions such as: Are the rights too strong or too weak? Are there any needs for new limitations or exceptions? Or should any of the existing limitations and exceptions be amended or revoked? All such questions relate to statutory rights and their interpretations. In practice these questions may not be very important because the substantive rights simply provide a basis for the development of private regulatory models that accommodate the needs of the parties affected by the rights and redefine the legal positions. Thus, in the intellectual property related industries often a layer of self-regulation is developed on top of the substantive rights. Self-regulation provides flexibility and modifies the one-size-fits-all characteristics of intellectual property law. This book and the underlying research project originate in an interest in why and how self-regulation of intellectual property rights in a knowledge society emerges and develops. In spite of the fact that self-regulation has a long history in law, including intellectual property law, it is still unclear what forces form the emergence and the further development of self-regulation and how it interacts with the framework conditions of statutory law.

In the first chapter of the book a model for the study of self-regulation is outlined (the model of 'User Generated Law'). The model is elaborated on the basis of Eric von Hippel's theory of user innovation which concerns the emergence of innovative products and services as results of processes driven by users. The central insights from the theory on user innovation are used to explain what drive the emergence and dissemination of various forms of self-regulation. Many examples of self-regulation in the intellectual property law based industries exist. Some of them are studied in this book and among other things it is evaluated to what extent the model of User Generated Law is a useful tool to explain and understand self-regulation of intellectual property rights in a knowledge society.

In March 2014, a workshop was held at the Centre for Information and Innovation Law in Copenhagen where some of the central concepts of the User Generated Law model were discussed and elaborated. The workshop was followed by the conference 'IP Governance by Private Collective Entities'. The chapters of this book are based on papers which were discussed at the workshop or presented at the conference. I truly thank the participants of the workshop and the conference and gratefully acknowledge their valuable contributions.

The book as well as the conference and workshop were supported by The Danish Council for Independent Research/Social Sciences [Grant No. 11-104442].

Thomas Riis
Copenhagen, 2015

1. User generated law: re-constructing intellectual property law in a knowledge society

Thomas Riis

1. INTRODUCTION

The exact elements of what constitutes a 'knowledge society' are still disputed. Yet the underlying notion that modern society and not least the modern economy are essentially based on the production and dissemination of knowledge is not contested. The most widely shared understanding deems that a knowledge society is characterized by a high absorptive capacity; by the possession of structures and cultures that facilitate dissemination and sharing of knowledge; and by the inclusion of learning communities which emphasize innovation. A knowledge society's main tool is information exchange via information and communication technologies. Information is a knowledge-generating tool; it is not knowledge itself. Knowledge relates to the practical use of information and involves a human experience.[1] Our contemporary knowledge society faces the crucial challenges of establishing structures and arrangements that support the creation of legitimate and productive knowledge and ensuring access to knowledge. Legal infrastructure is essential in shaping such structures and arrangements. Technological and economic development have been the major forces in creating a knowledge society (which by nature is a dynamic society) whereas the legal infrastructure which regulates behaviour in this knowledge society has not developed correspondingly.

Traditionally, law has been construed as being authoritatively determined by national legislative directives. In cases of uncertainty concerning the contents of these directives, national Supreme Courts have been envisaged as the source of legal certainty. This construction is ill-suited to meeting the needs of a knowledge society. In a knowledge society, law

[1] See the UNESCO World Report, *Towards Knowledge Societies* (2006).

must be capable of managing more complex and flexible relationships and there is often a high degree of heterogeneity in the demands for legal solutions. Additional characteristics of a knowledge society that challenge the traditional mode of legal regulation include the increase in cross-border activities – knowledge recognizes no borders – and the speed of technological and commercial development which rapidly makes previously well-functioning legal solutions obsolete or inadequate.[2]

A critique of the traditional regime of law production is not new; but such criticism has differed in terms of its angles and content. Normative statements on the quality of legal regulation presuppose a choice of value foundations. At the most general level, all sorts of acceptable legal models must arguably include a notion of justice and a regard for fundamental rights. At the instrumental level, a choice must be made on what policy objectives legal regulation is supposed to promote. In this latter instance, legal regulation is supposed to promote dynamic efficiency, innovation and growth in a knowledge society which is basically an objective of economic welfare.

Kobayashi and Ribstein note that scholars have often recognized the potential shortcomings of State-enacted laws due to the fact that public lawmakers are susceptible to powerful interest groups and have weak incentives to produce socially valuable legal innovations, in part because they share little of the public benefits of producing laws.[3] Kobayashi and Ribstein's focus is on various public choice problems in law production. This book adopts a different approach by examining how law production is determined by the intrinsic characteristics and needs of the actors in a knowledge society, thus shaping new framework conditions for the production of law by means of feedback loops. The book is a study in the development and elaboration of law and it is based on the premise that law which accommodates the needs of knowledge is characterized by:

1. *flexible norms* (reflecting both the complexity and rapid pace of development);
2. a *cross-border scope* (reflecting the global dimension);

[2] E.g. Gillian K. Hadfield, 'Producing Law for Innovation', in Kauffman Task Force on Law, Innovation and Growth, *Rules for Growth* (2011) pp. 36 et seq.

[3] Bruce H. Kobayashi and Larry E. Ribstein, 'Law as Product and By-product' (2013) 9 *Journal of Law, Economics & Policy* 521, p. 522. See also e.g. Gillian K. Hadfield, 'Producing Law for Innovation', in Kauffman Task Force on Law, Innovation and Growth, *Rules for Growth* (2011), pp. 23 et seq.

3. the capacity to be *industry-specific and subject-specific* (reflecting the heterogeneity of the demands for legal solutions).

Seen from this perspective, law can no longer be perceived as a closed, primarily autonomous system directed by national legislators and national courts.[4] This book examines how private regulatory models evolve either as new layers of law based on State-enacted law, or as sui generis legal systems. By examining concrete cases of private regulatory models we shall determine what conditions drive the formation of these alternative forms of legal regulation which can be subsumed under the concept of user generated law.

2. PRIVATE REGULATORY MODELS AND THE FRAGMENTATION OF LAW

Various actors often have divergent demands for legal solutions in a knowledge society context. In order to meet those demands they construct private regulatory models. However, a variety of private regulatory models, each governing a specific activity with a limited scope, leads to fragmentation of the law. Thomas Schultz addresses a key instance of this concerning law in cyberspace which is an essential part of a modern knowledge society. Schultz describes the State as having a decreased capacity to code power in this domain, and adds that: 'Cyberspace is carved up into different spheres of normativity, some of which are connected only remotely to other normative systems'.[5]

Private regulatory models have a long history and *lex mercatoria* has a prominent place in legal studies of such models. *Lex mercatoria* refers to the system of rules detached from national law and national courts used by merchants in the Middle Ages to govern commercial transactions in Europe. It was affirmed as a coherent system of transnational rules enacted by applying commercial customs and enforced by threat of

---

4 For a related perspective, see Jan M. Smits, 'Private Law 2.0: On the Role of Private Actors in a Post-National Society' (November 30, 2010), Hague Institute for the Internationalisation of Law and Eleven International Publishing, 2011; Maastricht Faculty of Law, available at http://ssrn.com/abstract=1779042 (accessed January 19, 2016).

5 Thomas Schultz, 'Private Legal Systems: What Cyberspace Might Teach Legal Theorists' (2007) 10 *Yale Journal of Law & Technology* 151, p. 193.

boycott and expulsion[6] and it was thus claimed to be a privately produced, privately adjudicated, and privately enforced body of law.

The traditional notion maintaining that *lex mercatoria* was actually a systematic law (standardized across Europe, synonymous with commercial law, unaffected by governments and sovereignty) has now been disputed.[7] Yet the notion does indicate a need spanning many centuries for privately produced law based on the idea that merchants were a better source of rules for governing commercial practices than local rulers. The comparison between *lex mercatoria* and regulatory models in the information society has been made by Trakman in connection with the law of domain names:

> The ICANN and WIPO policies, principles, and rules include precepts attributed to the Law Merchant … The ICANN and its main service provider, the WIPO, seek to promote a cosmopolitan and uniform system of rules that transcends local rules and nation states. … Many of the characteristics of the medieval Law Merchant are apparent in domain-name jurisprudence. In particular, domain-name disputes are resolved efficiently and at a comparatively low cost.[8]

The law of domain names comprises legal rules adopted by ICANN and relies on established trademark law principles; and as such it differs from *lex mercatoria* where the transnational rules were created by applying commercial customs.[9] However, other parts of privately produced regulatory models in our existent knowledge society can be said to have been composed by applying commercial customs (e.g. the collective management of patent rights, and to a certain extent the collective management of copyrights).

---

[6] Cf. Albrecht Cordes, 'The Search for a Medieval *Lex Mercatoria*' (2003) *Oxford University Comparative Law Forum*, 5, available at http://ouclf.iuscomp.org/articles/cordes.shtml#fn14sym, p. 17 (accessed January 19, 2016).

[7] E.g. Christopher R. Drahozal, 'Contracting out of National Law: An Empirical Look at the New Law Merchant' (2004–2005) 80 *Notre Dame Law Review* 523, p. 527; and Ralf Michaels, 'The Mirage of Non-State Governance' (2010) *Utah Law Review* 31, pp. 37 et seq.

[8] Leon E. Trakman, 'From the Medieval Law Merchant to E-Merchant Law' (2003) 53 *University of Toronto Law Journal* 265, pp. 287 et seq.

[9] Leon E. Trakman, 'From the Medieval Law Merchant to E-Merchant Law' (2003) 53 *University of Toronto Law Journal* 265, pp. 289 et seq.

3. USER INNOVATION

Schultz's description of the fragmentation of law is arguably pertinent to law in a knowledge society in general, but it does not explain how the law evolves. For that purpose, and with strong inspiration from Eric von Hippel's theory on user innovation, we shall develop a new perspective on law which we will call user generated law.[10] The theory concerning user innovation relates to the development of products and services and it explains why innovative products and services are developed by users under certain conditions while manufacturers create development under other conditions.

The ensuing attempt to apply a new perspective on law is based on the premise that the development of law in a knowledge society and the development of products and services have many common features. The 'users' in law are the persons subjected to the law. In cases where it is not optimal for these persons to rely on State-enacted law they may opt out and establish a private form of legal regulation, primarily by contractual means (the legal innovation). The creation of products and services and the creation of regulatory models are not identical processes. First, the possibilities of opting out of State-enacted law are in some areas of law (chiefly in public law) very restricted due to mandatory rules. In comparison, most innovative products and services can be created and marketed without significant legal constraints. In order to deal with that challenge the concept of 'autonomy spaces' is incorporated into the notion of user generated law.[11] Second, the concept of 'user' in regard to law may appear somewhat obscure. In principle, all persons are subjected to all parts of the law. However, far from all persons will have an interest in opting out of a certain part of the law; such an interest will only arise if the person is appreciably affected by the law in question. Thus, the users in user generated law are not simply the persons subjected to the law but rather those who are affected by it.

Another aspect of the user concept needs to be clarified. A person who has an interest in opting out of State-enacted law and creates a legal innovation does not necessarily do it by herself but will often commission a team of lawyers and other consultants to do the job. Even though the team contributes to the creation of the legal innovation (and quite possibly the innovation would not have come into existence if it were not

---

10 Eric von Hippel, *The Sources of Innovation* (Oxford University Press, 1988); Eric von Hippel, *Democratizing Innovation* (MIT Press, 2005).

11 On 'autonomy spaces', see para. 4.1 below.

for the team) the person who initiates and organizes the process that leads to a legal innovation is the 'user' for the purpose of user generated law.

When law is produced in a new way we need a new model in order to construe the process. Regarding products and services, von Hippel claims that new sources of innovation demand new management tools as well as a new organization,[12] and in the same vein it can be claimed that the prevalence of user generated law will demand new framework conditions for the production of law.

3.1 Heterogeneous Demands

It follows from the theory on user innovation that user innovations are developed as a result of heterogeneous and small scale demands. Users' needs for products and services are highly heterogeneous in many fields. Economies in the production process spur manufacturers to employ a strategy of developing products that are designed to meet the needs of one large market segment or a few large market segments. The resulting supply of products is characterized by a few different versions of the product that are supposed to meet the needs of all the users. In other words, manufacturers adopt a strategy of 'few sizes fit all'. Since users' needs are heterogeneous, this strategy will leave many users dissatisfied with the commercial products on offer. When a user does not find what they want on the market they have no other choice but to modify existing products or to develop entirely new products – namely, to innovate in order to meet the user's individual needs which the majority of consumers do not share.[13]

3.2 Expectation of Benefits (Profits)

Heterogeneous demand is not in itself a sufficient reason why user innovation will occur. The theory on user innovation is based on the traditional economic rationale maintaining that actors act if they think that it will be beneficial for them to do so – that is, if they expect an attractive return. Hence, a user will innovate if they foresee an in-house benefit from doing so and typically (and in contrast to the manufacturer)

[12] Eric von Hippel, *The Sources of Innovation* (Oxford University Press, 1988), p. 9.

[13] Eric von Hippel, *The Sources of Innovation* (Oxford University Press, 1988), p. 7; and Eric von Hippel, *Democratizing Innovation* (MIT Press, 2005), p. 5.

the user does not consider whether other users have similar needs. The manufacturer also considers the benefits, but it is typically a precondition for a manufacturer that many users have similar needs for the innovative product to be profitable.[14] Whether an innovation is made by a manufacturer or a user depends on the relative benefits of the innovations for the two parties. A user innovation may be made if it implies small or no benefits for the manufacturer, which is often the case where the innovative product or service is easily copied by other manufacturers (for instance due to the lack of practical and legal means of protecting the innovation).[15] This scenario suggests that users obtain benefits in ways which differ from manufacturers and thus that the incentive structures are different. It has been shown that in general patent protection is less necessary and more costly for user innovations than for innovations made by manufacturers.[16]

3.3 Asymmetric Information

Knowing about needs in the market place is crucial in manufacturing. However, information on users' needs is not equally distributed. Normally the manufacturer has inadequate information on users' needs. Users are the first to know about their own needs and the information on users' needs is not easily distributed to manufacturers. Eric von Hippel uses the term 'sticky information' and it creates a case of asymmetric information. Since existing information asymmetries cannot be erased easily or cheaply, each innovator will tend to develop innovations that draw on the sticky information they already have, because it is the cheapest course of action.[17] This is another reason why many users do not find what they want in the market and choose to innovate.

3.4 The Role of Lead Users

In envisaging final determinants for user innovation, von Hippel has identified a certain category of actors that he calls 'lead users'. Studies show that many users develop and modify products for their own use but

---

[14] Eric von Hippel, *The Sources of Innovation* (Oxford University Press, 1988), p. 7.

[15] Eric von Hippel, *The Sources of Innovation* (Oxford University Press, 1988), p. 63.

[16] Katherine J. Strandburg, 'Users as Innovators: Implications for Patent Doctrine' (2008) 79 *University of Colorado Law Review* 467.

[17] Eric von Hippel, *Democratizing Innovation* (MIT Press, 2005), p. 70.

innovation is concentrated among lead users. Lead users share two characteristics. First, they are ahead of the majority of users in their populations with respect to an important market trend and so are currently experiencing needs that will later be experienced by many users in that market. Consequently, lead users understand emerging user needs and markets better than manufacturers and ordinary users. Second, lead users anticipate relatively large benefits from obtaining a solution to their needs and may consequently innovate.[18]

In conclusion, four determinants for the emergence of user innovations can be identified: (1) heterogeneous demands; (2) expectation of benefits (profits); (3) asymmetric information between users and manufacturers; and (4) the existence of lead users.

After a user innovation has emerged a phase may follow in which the innovation is diffused through networked media and a community may form around the innovation. Finally, as the last phase, a manufacturer may adopt the innovation to develop and market a commercial version.

4. USER GENERATED LAW

In the following sections the structural similarities between product and service innovations and legal innovations will be investigated. It is anticipated that the circumstances and the actors involved in the development of legal innovations will to a high degree resemble the development of product and service innovations. If the two production processes can sustain a comparison in this way, the insights of von Hippel's theory can provide a better understanding of how user generated law develops.

The theory on user innovation has certain policy implications since von Hippel claims that in general user innovations are undervalued and that the obstacles to user innovations are not properly understood. As a consequence, it would be beneficial to society at large to address these obstacles and provide the best conditions for the promotion of user innovation. If user generated law entails the same societal benefits as user innovations, the model can contribute to the creation of a better legal process, and the theory can be used to identify the best legal institutional conditions for the promotion of user generated law.

A model of user generated law in a knowledge society relates to a variety of legal disciplines. In this work the concrete cases of private regulatory models are taken from the area of intellectual property law but

---

[18] Eric von Hippel, *Democratizing Innovation* (MIT Press, 2005), pp. 5, 22.

the methodological framework could be extended to other parts of law. Intellectual property law is essential to the legal infrastructure of a knowledge society. The underlying rationale of intellectual property law can be construed as a balancing mechanism that on the one hand provides economic incentives for the creation of new knowledge, information, and innovation, while on the other hand ensuring access for others to this new knowledge, information, and innovation. This is a balance between the interests of creators and the interests of users.

Due to factors such as the time lag[19] and inflexibility involved in the traditional model of legal regulation (statutory law and case law) this model and the notion of intellectual property law as a balancing mechanism have been challenged in today's knowledge society and a number of new non-legislative regulatory models have emerged. It is common to many of these regulatory models that the authoritatively determined regulation does not work as intended and private arrangements redefine the legal position and change the balance between the opposing interests.

The theory on user innovation suggests the following determinants of user innovation:

1. Heterogeneous demands.
2. Expectation of benefits (profits).
3. Asymmetric information between users and manufacturers.
4. User innovation is most likely to occur if there are lead users.

For the purposes of the user generated law perspective we shall study whether the emergence of private regulatory models within intellectual property rights depends on the same four determinants.

After studying the emergence of the private regulatory models we shall examine whether the models follow the same phases as those ascribed to user innovations:

Phase 1: Emergence
Phase 2: Diffusion
Phase 3: Adoption

---

[19] See e.g. Paul M. Romer, 'Process, Responsibility, and Myron's Law', in Olivier J. Blanchard, David Romer, Michael Spence, and Joseph E. Stiglitz (eds), *In the Wake of the Crisis: Leading Economists Reassess Economic Policy* (MIT Press, 2012), pp. 112 et seq.

'Emergence' refers to a situation where a regulatory model (the legal innovation) is created and used by the parties affected by it. 'Diffusion' simply means that the legal innovation is copied and used by other parties, and 'adoption' implies that the legal innovation is acknowledged by the legislator or other producers of State-enacted law as a regulatory model that works well.

4.1 Autonomy Spaces

Different applicable rule-sets in a knowledge society are formed by two major forces: the pressure of public policy protection as enunciated by the State and commercial efficiency as pursued by private actors.[20] Public policy protection is motivated by ideological as well as efficiency concerns. Public efficiency concerns include supporting private transactions, balancing information asymmetries, sustaining the production of public goods, and redressing externalities.[21] The same two major forces influence the development of new products and services. However, in regard to products and services the pressure of economic efficiency is by far the most dominant factor.

In law the situation is somewhat different because in some parts of State-enacted law public policy considerations are so strong that private actors only have very limited freedom to establish private regulatory models. In other parts of State-enacted law public policy considerations play a minor role which gives a large degree of freedom to establish private regulatory models. The State-enacted law defines a space within which persons may act autonomously which will hereafter be termed the *autonomy space*. In parts of State-enacted law where public policy protection plays a minor role, the autonomy space is wide and in parts of State-enacted law where public policy protection is dominant the autonomy space is narrow. In some regulated fields there are not really any autonomy spaces because the persons subjected to the law must simply comply. For example, all persons have to comply with the applicable, valid tax law rules.

Even in cases where persons cannot substitute a private regulatory model for an existent law there may be possibilities for the persons to opt out of the law by changing behaviour or institutional nature. For

---

[20] In the same vein, see Thomas Schultz, 'Carving up the Internet: Jurisdiction, Legal Orders, and the Private/Public International Law Interface' (2008) 19(4) *The European Journal of International Law* 799, p. 805.

[21] Cf. Anthony Ogus, *Regulation. Legal Form and Economic Theory* (Clarendon Press, 1994), pp. 29 et seq.

example, a production company that wants to avoid the high corporation tax in the country where it is established can move the company to another country with a lower corporate tax rate.[22] However, the concept of user generated law developed here shall be understood as privately produced law developed in autonomy spaces. User generated law emerges in these autonomy spaces. Outside the autonomy spaces private parties cannot enter into a valid mutual agreement or other regulatory model stating that another set of legal rules ought to apply to them.

In reality, the borders of autonomy spaces are diffuse. Parties are not actually prevented from acting outside autonomy spaces; but if they do they may be met with legal sanctions or remedies. Rational parties are expected to act if the benefits of the act exceed the costs. If the legal sanctions and remedies for not respecting the autonomy space are severe the likelihood that the parties will comply with normative law is relatively high. However, in certain fields (for instance where violations are difficult to detect or where enforcement is problematic) there may be no real legal effect of not complying with normative law. In those cases the *de facto* autonomy space may be much broader than the *de jure* autonomy space. The claim that actions are determined by the balancing of benefits and costs may be modified by the internalization of social norms. In the literature on behavioural theory and social norms it is noted that due to the existence of social norms people do not always appear to behave in a rational way and that behaviour may therefore deviate from economic predictions.[23] It has been demonstrated how obedience to the law may stem from other reasons than the threat of sanctions, namely that law violations have reputational consequences.[24] Accordingly, the discrepancy between *de facto* and *de jure* autonomy spaces may not be as large as predicted by mainstream economic reasoning.

Policy implications arise from the diffuse borders of autonomy spaces as well as from the fact that the *de facto* autonomy spaces may be larger than the *de jure* autonomy spaces. Provided that user generated law

---

[22] On the substitution of law in other ways than those contemplated here see, inter alia, Erin A. O'Hara and Larry E. Ribstein, *The Law Market* (Oxford University Press, 2009); Roger Van den Bergh, 'Towards an Institutional Legal Framework for Regulatory Competition in Europe' (2000) 53 *Kyklos* 435; and Norbert Reich, 'Competition between Legal Orders: A New Paradigm of EC Law?' (1992) 29 *Common Market Law Review* 861.

[23] E.g. Cass R. Sunstein, 'Social Norms and Social Roles' (1996) 96 *Columbia Law Review* 903.

[24] Tom R. Tyler, *Why People Obey the Law* (Princeton University Press, 1990).

(respectful of the relevant public policy concerns) performs better than State-enacted law, the legal framework for user generated law is improved by clarifying the State-enacted law which defines the autonomy spaces and by legal means to enforce the borders of the autonomy spaces.

5. PHASE 1: EMERGENCE

Von Hippel's empirical studies find that the functional source of innovation differs strikingly across the several types of product and process innovation he has explored.[25] This finding is not surprising and the same must be expected in law. User generated law is expected to emerge in some parts of law and not in others and must furthermore be expected to have a larger impact in some parts of the legal system than in others.

User generated law emerges where private actors expect such law to perform better than State-enacted law. Various reasons may potentially give rise to this situation. Gillian K. Hadfield has studied the privatization of commercial law and claims that politicians and bureaucrats do not evaluate and pursue innovations in law in the ways that entrepreneurs do – with the speed, flexibility, resources, and incentives of the market at their disposal.[26]

5.1 Heterogeneous Demands

The heterogeneous legal demands existent in today's knowledge society are reflected in Thomas Schultz's notion concerning law in cyberspace, according to which the internet will be increasingly carved up into distinct spheres or virtual spaces governed by different rule-sets.[27] It is reasonable to presume that demands for law are highly heterogeneous due to the multitude of different business models, user communities, transactions, and so forth which continuously come into existence in this knowledge economy and due to the diverse interests involved in these phenomena.

---

[25] Eric von Hippel, *The Sources of Innovation* (Oxford University Press, 1988), p. 28.

[26] Gillian K. Hadfield, 'Privatizing Commercial Law' (Spring 2001) *Regulation Magazine* 41.

[27] Thomas Schultz, 'Carving up the Internet: Jurisdiction, Legal Orders, and the Private/Public International Law Interface' (2008) 19(4) *The European Journal of International Law* 799, p. 805, see also pp. 828 et seq.

In the development of new products and services it is characteristically assumed that the manufacturer must find a need and fill it by executing new product development stages, provided that the demand for the new product is estimated to be large enough. In law it is different. When it comes to State-enacted law that creates autonomy spaces, such law is primarily based on public policy considerations which again are determined by the needs of society at large rather than the needs of the persons affected by the law. Often the purpose of State-enacted law that creates autonomy spaces is to prevent the persons affected by the law from doing what they would prefer to do. In such cases it is not very useful to speak about heterogeneous demands for law even though such demands do exist – for instance in regard to adequate standards for environmental protection and the scope of prohibitions on additives in foodstuffs – because it is not crucial for the legislator to satisfy the different demands and preferences of the groups of persons affected by the law. The legislator will simply adopt the law that is presumed to be best for society at large and create the legal framework that applies equally to all persons irrespective of their demands and preferences.

In conclusion, there are probably heterogeneous demands for all kinds of law; but since such claims are not necessarily valid or relevant in regard to public law that creates autonomy spaces the notion of user generated law developed here cannot explain this area of law.[28]

State-enacted law that creates autonomy spaces adds a further complication to the emergence of legal innovations because such law may be the result of two different processes. A *proactive* process is used when the legislator adopts law that defines the autonomy space before an actual legal need has emerged.[29] The reason for using a proactive process is that

---

[28] The delimitation of law that creates autonomy spaces as opposed to other parts of law bears some resemblance to the distinction made by Anthony Ogus between 'facilitative law', which is law that provides mechanisms for ensuring mutually desired outcomes, and 'interventionist law', which protects defined interests and/or supersedes voluntary transactions; cf. Anthony Ogus, 'Competition between National Legal Systems. A Contribution for Economic Analysis to Comparative Law' (1999) 48 *The International and Comparative Law Quarterly* 405, pp. 410 et seq.

[29] The mirror image of the proactive legislative process has been termed 'preemptive self-regulation', which refers to the situation where the relevant industries use some form of self-regulation to react to concern from the public and policy-makers expressed through such channels as the threat of increased regulation. See Jason M. Solomon, 'New Governance, Preemptive Self-Regulation, and the Blurring of Boundaries in Regulatory Theory and Practice' (2010) *Wisconsin Law Review* 591.

a future need for legal regulation is anticipated and the legislator determines the width of the autonomy space on the basis of efficiency and public policy considerations. In a *reactive* process the legislator has left a legal vacuum and user generated law develops in this vacuum spontaneously.[30] After the development of the user generated law two things can happen. Either the user generated law is perceived as being in conflict with the needs of society at large and the legislator decides to narrow down the autonomy space, or the user generated law is found to be in conformity with the needs of broader society and the State decides not to intervene in this private practice or institutionalizes it into State-enacted law. In the two latter situations the user generated law is said to be fully adopted.[31]

5.2 Expectation of Benefits

According to mainstream economic theory innovation is seen as having a positive impact on social welfare because innovation enables new and better products, cheaper products, or indeed both. Innovation thus increases product variety. As a starting point great product variety is assumed to be desirable because, compared to a situation with lesser product variety, it enables most consumers to acquire products which better satisfy their preferences. However, new products only come at a cost. The producer of a new product must pay fixed costs associated with the development and marketing of a new product. In order to recoup the fixed cost the producer must demand a higher price for the new product variety and the more product varieties the smaller market segment for each variety. Accordingly, the producer can only benefit from small scale economies in production.[32]

Seen from the point of view of consumers, the lowest product price is offered when there is only one product variety in the market. The individual consumer will be willing to pay a higher price for a new product variety that more closely corresponds to the preferences of the consumer. Since consumers have different preferences they also have different preferred product varieties. Each new product variety requires

---

30 This situation may reflect the observation made by Gillian K. Hadfield, 'Privatizing Commercial Law' (Spring 2001) *Regulation Magazine* 40, p. 45, according to which one of the striking features of the history of private legal regimes is that they appear only to emerge where there is an absence of public law.

31 See para. 7 below.

32 Eric von Hippel, *Democratizing Innovation* (MIT Press, 2005), p. 110.

development costs and if too many product varieties are developed the aggregated development costs exceed the aggregated added value for the consumers and there is a case of over-provisioning. If, on the other hand, the added value for the consumers of a new product variety exceeds the costs of developing the variety there is a case of under-provisioning.

To sum up, variety is a good thing for users and for society; but only to a certain point. Beyond that point the costs of variety outweigh the benefits. The unresolved issue in this context is whether the same basic trade-off between variety and cost also applies to privately produced regulatory models.

First, it is reasonable to assume that there are substantial fixed costs involved in the creation of a new private regulatory model. Irrespective of the type of model, it always requires human resources (often of a highly specialized and costly nature) to create a new regulatory model.[33] In addition, it is necessary to distinguish between regulatory models that do not require an institutional set-up (such as pure contractual arrangements) and models that do (such as copyright collecting societies which require an organization to collect remuneration). Obviously, the latter types of models require additional costs. The mere fact that fixed costs are involved in the development of a new regulatory model suggests that there is an upper limit to the optimal degree of variety in private regulatory models. Following the market economic rationale the entity that creates a new regulatory model must have an expectation that the fixed costs will be recouped. Von Hippel talks about innovators (either user or manufacturer) who expect a temporary profit as a precondition for innovating. The same can be said about user generated law but the notion needs to be expanded.

Normally, regulatory models are not sold in the same way as products. Instead, they generate value by being used.[34] For instance, a group of

---

[33] See, however, Robert G. Bone, 'Decentralizing the Lawmaking Function: Private Lawmaking Markets and Intellectual Property Rights in Law' (2014) 38 *International Review of Law & Economics* 132, p. 140: 'While it is ultimately an empirical question, ordinary experience suggests that creativity in law usually involves only modest upfront investment compared to other types of creativity. There are exceptions, of course, but modest investment seems likely in most cases.'

[34] User generated protective regimes have emerged even in fields where some intellectual protection is available. In one study it is suggested that the main reason for this is that the State-enacted intellectual property system is too rigid and too costly to use. See David Fagundes, 'Norms-Based Regulation of Intellectual Property: The Case of Roller Derby Pseudonyms' (2012) 90 *Texas Law Review* 1093, p. 1093.

companies may create a contractual model that reduces the commercial risks involved in a certain type of transaction. The contractual model generates value for the companies by reducing risks since risks represent costs. The more the contractual model is used, the more value it generates. In addition, it must be assumed that in some cases innovators can generate benefits of a non-economic nature that are sufficiently high to spur innovation. That will be the case if the incentive for the innovator is not an expected economic income but an increase in the innovator's reputation with her peers or in a community. The more the innovation is used the more the innovator's reputation is increased. Therefore, irrespective of the sort of benefits user generated law may create, it can be stated that a new regulatory model will only be created if it is expected to be sufficiently used (extensively or intensively).[35]

Some intuitive insights and anecdotal evidence can be gained from the open content licences provided by Creative Commons. Creative Commons offers standard open content licence agreements that right-holders can choose to use when they want to license their work. A right-holder is free to write her own licence agreement that perfectly conforms to her needs and such a licence is no less binding than a Creative Commons licence. Nevertheless, a large and increasing number of right-holders decide to use the Creative Commons licence instead of making a licence agreement themselves despite the fact that the Creative Commons licence may not be the optimal licence for many of the right-holders. For these right-holders the additional value of making their own licence contract does not exceed the cost of making such a contract (working hours, cost of legal advice, and so forth). Therefore, it is rational for them to use Creative Commons.

Creative Commons combines standard agreements with flexibility by offering six standard agreements to choose between. When the right-holders have a choice between more standard contracts, they get more precisely what they want. But why does Creative Commons not offer the

[35] According to von Hippel it is problematic if potential innovators do not measure benefits in commensurable ways: 'However, the model will not be practicable in fields where all potential innovators do not measure the rents they expect in commensurable ways. This is so simply because the hypothesis that underlies the model requires that one compare levels of expected rents across functional groups in order to predict the functional source of innovation. And this is only possible in fields where all classes of potential innovators with a significant potential interest in an innovation use commensurable measures.' Cf. Eric von Hippel, *The Sources of Innovation* (Oxford University Press, 1988), p. 71.

greater variety represented by 20 or 50 standard contracts? In that case each right-holder would get a standard contract closer to the right-holder's optimal contract. Arguably, the reasoning from product variety is not convincing in this respect because Creative Commons is an NGO not governed by profit motives and the costs of developing new contract versions are presumably not decisive. The cost of variety must be found among the right-holders who are the users of the contracts. A possible explanation could be that a large variety of contracts complicates the choice. The presence of many choices implies that the right-holder must use time considering each choice and perhaps seek legal advice to choose the best contract. The hypothetical situation where the right-holder could choose between an indefinite number of standard contracts equates cost-wise to the situation where the right-holder decides to write an individual licence contract.

The Creative Commons example above points to another issue where the creation of legal innovations may diverge from the creation of product and service innovations. In the theory on user innovation the person who creates the innovation is supposed to benefit from using or selling the innovation and that is not the case for an NGO such as Creative Commons. It may be argued that Creative Commons benefits from the widespread use of its licences by an increase in the organization's reputation in the community. However, since the organization does not follow the norms of the market it is reasonable to assume that the organization is primarily driven by a sense of altruism and therefore does not act in conformity to mainstream economic reasoning.[36] This may be an important issue when the theory on user innovations is applied to legal innovations since NGOs such as Creative Commons may turn out to be a major source of legal innovations.

---

[36] A similar explanation is given by David Fagundes regarding individual persons who have invested considerable time in creating an IP-like name registration system for the benefit of a sports league, cf. David Fagundes, 'Norms-Based Regulation of Intellectual Property: The Case of Roller Derby Pseudonyms' (2012) 90 *Texas Law Review* 1093, pp. 1138 et seq. See, however, the critical comments of Robert Ellickson, 'How Norm Entrepreneurs and Membership Associations Contribute to Private Ordering: A Response to Fagundes' (2012) 90 *Texas Law Review* 247; and the reply, David Fagundes, 'The Varieties of Motivation and the Problem of Supply: A Reply to Professor Ellickson' (2012) 90 *Texas Law Review* 311.

5.3 Asymmetric Information

In the development of new products and services manufacturers do not know emerging users' needs as well as users and, in particular, lead users do.[37] The same can be said for some areas of law; yet for other areas of law it is different.[38] State-enacted law that creates autonomy spaces is primarily based on public policy considerations and thus information on users' needs is not particularly relevant. When an autonomy space is narrowed down by law the purpose is to prevent the persons affected by the law from acting in certain ways when such actions create harmful effects on third parties (externalities) or violate moral norms in the given society. For that purpose, the State/legislator does not have to know about the exact needs of the persons affected by the law; the decisive information relates to the effects of the actions on third parties.[39] It has already been stated that law that defines autonomy spaces cannot be explained by the concept of user generated law. Hence, possible information asymmetries are only relevant concerning law that can emerge within autonomy spaces. Since information on legal needs within autonomy spaces is not equally distributed among the State/legislator and the parties affected by the law there is a case of asymmetric information.

One issue is that the State/legislator has inadequate information on users' legal needs that emerge within autonomy spaces; another issue is that such needs are presumably very diverse because they are by definition heterogeneous demands for law. Satisfying such heterogeneous demands is a very complex task and normally the users must be assumed to be able to deal with the complexities in a more efficient way. The State/legislator must aim to take into consideration the needs and preferences of all persons in a given society and adopt the best possible legal model which applies to all persons in that society. By comparison an individual user has the much simpler task of establishing a regulatory model that optimizes the individual user's needs and preferences.

---

[37] On lead users, see para. 5.4 below.

[38] Cf. Erin A. O'Hara and Larry E. Ribstein, *The Law Market* (Oxford University Press, 2009), pp. 14 et seq.; and Jan M. Smits, 'Private Law 2.0: On the Role of Private Actors in a Post-National Society' (November 30, 2010). Hague Institute for the Internationalisation of Law and Eleven International Publishing, 2011; Maastricht Faculty of Law, available at http://ssrn.com/abstract=1779042, p. 17 (accessed January 19, 2016).

[39] The needs of the persons affected by the law are not wholly irrelevant. If it turns out that a planned restriction on an autonomy space will have significant harmful effect on these persons, the restriction can be reconsidered.

Asymmetric information in relation to the creation of new regulatory models may also be present when one party (the legislator) has an abundance of information but is not able to distinguish between more and less relevant information. This may be an important factor in law due to lobbying in the legislative process. Lobbyists provide information with a specific view on the issues and the result may be an information overload that obscures rather than clarifies.

Legislators' lack of information may explain the emergence of a number of private protective regimes that complement protection under State-enacted intellectual property law. Emmanuelle Fauchart and Eric von Hippel have studied the emergence and functioning of a norm-based intellectual property system among French chefs which provides protection of recipes. They found the existence of a social norm that prohibits exact copying of recipes. According to another norm among the chefs, a chef who asks for and is given proprietary information by a colleague would not pass that information on to others without permission. Additionally, a third norm implied the right to be acknowledged as the author of a recipe one has created. The study found that violations of the norms were punished by shaming, loss of status within the community, and reduced future access to valuable community resources such as information.[40] This norm-based intellectual property system studied by Fauchart and von Hippel is not a legal model; they have defined their research object as a pure, norms-based intellectual property (IP) system that is based entirely upon social norms, possessing a functionality similar to that offered by law-based systems. Thus, it is user generated regulation but not user generated *law*. It does, however, illustrate the emergence of private regulation in a context where the absence of any State-enacted IP system for chefs' creations is explained by asymmetric information. The State does not know about the needs of such a system and the resulting benefits stemming from it.

Similar norm-based systems have also been shown to exist among stand-up comedians regarding the protection of jokes,[41] and among magicians regarding the protection of magic tricks. In the latter case, the IP system is supported by codes of conduct adopted by the magicians'

---

[40] Emmanuelle Fauchart and Eric von Hippel, 'Norms-Based Intellectual Property Systems: The Case of French Chefs' (January 2006) MIT Sloan Working Paper 4576-06.

[41] Dotan Oliar and Chris Sprigman, 'There's no Free Laugh (Anymore): The Emergence of Intellectual Property Norms in Stand-Up Comedy' (2008) 94 *Virginia Law Review* 1787.

organizations and a violation of the norms may lead to expulsion from the organization.[42]

In the same vein, a number of non-optimal and possibly superfluous State-enacted regulatory models can be explained by asymmetric information. The United States was the first jurisdiction in which specific rules for the protection of semiconductor products were adopted by the Semiconductor Chip Protection Act (SCPA) of 1984. The Act establishes a complicated protective regime based on registration of sui generis rights to so-called mask works fixed in semiconductor chip products. Foreign mask works are granted protection on the basis of a reciprocity principle; so in order to ensure protection of EU citizens' mask works in the United States, the EU adopted the Semiconductor Directive[43] that is based on registration as well and also has many other similarities with the SCPA. However, neither the SCPA nor the Semiconductor Directive seems to have any practical impact in the affected industries. Arguably, the first reason for this is that the object of protection (the design of the topography) does not correspond to the need of the producers whose commercial interests are closely connected to the function of the semiconductor. A second reason is that registration of a new topography in all countries possibly involves too much expenditure of money and human resources. Instead, producers of semiconductor products have found more efficient means of protecting their investments in the technological development.[44]

Another example of a different nature is the multilingual EU open source standard contract European Union Public Licence (EUPL)[45] that

---

[42] Jacob Loshin, 'Secrets Revealed: Protecting Magicians' Intellectual Property without Law', in Christine A. Corcos (ed.), *Law and Magic. A Collection of Essays* (Carolina Academic Press, 2010) pp. 123–41.

See also the emergence of a private intellectual property system in the US fashion industry, cf. Kal Raustiala and Christopher Sprigman, 'The Piracy Paradox: Innovation and Intellectual Property in Fashion Design'(2006) 92 *Virginia Law Review* 1687, pp. 1695 et seq.; and Robert P. Merges, 'From Medieval Guilds to Open Source Software: Informal Norms, Appropriability Institutions, and Innovation' (November 13, 2004), available at http://ssrn.com/abstract=661543 or http://dx.doi.org/10.2139/ssrn.661543, p. 19 (accessed February 3, 2016).

[43] Council Directive 87/54/EEC of 16 December 1986 on the legal protection of topographies of semiconductor products.

[44] See e.g. Gunnar W. G. Karnell, 'Protection of Layout Designs (Topographies) of Integrated Circuits – R.I.P.?' (2001) *IIC* 648.

[45] See the Commission's website at https://joinup.ec.europa.eu/software/page/eupl.

was launched by the European Commission[46] in January 2007. The standard contract is used by various EU Member States in public governed software programs, but has not had any substantial impact on the open source sector in general. A plausible explanation for the meagre success of the EUPL is simply that users do not have a need for it. More established and widespread open source standard licences have positive reputational effects that make it costly for software producers to switch to a new standard contract such as the EUPL.

5.4 The Role of Lead Users

According to von Hippel, lead users are users whose present strong needs will become general in the market place months or years in the future. Lead users play an essential role in a fast-moving world. Conversely, in a relatively slow-moving world, new versions of a product do not differ radically from their immediate predecessors. A new product is thus reasonably familiar and a typical user (and not necessarily a lead user) will be representative of the users' needs. In a fast-moving world typical users' real world experience is often rendered obsolete by the time a new product is developed and the manufacturer needs the experience of lead users who are in advance of product development.[47]

When a lead user modifies a product (i.e. makes an innovation) the market for the innovation is typically too small for a manufacturer to commercialize it. However, the lead user is at the leading edge of a market trend and when the market catches up it may be profitable for manufacturers to commercialize the innovation. In this way, successful innovations start up as user innovations and are subsequently adopted by manufacturers who commercialize them. As part of this process lead users can provide very useful information to manufacturers which they would not otherwise gather.[48] Manufacturers need not explore such users' needs very accurately. They need to ascertain how the innovative product is designed by lead users, not why it is designed in this way.

The lead user demonstrates a higher level of innovative activities because the lead user is the party who expects to gain the most from a new product or service.

---

[46] Strictly speaking, the Commission is not the EU legislator but it is an inherent part of the EU legislative process.

[47] Eric von Hippel, 'Lead Users: A Source of Novel Product Concepts' (1986) 32(7) *Management Science* 791, p. 796.

[48] Eric von Hippel, *Democratizing Innovation* (MIT Press, 2005), p. 108.

The prevalence of lead users in law is not as evident. An example of lead users in law may be the French authors who formed the first copyright collecting society, the French organization Société des Auteurs et Compositeurs Dramatiques (SACD) in 1777. Similar societies were later formed in other countries and in 1926 the performing rights societies formed the association International Confederation of Authors and Composers Societies (CISAC) to manage their common interests. The CISAC created, among other things, a model contract for reciprocal representation that set the standard for collective management of copyright in Europe until it was contested for being anti-competitive by the European Commission in a 2008 decision.[49]

When looking at the provision of standard contracts on open source and open content the entities that are ahead of the majority of users with respect to an important market trend are not users themselves in the sense that they are not developing the open licence contracts with the primary purpose of using the contract for their own activities and they are not selling the contracts to users. For instance, Free Software Foundation, which created the open source model contract *GNU General Public License*, and Creative Commons, which created the *Creative Commons Licenses* are non-profit organizations that have developed the model contracts in question for the use of others and their major mission is to disseminate the use of the contracts as widely as possible. What motivates the apparently altruistic work in such organizations falls outside the scope of this book. However, in this context the term 'lead user' is misleading. For the development of a model on user generated law the term 'lead actor' is a more exact term that shall, in addition to organizations, comprise inter alia communities and intermediaries who set the scene and are perceived as directly or indirectly representing user interests. Contrary to the lead user notion in the theory on user innovation, often lead actors are not motivated by an expectation of obtaining benefits from the creation of a legal innovation (cf. para. 5.2 above).

6. PHASE 2: DIFFUSION

The three phases in user generated law (emergence, diffusion, and adoption) indicate that the strongest societal impact arises from the user generated law which passes through the final phase and is adopted. Legal

---

49 Commission Decision of 16 July 2008 case COMP/C-2/38.698 – CISAC, [2008] OJ C 323/12.

innovations may be diffused through networked media in the same way as innovative products and services; and a community may be formed around the legal innovation. Numerous communities of this nature exist: for instance the non-profit organization ICANN in domain name law, collecting societies in copyright law, and patent pools in patent law.

In regard to new products and services the extent of diffusion is assumed to be closely related to the costs of copying, but diffusion may also be affected by other factors such as reputational effects and network effects. Some innovative products may be costly to copy; yet more importantly innovations may be protected by intellectual property rights which more or less effectively preclude others from copying it. Notably, though, legal protection of innovations is more often applied by manufacturers than by users. According to von Hippel, empirical research shows that new and modified products developed by users often do diffuse more widely than innovations made by manufacturers. The reason for the wide diffusion of user innovations is that user-innovators themselves often voluntarily publicly reveal what they have developed for all to examine, imitate, or modify without any payment to the innovator.[50] Since user-innovators often do not seek to maximize the economic return from others using the innovation, this suggests that user-innovators obtain benefits in other ways.

If a legal innovation becomes sufficiently diffused it will possibly obtain a positive reputational effect that reduces the uncertainties for new users and therefore be diffused even more. Here, too, the Creative Commons licences provide an example. Creative Commons licences are used widely and the extensive use may reassure new users that unexpected serious legal risks are not involved and that the licences in general seem to work well.

Pursuing the Creative Commons example and focusing on the copyleft provision[51] (in Creative Commons terminology: the 'share alike' provision) it is possible that there is even a network effect involved that increases diffusion. A network effect exists when one user of a product has a positive effect on the value of that product to other people. When a network effect is present, the value of a product increases with the number of other persons using the product. The copyleft provision imposes a duty on the licensee who remixes, transforms, or builds upon the licensed work to distribute the derivative work under the same licence

---

[50] Eric von Hippel, *Democratizing Innovation* (MIT Press, 2005), p. 77.

[51] A copyleft provision is also included in the GNU General Public License for instance.

as the original. The purpose of the copyleft provision is to ensure that subsequent users of a derivative work are offered the same freedoms to use as the author of the derivative work was offered in regard to the original work. If the author of the derivative work uses other contractual means than the corresponding Creative Commons licence there may be doubt as to whether copyleft compliance has been met. The corresponding Creative Commons licence is definitely compatible with the copyleft provision and the use of that licence facilitates subsequent licensing.

There are indications that when it comes to mass uses of privately produced regulatory models, reputational effects play a decisive role in the diffusion of the model. The name of the model functions like a trademark and may develop into a strong brand that further extends the dissemination of the model. Creative Commons and GNU General Public License are well-known names which not only inform prospective users that the licences work well and without unexpected legal risks, they have also developed into strong brands with values that are independent of the underlying legal standard contracts. Thus, some persons are using Creative Commons and GNU General Public License because it has symbolic value to them. In this way, the use of such contracts with well-known names is a means to signal to rest of the world that the user is associated with the communities surrounding the contracts.

7. PHASE 3: ADOPTION

According to von Hippel, a manufacturer may adopt the innovation in order to develop and market a commercial version as the last phase in the process. This is not a foregone conclusion because users can bypass manufacturers altogether.

The relevant legal innovation can be said to be 'adopted' in two situations. First, if the legislator and other producers of State-enacted law acknowledge the legal innovation by deciding that it works well and that there are no grounds for legal corrections of the model, then the innovation is adopted. Second, the legal innovation is adopted if it is incorporated into State-enacted law. For instance, the innovation may be adopted as statutory rules or the courts may apply the legal innovation as the default rule. Alternatively, the legal innovation may be incorporated into State-enacted law by means of customary law.

In reality it may prove difficult to determine whether privately created legal innovations have been adopted if the legislator has not acted in relation to the legal innovation. The lack of legislative intervention in relation to a legal innovation is not equivalent to the State's approval of the legal innovation because the legislator must be allowed a reasonable period of time to evaluate whether a legal innovation is working well or needs to be corrected. In the same vein, a reasonable period of time for evaluation is also needed for a legal innovation that previously worked well but, due to changes in the surrounding conditions, is not necessarily working well anymore.

The act of 'adoption' is not an either/or decision. The legal innovation may be fully accepted (adopted) and it may be fully rejected (non-adopted); yet presumably the most prevalent situations are those where the central part of the legal innovation is found to work well but at the same time there are minor legal corrections required (namely, an adjustment of the autonomy spaces).

8. THE INTERNATIONAL DIMENSION

Internationalization is a dimension that is not addressed in the theory of user innovation but is essential to conceptions of law in a knowledge society. Internationalization of cyber law has been highlighted by Thomas Schultz, arising from the simple fact that the internet is international by nature and is concerned with global economies. Schultz's characteristic of the internet seems pertinent to a knowledge society in general:

> our general understanding of the Internet forms one of the paradigms which underlie the general view of deterritorialization, transnationalism, state decline, and the replacement of national pyramids of normativity by global networks of spread-out normativity.[52]

Such an understanding is in conflict with the traditional process of law production characterized by a national legislator adopting statutes and national courts that interpret the statutes. Privately produced regulatory models have the potential to be truly global and as such to be independent of any nation states even though they rely on national courts for enforcement.[53]

---

[52] Thomas Schultz, 'Carving up the Internet: Jurisdiction, Legal Orders, and the Private/Public International Law Interface' (2008) 19(4) *The European Journal of International Law* 799, p. 801.

[53] Thomas Schultz, 'Private Legal Systems: What Cyberspace Might Teach Legal Theorists' (2007) 10 *Yale Journal of Law & Technology* 151, p. 154. See

The enforcement dimension of law creates links of different strengths to national legal systems. National courts must respect national mandatory provisions and differing legal cultures may affect legal interpretation. Hence (to offer just one example) it is possible that an alleged breach of the GNU General Public License could be litigated in courts of two different countries and produce opposite results. In principle, it must be assumed that a legal innovation enforced by the ordinary courts will have a relatively strong link to national legal systems compared to a legal innovation enforced by arbitration.

9. PROSPECTS FOR A MODEL ON USER GENERATED LAW

This book (and the underlying research project) developed from an observation that much law in our knowledge society is a matter of self-regulation; and in order to understand such law, the pertinent focus for legal study should shift to these legal phenomena rather than statutory intellectual property rights which have dominated the scholarly discussion on the legal infrastructure of today's knowledge society.

In this introductory chapter a preliminary attempt has been made to adapt the theory of user innovation to law, which is one way to explain and construe law in a knowledge society. Prima facie, there appear to be many similarities in the creation of innovative products and services vis-à-vis legal innovations. However, on a few points the theory on user innovation does not seem to reflect the legal world.

In the following chapters various examples of privately produced regulatory models will be studied. A primary purpose of the chapters is to examine whether a model of user generated law is a useful framework for analysing legal innovations created by their users. If that is the case, it should be possible to identify the drivers that create these forms of private regulatory models. The chapters will also examine the characteristics of the regulatory models that can be subsumed under the notion of user generated law in order to determine the impact of user generated law on the legal infrastructure of a knowledge society.

Law is different from products and services. Most importantly, law includes a number of inherent values (such as the rule of law founded upon consistency and predictability, or legitimacy and protection of

also Gunther Teubner, 'Breaking Frames: The Global Interplay of Legal and Social Systems' (1997) 45 *American Journal of Comparative Law* 149, p. 157.

minority interests), which are not relevant for the creation of innovative products and services. For instance, the producers of user generated law do not necessarily represent all persons affected by the law, which may create a legal situation where one group of people is shown preference on account of another group. If third persons are actually harmed by user generated law an externality has been created. Even in the absence of externalities, user generated law may create biases that are found to be unbalanced. Such externalities and biases may, in conformity to the prevailing political preferences, give rise to legal intervention by adjusting the autonomy spaces. This continuous interaction between legal innovations and the legal framework is not reflected in the theory on user innovation, which therefore needs to be developed and enriched when adapted to the legal world.

The interaction between legal innovations and the legal framework (the scope of the autonomy spaces) raises the question on how State-enacted law may be amended to facilitate the emergence and maintenance of efficient forms of user generated law. If the model of user generated law outlined here is adequate and useful in explaining and construing our knowledge society's privately produced regulatory models, it may also prove useful in providing policy prescriptions for the content of State-enacted laws that create the autonomy spaces.

2. Information abundance and knowledge commons

Michael J. Madison

1. INTRODUCTION

This chapter describes a fundamental conceptual and empirical challenge to the foundations of intellectual property (IP) law and then describes what to do in response.

The standard accounts of IP law describe systems of legal exclusion intended to prompt the production and distribution of intellectual resources, or information and knowledge,[1] by making those things artificially scarce. The argument here and below frames IP law instead as one of several possible institutional responses to the need to coordinate the use of intellectual resources given their natural abundance, and not necessarily useful or effective responses at that. The chapter therefore aims to shift the analytic framework from law to governance, and from IP law in isolation to IP law as part of commons, or resource management. Examples and illustrations are drawn from several domains of information and knowledge governance.

A more elaborate introduction to the argument can be laid out as follows. The several forms of IP law – patent, copyright, design rights, and so on – are specialized institutional responses to a subset of the many social dilemmas concerning knowledge and information resources. The standard economists' account of that subset, common to each of these legal fields, is a variant of the well-known "tragedy of the commons." Some relevant intangible or immaterial "thing" in some social environment (the "commons," in this account), such as a creative work or a novel invention, will be overused or overconsumed by those with access to that

[1] The chapter uses the phrases "intellectual resources," "information and knowledge," and "information and knowledge resources" interchangeably. Each phrase is intended to include propositional knowledge, technical and scientific knowledge, art and culture, data, and informal, tacit, and customary knowledge.

environment, in the absence of legal devices that limit access to it and permit the thing's producer to exclude unwanted users, or charge a fee for use, or both. Non-paying users are characterized pejoratively as "free riders." This dilemma of overconsumption prompts the related dilemma of underproduction. Because information and knowledge resources are naturally abundant – they are, in their intangible forms, public goods – it is said that only exclusion of free riders permits producers to recover their costs of production and a reasonable profit. In the absence of cost recovery, these resources will not be produced in sufficient quantity or quality. IP law solves these dual dilemmas, by creating legal protections for creative works, inventions, designs, and the like. Access and consumption of these resources is restricted, in the discretion of the producer (that is, the IP rights owner). In sum, naturally abundant intellectual resources must be made artificially scarce to ensure their continued production and distribution.[2]

As applied to knowledge and information resources, this standard account is subject to well-known and critical flaws. Most important, because knowledge and information resources are public goods – that is, because they are nonrival and nondepletable – the tragic dilemma of overconsumption is non-existent.[3] Knowledge resources are by definition abundant; consumption or use of the resource by one person does not diminish the pool of that resource that is available to anyone else. A scarce resource can be overconsumed. An abundant one cannot be. IP rights create scarcity in the face of abundance, but in doing so IP systems may produce the very overconsumption problem that IP rights are, in theory, intended to solve. Moreover, in certain respects existing IP law makes this artificial overconsumption problem worse rather than better, by imposing legal standards for protection of copyright works and inventions that are so low, often, that cultural and technical worlds are

---

[2] For present purposes I mostly set aside the important alternative solution to the underproduction dilemma. In the text, IP law is a creature and feature of an exchange-based market. As an alternative, the state may, and often does, provide information resources either directly (via procurement and production of those resources itself) or indirectly (via funding resources, via tax subsidies, and otherwise).

[3] For an extended version of this critique, see Brett M. Frischmann, *Infrastructure: The Social Value of Shared Resources* (Oxford University Press, 2012).

overrun by an overabundance of IP rights.[4] Law gives society an abundance of artificially scarce resources.

Social dilemmas concerning the production and distribution of information and knowledge resources are important and should not be ignored, and in appropriate settings IP laws turn out to be useful and well-justified responses. But inverting usual suppositions about scarcity and abundance means likewise inverting usual suppositions about the importance of IP law, rights of exclusion, and other conceptual frameworks for managing intangible resources. Social dilemmas concerning production and distribution of intellectual resources may be less significant, often, when compared with social dilemmas concerning coordination and combination of those resources. The experience of user-innovation communities[5] and the lessons of recent scholarship on norm-based creative communities[6] teach that intellectual resources may be provided and distributed via robust systems that have little or no basis in formal IP law. Yet coordination and combination of those resources may be extraordinarily challenging, as they often overlap and/or interact with one another as they are consumed and re-used. Few intellectual resources today exist in splendid isolation from other intellectual resources; re-mixing within and across scales, genres, traditions, and histories is the historical norm rather than the twenty-first-century or digital exception.[7]

As necessary solutions to relevant social dilemmas, IP systems may be the exception rather than the rule. Governance systems, in which the production, distribution, conservation, and coordination of abundant resources are managed via blends of law, technical rule, custom, convention, and social norm, are likely the more productive framework for understanding and interpreting those solutions.

That conceptual or theoretical beginning is subject to an all-important proviso. The points outlined above raise empirical questions as well as theoretical provocations. The remainder of this chapter is devoted primarily to the empirical aspects of this topic. Perhaps we have IP laws where

---

[4] For a related view, see Michael A. Heller and Rebecca S. Eisenberg, 'Can Patents Deter Innovation? The Anticommons in Biomedical Research' (1998) 28 *Science* 698.

[5] E.g., Eric von Hippel, *Democratizing Innovation* (MIT Press, 2005).

[6] E.g., Kal Raustiala and Christopher Sprigman, *The Knockoff Economy: How Imitation Sparks Innovation* (Oxford University Press, 2012); Aaron Perzanowski, 'Tattoos and IP Norms' (2013) 98 *Minn. L. Rev.* 511.

[7] This is consistent with Lawrence Lessig's work, even though he frames his argument in terms of Internet exceptionalism. See Lawrence Lessig, *Remix: Making Art and Commerce Thrive in the Hybrid Economy* (Penguin Press, 2008).

they are unneeded; perhaps we have IP laws where they are needed but that function in ways other than intended or desired. A way systematically to investigate those questions from an empirical perspective, with due attention to context and nuance, is needed. This chapter outlines such a method.

The chapter takes as its central organizing principle the idea of knowledge commons. The phrase "knowledge commons" captures the idea of governance of intellectual resources, including copyright works and patented inventions and also including public domain material, data, tacit knowledge, and know-how. The term "commons" denotes the proposition that in any particular context or environment, those resources are likely to be governed by some combination of positive law and informal devices.[8] The result may be a regime of more or less strict exclusion; the result is often, instead, a regime of knowledge and information sharing, where the sharing has an identifiable social and cultural structure or discipline. Call this "managed openness." Commons, according to this usage, does not mean "open to all, on unregulated terms," even where the knowledge resource is formally part of a public domain. Commons means structured sharing. Even public domain resources are governed via structures that can be investigated and described.

The point of linking information abundance with knowledge commons is that knowledge commons represents a method of understanding governance of abundant information resources. Sharing strategies, as forms of knowledge commons, may exist as responses to social dilemmas other than the coordination and combination dilemmas highlighted above. This chapter, however, draws attention to those coordination and combination dilemmas precisely because they so clearly illustrate the weaknesses of the standard economic justifications for IP laws.[9] The chapter does not take a strong normative position regarding commons in general. Instead, it offers knowledge commons as an analytic framework for collecting research and data regarding governance in the knowledge and information context. IP laws may play a role in knowledge commons

---

[8] See generally Brett M. Frischmann, Michael J. Madison and Katherine J. Strandburg (eds), *Governing Knowledge Commons* (Oxford University Press, 2014), discussed in the following sections.

[9] Julie Cohen frames this point specifically in terms of copyright law. See Julie E. Cohen, 'Copyright as Property in the Post-Industrial Economy: A Research Agenda' (2011) *Wisc. L. Rev.* 141, 155 ("[C]opyright is valuable not (only) because it is individual and atomistic ... but also because it facilitates combination and coordination.").

governance. The question to be addressed – rather than simply assumed – is how and when that is the case.

Two limitations guide the presentation in order to sharpen it. First, some examples of commons as solutions to coordination and combination dilemmas are drawn in parallel with scholarship on user-innovation communities. That work describes how end-users of knowledge goods – meaning tangible or material embodiments of knowledge resources – explore and exploit access to those goods, via use and experimentation, and develop new or improved or different applications and forms, all without guidance, commands, or incentives from IP laws or IP rights holders. Such user-innovation communities are particularly robust in technical domains and in consumer product or consumer technology domains. Second, some examples are drawn with reference to law itself, as an intangible and therefore widely shared intellectual resource;[10] user-innovators may develop new models of governance to accompany their modes of innovation.[11] Combining the three perspectives – knowledge commons, user-innovation, and law as a shared intellectual resource – one may ask the following question. Can knowledge commons help us understand the dilemmas of abundance, meaning both governance by law (as in the case of IP systems) and also governance of law? This chapter explores answers.

The next section of this chapter introduces the knowledge commons concept in some additional detail and provides some initial illustrations.

---

[10] For provocative accounts of law as a shared information resource subject to coordination dilemmas, see Gillian K. Hadfield, 'Legal Infrastructure and the New Economy' (2012) 8 I/S: *A Journal of Law and Policy for the Information Society* 1; Gillian K. Hadfield and Barry R. Weingast, 'What is Law? A Coordination Account of the Characteristics of Legal Order' (2012) 4 *J. Legal Analysis* 471.

[11] See Katherine J. Strandburg, 'Legal But Unacceptable: Pallin v. Singer and Physician Patenting Norms', in Rochelle C. Dreyfuss and Jane C. Ginsburg (eds), *Intellectual Property at the Edge: The Contested Contours of IP* (Cambridge University Press, 2014).

2. KNOWLEDGE COMMONS GOVERNANCE

Following Elinor Ostrom's groundbreaking work on institutions for resource management in the natural resource and environmental contexts,[12] Frischmann, Madison, and Strandburg describe knowledge commons generally as governance solutions for shared resources subject to social dilemmas.[13] In the first place a resource is identified or created; use of that resource is purposefully shared by some population of producers and/or consumers. In the second place there exists a number of possible social dilemmas associated with the shared production and/or use of that resource, deriving generally from interests in social collaboration and cooperation. Commons address one or more of those dilemmas. Commons are forms of governance, or management, of shared resources.

With respect to natural resources, Ostrom and her colleagues and collaborators demonstrated the viability of a range of sustainable, durable commons governance strategies preserving the resource over time, implemented by local groups and communities using well-structured convention and custom. Commons are collectively managed, and they are often marked by the absence of formal, market-based property law systems. In their re-purposing of Ostrom's work, Frischmann, Madison, and Strandburg set out a research framework to investigate the viability of equivalent commons governance strategies with respect to knowledge, scientific, and cultural resources. Knowledge commons governance may differ from natural resource commons governance in key respects, beginning with the fact that knowledge commons resources, unlike forests or fisheries, are naturally nonrival or nondepletable and therefore naturally or inherently shareable. The case for sustainable commons governance is neither inherently stronger nor weaker as a result. Instead, cases of knowledge commons must be researched from the beginning, rather than analyzed solely by analogy to natural resource commons.

Drawing attention to information or knowledge abundance rather than scarcity offers only an introduction to the reframing that this chapter proposes. Nuances matter. First, the challenges of abundance have been noted before, in terms of economic theory,[14] in terms of cultural

---

[12] Elinor Ostrom, *Understanding Institutional Diversity* (Princeton University Press, 2005); Elinor Ostrom, *Governing the Commons: The Evolution of Institutions for Collective Action* (Cambridge University Press, 1990).

[13] See Frischmann et al., note 8 above.

[14] See Mark A. Lemley, 'IP in a World without Scarcity' (2015) 90 *N.Y.U. L. Rev.* 460 (focusing on production and distribution issues in IP law but referring only indirectly to governance of coordination dilemmas).

theory,[15] and in terms of social theory.[16] Earlier work suggests that abundance in any specific context may mean "lots," or it may mean "too much"; the distinction may have powerful consequences as that context is fully described in terms of the social dilemmas that are present. Second, abundance in any specific context may be relative rather than absolute. A resource may be abundant with respect to its use by an individual or a single agent or with respect to its use relative to a pair of individuals or agents (one person or a pair may be overwhelmed by information), and in this sense an intellectual resource is an individual resource. Alternatively, a resource may be abundant with respect to its use by a group, community, or population (software developers may be overwhelmed by information), and in this sense an intellectual resource is a social resource. Again, the social dilemmas are described differently in the two cases, and different stable institutional solutions may be present. Third, the fact that intangible intellectual resources are abundant, because of their nondepletable character, should not obscure the fact that knowledge and information often take specific tangible or material forms, which may be independently depletable and therefore scarce. Their scarcity should be understood as a distinct but related phenomenon, complicating the description of relevant social dilemmas and their solutions.[17]

Drawing attention to social dilemmas concerning intellectual resources as coordination and combination problems, and suggesting that the knowledge commons concept may unify research into durable and effective institutional solutions, complements rather than substitutes for long-standing research in game theory and related disciplines on theories of coordination via convention and custom. The best known work in this genre is Schelling's theory of focal points as convention-based solutions to what is sometimes referred to as "the meeting place problem."[18] Focal point theory, and related work on conventions, customs, and social norms, share with the knowledge commons concept an acceptance of the possibility of multiple stable institutional solutions to a given social

---

[15] See Grant McCracken, *Plenitude 2.0 – Culture By Commotion* (rev. ed., Periph.: Fluide, 1998); Grant McCracken, 'The Politics of Plenitude' (1998) *Reason* (August/September), available at http://reason.com/archives/1998/08/01/the-politics-of-plenitude (accessed January 20, 2016).

[16] See Andrew Abbott, 'The Problem of Excess' (2014) 32 *Sociological Theory* 1 (focusing on problems of coordination).

[17] See Michael J. Madison, 'Of Coase and Comics, or, the Comedy of Copyright' (2009) 95 *Va. L. Rev*, In Brief 27.

[18] Thomas C. Schelling, *The Strategy of Conflict* (Harvard University Press, 1960).

dilemma; an acceptance of multiple inputs into those solutions (state-based rules, hierarchies, markets and private ordering, and custom, convention, and social norm); and a special interest in shared or common knowledge as prerequisite for their emergence.[19] The knowledge commons concept is not limited to game theoretic environments, however.

3. AN ILLUSTRATION: LAW ITSELF AS KNOWLEDGE COMMONS

Against that background, law itself consists of a potential case of knowledge commons, in the sense that law in a general sense or law in any particular social context consists of a shareable knowledge resource that is potentially subject to social dilemmas. Law illustrates particularly clearly how the prototypical social dilemma for shared knowledge resources may be the problem of coordination and combination.[20] If multiple individuals or small groups could invent and apply their "own" law at will, with no discipline to enforce what is valid, legitimate, and enforceable, then – arguably – society could not function. Society runs the risk of excessive conflict as partisans of different rule-sets interact but in legally incompatible ways. Despite the many criticisms of systems of law-making and law enforcement, it is rare to hear the criticism made that the dominant social dilemma regarding law (or good law, or just law, or efficient law) is that it is systematically overconsumed and underproduced.[21] The problem is typically not too little law, but too much.

---

[19] On the respective roles of common knowledge and salience in the emergence of conventions and social norms, see David K. Lewis, *Convention: A Philosophical Study* (Harvard University Press, 1969); Edna Ullman-Margalit, *The Emergence of Norms* (Clarendon Press, 1977). The idea of law as a solution to coordination problems has been imported into legal scholarship by a number of scholars. See, e.g., Steven J. Burton, 'Default Principles, Legitimacy, and the Authority of a Contract' (1993) 3 *S. Cal. Interdisc. L.J.* 115; Marcel Kahan and Michael Klausner, 'Standardization and Innovation in Corporate Contracting (Or "The Economics of Boilerplate")' (1997) 83 *Virginia L. Rev.* 713; Richard H. McAdams, 'A Focal Point Theory of Expressive Law' (2000) 86 *Virginia L. Rev.* 1649.

[20] See Hadfield, note 10 above.

[21] The criticism is made, but it is rare. Even if underproduction of law is a relevant social dilemma, it does not necessarily follow that private rights of exclusion are the appropriate solution. Permitting producers of law to appropriate private returns by granting them rights of exclusion in legal resources often – though not always – conflicts with basic notions of social justice and equality

Positive law-making by executive and legislative authorities can be understood as a case of solving this social dilemma via centralized, top-down, hierarchical authority. Law is a kind of shareable resource provided by a single producer, with its development, extension, and enforcement coordinated – via disciplinary subdivisions (contract or obligation, property, tort, criminal law, and so on) and via institutional subdivisions (courts, legislatures, and agencies at national and local levels) – partly by the state and partly (in democratic systems) by private actors.

Does knowledge commons as governance offer a stable alternative to what I have just described as government coordination of law?[22] The idea of "law" here has to take on a different meaning; clearly it is at least unorthodox and at worst incoherent to speak of formal, positive law as being collectively managed via convention and custom in local communities. Re-characterizing law as a form of governance, or the shared expectations, customs, conventions, and norms by which members of a community are governed and/or govern themselves, makes the question more tractable.[23] New and stable law in that sense can emerge from and be governed from below (governance of governance, as it were), that is, from user or community practice, or as practice combined with formal rules, rather than exclusively from above, from law-making institutions or hierarchies of individuals and firms organized in markets. Commons strategies may emerge to coordinate governance of different sorts, among different communities and/or among different intellectual resources.

Two brief examples illustrate specific knowledge commons solutions to social dilemmas concerning problems of coordination and combination

---

before the law. See *Wheaton v. Peters*, 33 U.S. (8 Pet.) 591 (1834) (rejecting a claim of copyright in the opinions of the Supreme Court of the United States); 17 U.S.C § 105 (2012) (excluding works of the US government from copyright). Crown copyright in the United Kingdom suggests that this principle has limits, even in democratic countries.

22 The question has analogues in political theory. See Yochai Benkler, *The Wealth of Networks: How Social Production Transforms Markets and Freedom* (Yale University Press, 2006); James C. Scott, *Seeing Like a State: How Certain Schemes to Improve the Human Condition Have Failed* (Yale University Press, 1998); Fred Turner, *From Counterculture to Cyberculture: Stewart Brand, the Whole Earth Network, and the Rise of Digital Utopianism* (University of Chicago Press, 2006).

23 It might be more appropriate to treat formal, positive, bureaucratized law and evolutionary, evolving, community-managed governance as two poles of a spectrum, although it is plausible to view them as occupying a hierarchical relationship as well as an oppositional or complementary one.

of different sorts, each involving the governance not only of conventional intellectual resources (creative works, patentable inventions) but also governance of forms of governance.[24]

Intellectual property pools. A patent pool is an agreement by two or more patent holders to aggregate and share their patents by cross-licensing.[25] The patents in question typically relate to complementary technologies, where one holder's exercise of patent rights "blocks" a different holder's exercise of related rights. Pooled patents are typically available to all members of the pool and are available to nonmembers on standard licensing terms. A well-known example of an early patent pool in the United States is the Manufacturer's Aircraft Association (MAA), which formed in 1917 and encompassed nearly all American aircraft manufacturers. The Wright Company and Curtiss Company held major patents on aircraft technology, but Wright and Curtiss did not hold all the relevant patents, and for any given manufacturer the cost of licensing a single needed patent from a competitor might have made manufacturing an airplane prohibitively expensive. During World War I, the United States government needed airplanes at reasonable costs and in a short time. As a result, the government facilitated the implementation of the MAA, a private corporation. The MAA entered into an agreement with airplane manufacturers, through which the manufacturers pooled their patents and their potential claims for exploitation of the patents by rivals and agreed to cross-licensing of the patents to one another on what was, essentially, a royalty-free basis.[26] Largely because of this functioning commons of patented inventions, airplanes were built, and the war was won.

The MAA was not the first patent pool; that distinction likely belongs to the Sewing Machine Combination, constructed in 1856 among the manufacturers of sewing machines and owners of related patents. And it is possible to tell the story of the MAA, and the Sewing Machine

---

[24] These examples are drawn from Michael J. Madison, Brett M. Frischmann and Katherine J. Strandburg, 'Constructing Commons in the Cultural Environment' (2010) 95 *Cornell L. Rev.* 657.

[25] See Carl Shapiro, 'Navigating the Patent Thicket: Cross Licenses, Patent Pools, and Standard Setting', in Adam B. Jaffe et al. (eds), *Innovation Policy and the Economy*, Vol. 1 (MIT Press, 2001).

[26] See *Mfrs. Aircraft Ass'n, Inc. v. United States*, 77 Ct. Cl. 481 (1933); Harry T. Dykman, 'Patent Licensing Within the Manufacturer's Aircraft Association (MAA)' (1964) 46 *J. Pat. Off. Soc'y* 646; Robert P. Merges, 'Contracting into Liability Rules: Intellectual Property Rights and Collective Rights Organizations' (1996) 84 *Cal. L. Rev.* 1293.

Combination, and other patent pools, as stories of successful private ordering grounded in exchanges of the IP rights documented by patents.[27] But telling the story in that way overlooks two key features that align patent pools generally with the knowledge commons concept. First, the very purpose of a patent pool is knowledge sharing, or structured openness regarding the patented inventions, rather than exclusion, as a solution to problems of an abundance of patents. Second, the knowledge commons solution depends on user (or patentee) creation of a foundational legal infrastructure, the cross-license that implements the commitment to sharing in a way that bridges, or coordinates, three sets of laws and rules: the default, positive patent regime and the numerous patents that are subject to the rules of the pool; the norms and rules of antitrust and competition law, governing lawful behavior by market competitors;[28] and the set of terms, expectations, and practices that governed the pool.

Open source software. The Linux operating system, an alternative to Windows and Mac OS (the Macintosh operating system), was produced and is still maintained by a volunteer collaborative of individual programmers. The Linux collaborative is linked loosely by communications technologies, by members' voluntary allegiance to the project, and by the terms of an open source license. Unlike proprietary computer programs, which are distributed to users in object code or executable format only, open source programs such as Linux are made available in source code form so that members of the community may modify their copies and, under the terms of the governing license, publish their modifications for use by others. Members of the community may also volunteer their modifications for inclusion in the standard Linux code base. Each member of the Linux community may use material in the Linux commons and may contribute material back to the Linux commons. Each individual member of the community contributes code to the accumulated archive of the Linux kernel, which is the core of the operating system.

---

[27] See Adam Mossoff, 'The Rise and Fall of the First American Patent Thicket: the Sewing Machine War of the 1850s' (2011) 53 *Arizona L. Rev.* 165. Carol Rose has argued persuasively that property law and property rights are constructed as stories: e.g., Carol M. Rose, 'Game Stories' (2010) 22 *Yale Journal of Law and the Humanities* 369.

[28] Early cases on patent pools and antitrust law shifted from uncritically accepting patent pools as matters of freedom to exploit patent rights: see *E. Bement & Sons v. National Harrow Co.*, 186 U.S. 70 (1902); to subjecting patent pools to antitrust scrutiny: see *Standard Sanitary Manufacturing Co. v. United States*, 226 U.S. 20 (1912).

The rules governing the use of open source material and contributions to the open source commons are partly formal and partly informal. Formally, the software is governed by copyright law, and its use is managed by the terms of the General Public License. Informally, the integrity of Linux as an identifiable and stable program depends on a thin hierarchy of informal authority, which extends from Linus Torvalds at the top to the body of individual developers at the bottom.[29] The result is a complete, complex, and successful industrial product that is built and maintained not by a traditional, hierarchical, industrial firm, but by a loose-knit community.

As with a patent pool, the integrity and durability of the Linux project is due not only to its members' shared commitment to building and maintaining the program and to their contributions of time, talent, and code, but also to innovations in the legal form that governs access to the code, use of the code, modification and extension of the code, coordination of different portions of the code with each other, and distribution of the code, all in great detail. The open source software license is itself a widely shared form of user-innovation in law, borrowing much of the terminology and structure of a proprietary software license and its relationship to positive copyright law but turning that license inside out, to ensure that the program is shared rather than kept secure from misappropriation.[30] In this case social dilemmas arise not only with respect to the need to coordinate the technical contributions of many different contributions of code but also the need to coordinate the copyrights associated with each of those contributions. As with the patents contributed to a patent pool, in an open source project there may be dozens or even hundreds of distinct contributions and associated sets of IP rights. In isolation, each contributor possesses a separate copyright and therefore has the presumptive right to block unauthorized reproductions and adaptations of the work governed by that copyright. The open

---

[29] A pair of recent books thoroughly examines the organizational structure of open source software projects. See Charles M. Schweik and Robert C. English, *Internet Success: A Study of Open-Source Software Commons* (MIT Press, 2012); Christopher M. Kelty, *Two Bits: The Cultural Significance of Free Software* (Duke University Press, 2008).

[30] Any conventional IP license can be understood as a kind of user-innovation with respect to adapting the default rules of IP law to the specific needs of the parties to the license. Open source software licenses are distinctive in the sense of the scale of their application and utility, because they serve effectively as governance not merely for the code and its developers and users but for the open source community as that group identifies itself. See Michael J. Madison, 'Reconstructing the Software License' (2003) 35 *Loy. U. Chi. L.J.* 275.

source license serves as a shared legal infrastructure that integrates those abundant legal rights, based on formal copyright law, into a single vehicle that is aligned with the substantive norms and expectations of the community.

In short, commons governance in both contexts emerges from user practice but borrows explicitly and directly from formal, positive law. Open source software development communities are organized around and are coordinated by open source software licenses which, the members of both these communities and their commercial partners generally assume, are enforceable with respect to contract law, copyright law, or both.[31] The software development community usually has a social existence that is distinct from the form and terms of its governing license. The community governs itself according to a set of informal but shared norms. Those norms are codified in part and extended in part in the formal license document. The license therefore has a legal existence that is distinct from the full social context of the software development community. But these two phenomena – the social world of the open source software developer and the legal world of the open source software license – are both necessary to the governance of an open source software project. A particular open source software project is a case of commons, a shared resource subject to coordination and combination dilemmas and governed by collectively-produced "law" with material and immaterial dimensions, and social and legal dimensions: the group, the code, and the license.

The next part generalizes, elaborating the knowledge commons concept for potential application to empirical investigation of particular cases. The central point introduced below is that understanding knowledge commons requires empirical as well as theoretical investigation, and effective empirical inquiry requires a systematic approach. The next section describes knowledge commons as a research framework, therefore, rather than as a model, theory, or prescription.

---

[31] Enforceability is generally assumed, although there is relatively little law on point. The leading US case is *Jacobsen v. Katzer*, 535 F.3d 1373 (Fed. Cir. 2008).

4. A RESEARCH FRAMEWORK FOR UNDERSTANDING KNOWLEDGE COMMONS GOVERNANCE

The point of any research framework is to permit research and data collection to proceed under a common set of assumptions and questions, even if specific research methods and disciplinary foundations may vary from researcher to researcher or field to field. The framework is neither theory nor model. Strong theorizing and modeling may follow the research but only light and tentative theorizing, if any, should precede it.

The framework as described is borrowed from a recent book by Frischmann, Madison, and Strandburg titled *Governing Knowledge Commons.*[32] That book presents the framework and applies it to a set of case studies of institutions defined in part by knowledge sharing practices with respect to one or more knowledge resources. While the framework is designed for application at the institutional level, which are referred to as commons, the intuitions and preliminary investigation that animated its development are applicable more broadly. Knowledge resources come in many forms. Information and knowledge are principally immaterial, intangible resources, but they may be embodied in material forms, in flows of knowledge as well as in forms, and in labor and skill and time as well as in embodied creation.[33] The balance of this section gives a fuller account of the framework; the next section introduces some novel commons problems to illustrate the breadth of its potential application.

The knowledge commons framework builds on a series of related intuitions. Commons governance means knowledge and information management characterized by domains of managed openness and sharing of relevant resources, and the first intuition is that commons governance is in broad use in day-to-day practice in a variety of domains and across a variety of scales. Documenting evidence to justify that intuition is a primary goal of the framework. The second intuition is that such structured openness in the management of both natural and cultural resources is likely to lead to socially beneficial and/or socially productive outcomes. Salient among the class of cases where commons governance is successful and sustainable are contexts where social interest in positive spillovers from bilateral market transactions is high. Commons may

[32] Frischmann et al., note 8 above.

[33] See Michael J. Madison, 'Creativity and Craft', in Shubha Ghosh and Robin Paul Malloy (eds), *Creativity, Law, and Entrepreneurship* (Edward Elgar Publishing, 2011).

sustain the production of spillovers when the market otherwise may not.[34] Testing that intuition by applying the framework to case studies is the second goal of the framework. Note that describing the commons framework in terms of spillovers from bilateral market transactions runs a substantial risk of characterizing an information context in "scarce resource" terms rather than in "abundant resource" terms; care must be taken in applying the framework to understand the nature of the resources in question. The final intuition is that a standard framework for identifying and assessing commons across a variety of domains can support the development of more sophisticated tools for realizing the potential for commons solutions in new institutional settings and for distinguishing commons solutions from other solutions in settings where some other approach, such as an approach grounded in IP law, might be preferred. Applying the knowledge commons research framework is an exercise in analyzing colloquial commons institutions, such as "scientific research" taken in the aggregate, in a nuanced way via comparative institutional analysis.

Examining constructed commons in knowledge and information contexts builds on the Institutional Analysis and Development (IAD) framework pioneered by Ostrom and her colleagues, but it adds some important modifications. The IAD framework has been used principally to structure analysis of solutions to collective action problems in natural resource contexts (so-called action arenas, or action situations) such as forests, fisheries, and irrigation systems. IAD analysis is premised largely on choice-processing, goal-oriented behavior by self-interested individuals. It looks to explain sustainable collective action that produces measurable, productive results. The insight from applying the IAD framework to a large number of governance institutions and resources is that commons solutions can be as stable and robust as market-oriented solutions to classic "tragedy of the commons" overconsumption dilemmas involving depletable natural resources. Shared governance can lead to sustainable fisheries and forests and to regular supplies of usable water.

The knowledge commons framework differs from the IAD framework in certain key respects. It does not assume the agency of rational, choice-selecting, self-interested individuals, as the IAD framework tends to do. It accepts the role of historical contingency and of both inward- and outward-directed (selfless or other-oriented) agents in the evolution

---

[34] See Brett M. Frischmann, Michael J. Madison and Katherine J. Strandburg, 'Governing Knowledge Commons', in Frischmann et al., note 8 above.

of collective or commons institutions. At the front end of the analysis, it requires understanding the contingency of the underlying resources themselves. Natural resource commons largely take the existence of their resources for granted: fish, trees, water, and the like. Knowledge commons identify resource design and creation as variables to be described and analyzed. As intellectual resources (that is, as forms of knowledge and information), patents, copyrights, and underlying inventions, creations, and data are shaped by a variety of institutional forces rather than by nature. Critically, the knowledge commons framework does not assume that the relevant resources are rival and depletable. The knowledge commons framework generally assumes precisely the contrary: that intangible information and knowledge resources are nonrival, nondepletable public goods. The dilemma to be solved is not primarily a classic "tragic commons" overconsumption problem. Instead, it is more likely (in part) an underproduction problem and (in part) a coordination problem. As noted above, this chapter directs primary attention to coordination dilemmas, but in applying the framework to any particular case, care must be given to describing the authentic character of the social dilemmas present.

Against that background, the knowledge commons framework proposes to undertake comparative institutional analysis by evaluating cases of commons resources via a series of questions, or clusters, to be applied in each instance.[35]

The case study investigation begins with a general description of the history and character of the problem that is being addressed by governance in the specific case or context. This may be an explanation that is internal to the governed institution(s) (problems and explanations may emerge from stories told by participants, either today or historically, or both), or an explanation that is external to the governed institution (such as the public goods account of the rise of IP law).

One should ask whether the relevant resource or case is characterized from the outset by patent rights or other proprietary rights, as in the case of a patent pool, or by a legal regime of formal or informal openness, as in the case of public domain data or information collected in a government archive. A particular regime might involve sharing data and information, or sharing rights in information, or sharing both. The character of the commons solution might involve coordinating holders of

---

[35] A brief overview and schematic of the framework is available at http://knowledge-commons.net/publications/gkc/research-framework/ (accessed January 20, 2016).

different IP interests or holders of different public domain knowledge resources, for example.

Answering that question sets a baseline against which a commons governance regime has been constructed. Within that regime, one next asks definitional questions. What are the relevant resources, taking into account both intangible and tangible resources and their individual or social character? What are the relationships among these resources, the baseline, and any relevant legal regime (for example, what a scientist considers to be an invention, what patent law considers to be an invention, and the boundaries of the patent itself are three related but distinct things)? What are the boundaries and constitution (membership) of the community or communities that manage access to and use of those resources? How is membership acquired (this may be informal, formal, or a blend of the two), and how is membership governed? What is good behavior within the group, what is bad behavior, who polices that boundary, and how?

Next are questions concerning explicit and implicit goals and objectives of commons governance, if any such goals and objectives exist (it is possible that commons governance regimes emerge from historical contingency rather than via planning). Is there a particular resource development or management dilemma that commons governance is intended to address, and what commons strategies are used to address that dilemma?

How "open" are the knowledge and information resources and the community of participants that create, use, and manage them? *Governing Knowledge Commons* argues that commons governance regimes involve significant measures of resource and community sharing and openness. Their details should be specified, along with their contributions to the effectiveness of commons. Some commons and commons resources have precise and fixed definitions of both resources and community membership. Either resources or membership or both may be more fluid, with boundaries defined by flexible standards rather than by rules.

A large and critical cluster of questions concerns the dynamics of commons governance, or what Ostrom refers to as the "rules-in-use" of commons: the interactions of commons participants and resources. Included in this cluster of questions are: (1) details of stories of the origins, histories, and operations of commons; (2) formal and informal (norm-based) rules and practices regarding distribution and coordination of commons resources among participants, including rules for appropriation and replenishment of commons resources; (3) the institutional setting(s), including the character of the regime possibly being "nested" in larger scale institutions and being dependent on other, adjacent institutions; (4) relevant legal regimes, including but not limited to IP law; (5) the structure of interactions between commons resources and participants and institutions adjacent to and outside the regime; and (6) dispute resolution and other disciplinary mechanisms by which commons rules, norms, and participants are policed.

At this point it becomes possible to identify and assess outcomes. In Ostrom's IAD framework, outcomes are typically assessed in terms of the resources themselves. Has a fishery been managed in a way that sustains fish stocks over time? Do commons participants, such as the members of a fishing community, earn returns in the commons context that match or exceed returns from participation in an alternative governance context? In knowledge commons, resource-based outcome measures may be difficult to identify and assess. Sustaining the resources and their uses, individually or in combination, may be the point. In a patent pool, pooled resources may constitute components of larger, complex products that could not be produced but for the pooling arrangement that reduces transactions costs among participants. Outcomes take different forms. It may be the case that patterns of participant interaction constitute relevant outcomes as well as relevant inputs. Agency, in a manner of speaking, may be less important than identity; the group and its participants, in a particular institutional setting, may be ends as well as means. Levels and types of interaction and combination matter. Participant interaction in the context of a shared resource pool or group may give rise to (or preserve, or modify) an industrial field or a technical discipline. In that specific case, such spillovers may be treated as relevant outcomes.

Having identified relevant outcomes, it becomes possible to look back at the problems that defined commons governance in the first place. Has the regime solved those problems, and if not, then what gaps remain? How do the outcomes produced by commons governance differ from outcomes that might have been available if alternative governance had been employed? Has commons governance created costs or risks that should give policy makers and/or institution designers pause? Costs of administration might be needlessly high; costs of participation might be high. A collection of industrial firms that pool related patents in order to produce complex products may engage in anticompetitive, collusive behavior. Commons governance may facilitate innovation; it may also facilitate stagnation.

5. THE KNOWLEDGE COMMONS RESEARCH FRAMEWORK APPLIED

The social worlds of knowledge and innovation are filled with cases of commons, in which users (or consumers, or participants, or others) are responding to social dilemmas and generating or making sets of governance rules and standards for themselves. This chapter lacks the space to fully apply and specify the framework with respect even to one rich case study; instead, it suggests how the knowledge commons framework may inform further research, particularly with respect to the related ideas of user-innovation and law as a shared commons resource.

5.1 Galaxy Zoo[36]

Example one is a case in which commons governance emerged to coordinate an astonishingly and apparently unmanageably large information resource.

Galaxy Zoo supplies a wildly successful model of what popular media refer to at times as "citizen science" and at other times and in other respects as peer production or "crowdsourcing." Academic researchers in astronomy in 2007 created a website that invited any and all comers to undertake the task of classifying approximately 900,000 galaxies, by looking at images downloaded from a recent sky survey. The classification exercise involved only a handful of relatively simple criteria and could be undertaken by non-experts after a brief online tutorial. The sponsoring researchers expected to rely on the results as part of preparing traditional scientific papers. (In the main, that has been the case, with some exceptions.) The researchers' initial modest expectations regarding the number of visitors to the site and the quality of their contributions were rapidly and vastly exceeded. The project was quickly extended both in depth and in breadth. The socio-technical "zoo" architecture that evolved in conjunction with the original Galaxy Zoo project has been refined and applied to additional and similarly-structured scientific research projects, all of them collected since December 2009 under the umbrella name, the "Zooniverse."

Galaxy Zoo began as a single solution to a pair of research problems. One of these was the domain of Kevin Schawinski, who in the mid-2000s

---

[36] This subsection is based on Michael J. Madison, 'Commons at the Intersection of Peer Production, Citizen Science, and Big Data: Galaxy Zoo', in Frischmann et al., note 8 above.

was a graduate student in astronomy at the University of Oxford. Schawinski was researching the evolution of elliptical galaxies, that is, he was pursuing morphological analysis of galaxies, distinguishing elliptical from spiral-shaped galaxies. Galaxy morphology is closely linked to color. Most spiral galaxies have a distinct blue tinge, which is associated with the younger, hotter stars in their spiral arms. Elliptical galaxies usually appear red, indicating the older ages of their stars and low levels of star formation. Blue ellipticals suggest the existence of gas reservoirs sufficient to support significant levels of star formation and are therefore of special interest to researchers. Schawinski aimed to examine a massive amount of digital astronomical data recently made available by the Sloan Digital Sky Survey (SDSS), a project of an international consortium of seven universities, other participating research institutions, several governments, and the Alfred P. Sloan Foundation. The SDSS had undertaken the largest comprehensive electronic map of the northern sky produced to date. Using a special purpose telescope on Apache Point, New Mexico, beginning in 2000 it imaged 10,000 square degrees of the sky, 70 million stars, and 50 million galaxies, resulting in approximately 15 trillion bytes of data, all of which were made publicly available as images to the research community. Schawinski planned to review and classify approximately 900,000 galaxies disclosed in the SDSS data. He tried, briefly, to do this himself, but he abandoned the effort because it was simply too time-consuming.

The second problem was the domain of another Oxford researcher, a post-doctoral fellow named Chris Lintott. Lintott was trying to understand spiral galaxies, also within the SDSS dataset. Whereas Schawinski was after blue ellipticals, Lintott was after red (that is, mostly dead) spirals. (In each instance, the existence of these galaxies would suggest new research problems having to do with galaxy evolution and the birth and death of stars.) Schawinski's conversations with Lintott yielded the idea that the classification exercise that interested each of them could be out-sourced, in a manner of speaking, to the public. Borrowing insights and some elementary technology from other, recent online scientific "crowdsourcing" efforts, notably Stardust@Home, the first, public, Galaxy Zoo website (http://www.galaxyzoo.org) made the SDSS image data available online beginning in July 2007. The images were accompanied by a brief tutorial describing the classification dimensions that visitors were invited to learn and apply. (The phrase "Galaxy Zoo" evokes the idea of a zoo of galaxies – a somewhat unruly collection of "animals" with distinct appearances.) A handful of simple questions were asked, directed to morphological issues. Based on a brief online tutorial, users were asked: Is this an elliptical galaxy or a spiral galaxy, or something else? If it is a spiral galaxy, which way does it appear to be rotating? Related publicity (principally through the BBC) described the launch of the project and pointed visitors to the website.

The project was a tremendous success almost overnight, in several senses related to knowledge commons governance and the challenges of solving coordination problems. First, the data classification problem that Galaxy Zoo was intended to solve was solved far more quickly and thoroughly than the organizers anticipated. Within 24 hours of launch, the site was receiving 70,000 classifications per hour. More than 50 million classifications were received by the project during its first year, from almost 150,000 people. Galaxy Zoo is now the world's largest database of galaxy shapes. The organizers, principally Lintott and Schawinski, built a technical platform that successfully coordinated the individual (and typically quite small) analytic contributions of thousands of non-expert contributors.

Second, the model of citizen science data analysis that Galaxy Zoo introduced appears to be socially productive at least in the sense that it has been accepted by the community of professional astronomers. The original Galaxy Zoo project has been succeeded by follow-on astronomical research projects using closely related protocols: Galaxy Zoo 2, which asked participants to classify more finely a subset of 250,000 galaxies from the original SDSS Main Galaxy Sample, using a different and more detailed set of questions; Galaxy Zoo: Hubble, which asked participants to classify a different group of older and more distant galaxies using data derived from images obtained through the Hubble Space Telescope; and now Galaxy Zoo Quench, which offered volunteers the opportunity to both classify and analyze galaxy data. In the case of the original Galaxy Zoo, Galaxy Zoo 2, and Galaxy Zoo: Hubble, the zoo-produced data either has been incorporated into a continuing series of scientific research papers published in scholarly journals or is being prepared for publication. (Galaxy Zoo Quench is still in progress.) More than 30 peer reviewed papers have followed from analysis of the original Galaxy Zoo data.

Third, the large scale data analysis and coordination exercise prompted by the original Galaxy Zoo has had unanticipated spillover benefits. Not only have the analytic contributions of Galaxy Zoo volunteers been coordinated successfully, but the thousands of volunteers have coordinated with each other by organizing themselves into a self-governed online forum, creating and sustaining a community that is adjacent to, and in some respects overlaps with, the community of professional astronomers. Through their forum, member "Zooites," that is, amateur Galaxy Zoo participants, have made a number of important discoveries based on the original SDSS data shared via Galaxy Zoo. Those discoveries have themselves been the bases for a number of scholarly papers. All of these Galaxy Zoo projects are now part of the larger cluster of citizen science projects known as the Zooniverse. Nearly 200,000 people are registered users of one or more Zooniverse projects, and more than 800,000 have participated in one way or another. This represents knowledge coordination and knowledge commons governance on an extraordinarily large scale.

5.2 Best Practices Projects

Example two is more law-specific on its surface and more subtle in its illustration of shared governance as a solution to a social dilemma. The Galaxy Zoo commons exists as a self-governed community with virtually no explicit reference to IP law or other positive law. Commons governance may arise more clearly in the shadow of formal, positive law. Research on informal social norms and customary practices in a diverse range of creative communities illustrates in part. French chefs, magicians, fashion designers, tattoo artists, stand-up comedians, graffiti artists, and even online pornographers have originated sets of social norms to govern their respective communities specifically in the absence of, and sometimes in opposition to, relevant IP law.[37]

In these cases of "substitute IP," there is a complex relationship between governance norms that guide production, appropriation, and re-combination of the relevant creative things, on the one hand, and group identity and membership, on the other. In some respects, commons governance serves as a guide to solving social dilemmas with respect to the objects of the group (producing and sharing magic tricks for magicians, or jokes for stand-up comedians) but also as a framework for constituting the group itself. Often, production of the intellectual resource (the recipe for the French chef) is not the subject of a social dilemma. The dilemma lies in coordinating distribution of and access to the resource among members of the group. The group or community is both the source and the product of norm-based governance as an emergent or "user-generated" phenomenon. It is not merely the case that magicians follow a sort of private, customary, and informal code with respect to the

[37] Much of the leading work in this area is collected in Aaron Perzanowski and Kate Darling (eds), *Creativity Without Law: How Communities and Markets Challenge the Assumptions of Intellectual Property* (NYU Press, forthcoming).

secrecy of their tricks. It is also the case that the identity of a magician is defined in part by participation in that code.[38]

In a related but distinct class of cases, the relationship between governance and group appears to be more direct. In these cases it appears more clearly that governance itself is the shared commons resource, rather than creative works or ideas or other forms of knowledge. Members of these groups are coordinating their respective responses to possible threats that they will suffer claims of IP rights infringement by third party rights holders and developing a shared governance norm as a result.

Since 2005 scholars at American University's Washington College of Law and Center for Media and Social Impact (formerly the Center for Social Media) have produced and published a series of Statements of Best Practices in Fair Use for a variety of creative communities. The purpose of each of these Statements is to identify and document a set of expectations and practices within specific communities that would guide their creative practice in avoiding unnecessary entanglement with potential liability for copyright infringement. In the context of US copyright law, the purpose is to provide a "soft" guide to fair use. The Statements are not negotiated with rights holders, and it is not intended that compliance with the guidelines in the Statements should be binding, as contractual obligations would be, should formal copyright disputes ever arise. The guides are predictions, grounded in relevant precedent, that, should a dispute later arise, conduct in conformity with the relevant Statement would also turn out to be persuasive to a judge. Creators are given some significant confidence before the fact that their creative practices are lawful, without clearing those practices with rights holders. There is hope but no promise that a future court would excuse accused infringement if the defendant alleged good faith compliance with one of these Statements.

The production of each of these Statements, intended as guides for non-lawyers, follows a similar path: partnership with entities and organizations that represent members of the relevant community; a lengthy series of interviews and meetings with members of the community to determine the community's own understanding of its interests and practices relative to the uses of copyrighted works; and preparation of documents and related materials that fix that understanding in writing,

---

38 Jacob Loshin, 'Secrets Revealed: Protecting Magicians' Intellectual Property without Law', in Christine A. Corcos (ed), *Law and Magic* (Carolina Academic Press, 2010).

with appropriate illustrations and guidelines, in the context of background copyright doctrine. The results are then published back to the community and otherwise distributed publicly. To date, the objects and subjects of these Best Practices Statements have included documentary filmmakers, producers of online video, media literacy educators, communication scholars, producers of open courseware, poets, dance archivists, research librarians, journalists, and librarians and archivists working with orphan works. This is an eclectic group of interests, and each project is time-consuming and labor-intensive.[39]

These Statements both comprise and reflect user-generated shared governance of a distinct sort. The members of a given community of practice are sharing their respective experiences with one another, not in order to produce new or more complex creative products but instead in order to construct a form of collective discipline that is possible only by virtue of that sharing. The shared social resource is governance relative to IP practice; the IP resources themselves are not necessarily social or shared. The Statements are also collective advocacy of a very concrete if unorthodox character. They seek not only to document existing practices within the group, but to create an aspiration, an ideal to which the members of the group might conform. In that sense, the Statements are commons-based law reform, or a kind of law themselves: rules and standards that not only emanate from and govern the group, but also rules and standards by which the group is willing to be judged by external authorities, in alignment with but distinct from the standards otherwise given by positive IP law. Those other authorities might include courts, as noted above, who might look to compliance with a Statement of Best Practices in determining whether or not an act of accused infringement should be excused as fair use. Those other authorities might include other institutional gatekeepers, such as Internet service providers or liability insurance carriers, which might rely on compliance with a Statement of Best Practices by a client, customer, or partner as evidence that doing business with that party would not pose an unnecessary risk.

Although some anecdotal evidence suggests that this shared governance has been successful, in the sense that relevant creative communities have benefited in terms of being able to produce additional creative work,[40] the Statements of Best Practices have not been free from debate. The claim that creative groups are normative, law-giving groups is

---

[39] The Statements are collected at http://www.cmsimpact.org/fair-use/best-practices (accessed January 20, 2016).

[40] See Patricia Aufderheide and Peter Jaszi, *Reclaiming Fair Use: How to Put Balance Back in Copyright* (University of Chicago Press, 2011); Pat

strengthened by evidence that creative communities are themselves normative in terms of being the *loci* of creative production.[41] It is also strengthened, curiously, by published skepticism of the Best Practices Statements.[42] Relevant content owners have been skeptical of the Statements on the ground that they are unilateral, rather than understandings negotiated bilaterally with copyright owners. Some scholars have expressed concern that the Statements tend to lock in backward-looking, customary practices[43] and crowd out the radical creator who is untethered to community norms. In both instances, critics would prefer that the Statements adopt a specifically descriptive perspective and avoid any connotation of normativity. In both instances, critics appear to prefer that governance be documented via bilateral and/or individual determination and adjudication with respect to individual intellectual resources, rather than collectively with respect to social intellectual resources. Critics resist the idea that the Statements carry the force of a kind of user-created law; the resistance itself highlights the governance power that the Statements exert. There is, to be sure, a kind of strength in numbers.

The purpose of this brief review of the Best Practices Statements is not to resolve the normative question but to point out in a preliminary way how these forms of governance may be analyzed using the knowledge commons framework, borrowing insights from the user-innovation literature and focusing specifically on law as a shared – and abundant – information resource. Further and more detailed exploration of this and

---

Aufderheide and Peter Jaszi, 'Fair Use and Best Practices: Surprising Success' (2007) *Intell. Prop. Today* 26.

[41] See Michael J. Madison, 'A Pattern-Oriented Approach to Fair Use' (2004) 45 *Wm. & Mary L. Rev.* 1525.

[42] The *Journal of the Copyright Society of the USA*, the leading professional journal of the American copyright law community, recently devoted an entire issue of the journal to papers assessing the Best Practices "movement." The symposium papers include Peter Jaszi, 'Getting to Best Practices – A Personal Voyage Around Fair Use' (2010) 57 J. *Copyright Soc'y U.S.A.* 315; Michael J. Madison, 'Some Optimism About Fair Use and Copyright Law' (2010) 57 *J. Copyright Soc'y U.S.A.* 351; Jennifer E. Rothman, 'Best Intentions: Reconsidering Best Practices Statements in the Context of Fair Use and Copyright Law' (2010) 57 *J. Copyright Soc'y U.S.A.* 371; Michael C. Donaldson, 'Fair Use: What a Difference a Decade Makes' (2010) 57 *J. Copyright Soc'y U.S.A.* 331; Jay Rosenthal, 'Best Practices' (2010) 57 *J. Copyright Soc'y U.S.A.* 389.

[43] The risk of locking-in normatively unattractive bargains over rights is described in James Gibson, 'Risk Aversion and Rights Accretion in Intellectual Property Law' (2007) 116 *Yale L.J.* 882.

other cases should, in time, produce better and generalizable knowledge about commons governance.

6. CONCLUSION

This chapter has highlighted the distinction between information abundance and information scarcity when considering the law and public policy governing intellectual resources, and it has argued that investigation of the information and knowledge landscape has been overly concerned with the latter, at the expense of the former. The result has been overemphasis of the tragedy of the commons story as a metaphor for social dilemmas regarding information and knowledge, an overemphasis on solving alleged problems of information and knowledge production and distribution, and an over-reliance on systems of IP rights as solutions to social dilemmas involving intellectual resources. Highlighting information and abundance, by contrast, leads to increasing attention to questions of coordination and combination with respect to the use and re-use of intellectual resources. Stories other than the tragedy of the commons may come to prominence; strategies of sharing rather than exclusion may take a prominent place in the policy makers' cupboard of institutional solutions. But the ultimate question is empirical rather than theoretical. How should social worlds make sense of the availability of lots of information, rather than too little?

Answering that question leads to the suggestion that the knowledge commons framework offers an important and useful research tool for investigating the institutional dynamics of specific contexts for sharing knowledge resources. In some cases, formal IP systems are appropriate and important pieces of the governance of knowledge and information. In other cases, formal IP systems are effectively irrelevant. In many cases, the question for research is the respective roles of IP and other governance mechanisms. Research from the field of user-innovation studies, and attention to the shared character of law itself as a knowledge resource, suggest productive ways in which coordination dilemmas can be highlighted and solved using knowledge commons strategies. Applying the knowledge commons framework to a robust set of case studies will, in time, yield better information.

Knowledge commons, or structured information sharing, does not operate on a simple uniform or standard principle. Research to date confirms as much.[44] And knowledge commons strategies are no more a panacea for social dilemmas concerning information and knowledge resources than are formal IP systems themselves. Applying the knowledge commons framework to a robust set of case studies will, in time, yield better guidance for designing and deploying effective commons governance in knowledge and innovation settings.

---

44 Brett M. Frischmann, Michael J. Madison and Katherine J. Strandburg, *Conclusion*, in Frischmann et al., note 8 above.

3. Collective agreements for the clearance of copyrights – the case of collective management and extended collective licences

Thomas Riis, Ole-Andreas Rognstad and Jens Schovsbo

1. COLLECTIVE AGREEMENTS

For many years copyright exclusivity has not only protected against direct copying of works but also against public performance and secondary uses of works. As a result, the mass use of music in radio and television, the photocopying of literary works in schools, or the provision of access to website material by public libraries all require the permission of the right holders (unless permitted by a specific limitation or exception).

For more than a century copyrights have been cleared through collective management organizations (CMOs) by means of collective agreements. Collective management of copyrights has proved to be mutually beneficial for copyright holders and users of copyrightable works. Mass use of copyrightable works (e.g. by a broadcaster) normally involves an extremely high number of copyrights which in practice are impossible to clear on an individual basis. Even if the broadcaster was able to identify the relevant right holders, the difficulties of contacting each right holder and negotiating an agreement would be insurmountable. Hence, a collective solution is needed. CMOs manage copyrights collectively on behalf of individual right holders. From the users' perspective the clearance of rights becomes much easier because users only need to contact and negotiate with one or a few parties (the CMOs), and from the right holders' perspective the CMOs facilitate the exercise of copyrights by pooling a large number of individual licences into one collective licence and then by monitoring the users of the copyrightable works and ensuring that the users comply with the licence. Basically, collective management of copyrights exploits economies of scale and scope in negotiating, monitoring and enforcing copyrights by reducing the transaction costs. The benefits of this process are assumed to be shared between the parties.

From a legal perspective, collectivization is fundamentally challenging because of the property right structure of copyright protection. The central piece of international copyright protection (viz. the Berne Convention from 1883) is based on a system of exclusivity.[1] Viewed through this lens, collective systems of rights administration which go beyond mere mechanisms for the administration of right holders' rights may be problematic. This position also has an ideological dimension which asserts that copyright law ought to facilitate individual transaction and the free exercise of choice by authors over the uses of their works. For this reason, collectivization is looked upon with some suspicion.

2. THE EMERGENCE OF CMOS

The need for collective solutions in the exercise of copyrights has a long history. The predecessor of modern CMOs came into existence in eighteenth-century France. The playwrights Pierre August Caron de Beaumarchais and Michel Jean Sedaine, in collaboration with the writer Jean-François Marmontel, conducted a campaign against the French theatres in order to make these theatres acknowledge and respect the authors' economic and moral rights in dramatic works. In 1777, this campaign resulted in the formation of the French copyright organization *Bureau de Legislation Dramatique* which worked as a political pressure group prior to and during the French Revolution. The work of the organization culminated in the Decree of 9 July 1791 according to which living authors were granted an exclusive right to the performance of works at public theatres. A new organization was formed with the purpose of collecting remuneration from the theatres on behalf of the individual authors. In 1829, the organization was merged with a similar organization and took on the name *Société des Auteurs et Compositeurs Dramatiques* (SACD), which became the first CMO in the modern

[1] Berne Convention for the Protection of Literary and Artistic Works, Art. 9(1), 24 July 1971, 25 U.S.T. 1341, 828 U.N.T.S. 221 (hereinafter Berne Convention) ("Authors of literary and artistic works protected by this Convention shall have the *exclusive right* of authorizing the reproduction of these works, in any manner or form") (emphasis added).

understanding of the term. While the 1791 Decree also granted performing rights to musical works, remuneration was not collected from concert organizers or other users who performed musical works publicly. A conflict between composers and users of musical works ensued and it came to a head in 1847 when the lyricist Alexandre Bourget and the composer Parizot brought action against the owner of the fashionable Café Concert "Ambassadeurs" in Paris for performing their works without paying remuneration. The action succeeded and prompted the formation of a CMO devoted to the management of performance rights for musical works, and subsequently in 1851 *Société des Auteurs, Compositeurs et Editeurs de Musique* (SACEM) was established.[2]

The development of the first CMOs demonstrates that the legal recognition of substantive and clearly defined copyrights is a prerequisite for the formation of institutions that exercise copyrights collectively. At the beginning of the nineteenth century, mass use of copyrightable works related to performances and hence the CMOs only managed performing rights. Since then, modes of exploitation have expanded and new CMOs have been formed to manage other rights. The right holders themselves have been (and remain) central stakeholders in the copyright-based industries and they have been the drivers for the formation of the organizations.[3]

Members of CMOs assign their rights to the organization, meaning that the organization is entitled to exercise the rights and that, by means of reciprocal representation agreements, a CMO is also entitled to exercise the rights of members from foreign sister organizations. However, while a network of reciprocal representation agreements assists functionality in some ways, adopting the traditional mode of collective management and adhering to the usual CMO processes creates one important limitation when it comes to clearing rights in an efficient manner: the CMO is not entitled to clear the rights of unrepresented right holders (i.e. rights holders who are not members of the CMO or another CMO covered by a reciprocal representation agreement). Irrespective of a valid collective licence, the users cannot be sure that all works and all right holders are covered by the licence agreement and hence that all relevant rights have

---

[2] Gavin McFarlane, *Copyright: The Development and Exercise of The Performing Rights* (John Offord, 1980), pp. 48 et seq, 56; and Martin Kretschmer, 'The Failure of Property Rules in Collective Administration: Rethinking Copyright Societies as Regulatory Instruments' (2002) *E.I.P.R.* 126, p. 127.

[3] See also Martin Kretschmer, 'The Failure of Property Rules in Collective Administration: Rethinking Copyright Societies as Regulatory Instruments' (2002) *E.I.P.R.* 126, p. 129.

been cleared. Consequently, the users run the risk of copyright infringement. Extended collective licences solve this so-called "outsider problem".

3. THE EXTENSION EFFECT (EXTENDED COLLECTIVE LICENCES)

The concept of an extended collective licence (ECL) originates in Nordic copyright law where it has been seen as an expedient means of clearing rights in regard to mass uses of copyrightable works.

The ECL is based on the notion that the copyright holder holds exclusive rights to the work and that this exclusive right sometimes, for practical reasons, will need to be managed collectively. Collective management will on the one hand presuppose an individual membership agreement between a right holder and the CMO and on the other hand an agreement between the CMO and a user. The special trait of the ECL is the "extension effect" which gives the collective management arrangement effect even for works of *right holders who are not members* of the CMO (or any organization that the CMO has entered into representativity agreements with). Thus, for these right holders the exclusivity rule is converted into a liability rule as a result of the combination of the collective agreement and the statutory provision triggering the ECL. Its intriguing structure lies in the fact that it is based on user involvement yet simultaneously involves a transformation of the legal norm from one based on exclusivity to a liability rule.

In order to function, the ECL model requires organizations (CMOs) which represent right holders. On behalf of their members CMOs enter into agreements with users of copyright protected works specifying the permitted use of the works and the applicable conditions. Due to the statutory provisions on the extended collective licences, the effects of the collective agreements are extended to the right holders who are not represented by the collective organizations. The ability to "represent" a right holder is crucial since it is that ability which enables the organization to rely on the extension effect. In order to understand this legal model a distinction must be made between the CMO/copyright user collective agreement and the statutory provision that provides the extension effect. The CMO is entitled to administer the rights of its members by means of individual assignments from authors, and it negotiates and enters into agreements with users. This is obviously a *user generated regulatory model* as opposed to the extension effect which does not have any user involvement. The user of the regulatory model (which in this case is the CMO) and the users of copyrightable works state in the collective agreement whether it shall be extended to unrepresented right holders. However, when the extension effect is activated – in some of the Nordic countries via governmental approval – the agreement is effective for other parties. It follows that – in regard to right holders who are not represented by the collective organizations – extended collective licences have the same effect as compulsory licences.[4]

As detailed elsewhere, ECLs function in different ways and there are major variations concerning central issues such as representativity, schemes of approval, distribution of remuneration, and the possibility of opting out. Consequently, "ECL" is not an unambiguous term that signifies a specific model of copyright clearance.[5]

Solving the outsider problem is the ECL's strength as well as its weakness. Its strength arises from enabling a more efficient clearance mechanism, while its weakness stems from the way it affects the exclusive nature of copyright and hence harms the legitimacy of the regulatory model.

The ECL model owes its effectiveness to a legislator's willingness to accept a third-party effect of the collective agreements entered into by representative CMOs. As a study in user generated law, the most striking feature of the ECL is that a voluntary collective agreement is given effect by means of law to persons who are not parties to the agreement.

4. EMERGENCE

4.1 The First ECLs

ECL rules were first introduced in the Nordic Copyright Acts in 1960–61.[6] Originally, they dealt only with broadcasting. The broadcasters

---

4 In the preparatory work that led to the Danish Copyright Act of 1961 where the first extended collective licence was introduced, the term "extended collective licence" (*aftalelicens*) was not used; instead the regulatory model was termed "a modified compulsory licence" (*modificeret tvangslicensbestemmelse*), *Folketingstidende* 1959-50, Tillæg A, sp. 2723.

5 Thomas Riis and Jens Schovsbo, 'Extended Collective Licenses in Action' (2012) 43 *I.I.C.* 930.

6 The honour of having invented the system is normally attributed to the Swedish law professor Svante Bergström who, according to Gunnar Karnell, 'Avtalslicenskonstruktionen, principiella och praktiska frågor' (1981) 50 *Nordiskt Immateriellt Rättsskydd* 255, used the term for the first time regarding copyright in Svante Bergström, 'Program för upphovsrätten', in *Rättsvetenskapliga studier*

faced the complex problem of clearing the innumerable rights involved in their broadcast. Prior to the introduction of ECLs to a certain extent the broadcasters entered into collective agreements with copyright organizations. However, apart from rights to musical works the collective agreements did not authorize using the work of authors who were not represented by the organizations (in particular, foreign authors). In some of the agreements, the copyright organization would indemnify the broadcasters against possible claims from unrepresented right holders. Nevertheless, large scale infringement was the result.[7] The broadcasters pushed for the introduction of a compulsory licence mandated by the Berne Convention. The authors were strongly against a compulsory licence that would deprive them of the entitlement to exclude users from using the works. The entitlement to exclude was considered an essential element of the authors' bargaining power vis-à-vis the broadcasters.[8] Additionally, the entitlement to exclude contained a moral dimension in cases where the author for some reason harboured regrets regarding particular uses of the work.

In 1939, the four Nordic governments convened a committee for the purposes of reviewing the Copyright Acts and proposing a new common copyright law. Due to the Second World War, the Committee did not deliver its report until 1951. During this process, the broadcasters asked for a compulsory licence. The Commission rejected a model based on compulsory licences since it believed that a compulsory licence would be an excessive encroachment on the rights of the authors. At this juncture, the Committee did not find that a great need for such a rule existed.[9] That position had changed by the end of the 1950s when all the Nordic governments seemed to agree on a need for legislative intervention.[10]

ägnad minnet av Phillips Hult (Almquist & Wiksell, 1960), p. 74. Bergström used the term *"utsträckt generellt tilstånd"* (p. 76) for what we here call "ECL-rules", and Bergström's version actually translates into "Extended Collective Licences". Svante Bergström was a copyright expert but also worked in the field of labour law, and in 1948 he wrote his doctoral thesis on "collective agreements" (*Kollektivavtalslagen, studier över dess huvudprinciper* (Almquist & Wiksell, 1948). In his 1960 publication, Bergström clearly stressed the importance of the building of authors' organizations and would seem to regard ECLs as an important part of such an endeavour.

[7] *Folketingstidende* 1959-50, Tillæg A, sp. 2722.

[8] Ole-Andreas Rognstad, 'Avtalelisenser' (2004) 73 *Nordiskt Immateriellt Rättsskydd* 152.

[9] "Udkast til lov om ophavsretten til litterære og kunstneriske værker", J.H. Schultz A/S, Copenhagen 1951, p. 89.

[10] *Folketingstidende* 1959-50, Tillæg A, sp. 2723.

The first ECL on broadcasting was a compromise solution that balanced the opposing views of the parties. It included an opt out provision for the benefit of the individual author, according to which an author was entitled to prevent the broadcast of his or her copyrighted work (both single or multiple works). Thus, the ECL was designed as a regulatory model that cleared all the relevant rights yet still, at least in principle, maintained the entitlement to exclude. On these terms, the relevant copyright organization could reject a proposed agreement in the process of negotiation. In addition, even after the establishment of a collective agreement, an individual right holder could prohibit a specific work from being broadcast. However, in practice the individual right holder's entitlement to exclude is questionable because usually the right holder will have no way of finding out that the work is going to be broadcast.[11]

The next area to be covered was photocopying in schools and by enterprises. The proposal to regulate this area using ECL rules was put forward in 1974 by the joint Nordic Copyright Committee[12] and this marked the beginning of a coordinated use of ECL rules as an integrated part of Nordic copyright law. The debate in the 1970s was fuelled by a need to "do something about" the explosion of photocopies in schools and it contains some interesting elements which would seem to illustrate the cultural background to ECLs in Nordic law. As such, the 1974 Committee considered carefully whether photocopying should be regulated by compulsory licences. This solution was rejected, however, with the remark that the Committee considered it as very likely that collective agreements would be set up by the organizations. Against this background, compulsory models were considered unnecessary for the job.[13] Therefore, the method of the legislator was to build on agreements and to use the Copyright Act to solidify these by dealing with the outsider problem via the "extension" component offered by the ECL agreement.

Since this time, ECL provisions have spread to other forms of mass use of copyrightable works. In the Nordic countries – with minor variations between the countries – they now cover the following areas:

---

[11] Felix Trumpke, 'The Extended Collective License – A Matter of Exclusivity' (2012) 82 *Nordiskt Immateriellt Rättsskydd* 264, p. 280.

[12] Upphovsrätt I – Fotokopiering och bandinspelning särskilt inom undervisningsverksamhet (Nordisk Utredningsserie 82–93 ((NU) 21/73, Stockholm 1974).

[13] Ibid., p. 82.

- reproduction within educational institutions or by business enterprises;
- digital reproduction by libraries;
- recordings of works in broadcasts for the visually impaired, etc.;
- reproduction of works of art which have been made public;
- broadcasts by certain national TV companies;
- broadcasts by certain national TV companies of works in their archives;
- cable retransmission to more than two connections; and
- "other forms of use" within specific areas covered by an agreement between an organization which represents a significant number of right holders and users (i.e. the "general" ECL rule).

The "general" ECL rule is particularly interesting, problematic and far-reaching.[14] The rule was introduced in Denmark in 2008; in Sweden in 2013; and then in 2015 in Norway. The discussions that led to the rule were set off by a debate on the need to find solutions for dealing with orphan works. A further, particularly important driving force was the need for a framework relating to the digitizing of the "cultural heritage" in libraries, museums and the public Danish broadcasting company ("DR"). The result, however, was a general rule which can be used as a "supplement" to the specific rules on ECLs and in all cases where right holders' organizations and users find the use of an ECL agreement to be helpful and can agree on such a solution and the terms for use. Due to this rule, access to ECLs has been opened completely and the decision regarding whether or not to operate an ECL has been left to the discretion of the organizations and users. As a consequence, all areas of copyright licensing which involve a multitude of right holders may fall prey to ECL agreements.

The collective agreements underlying ECLs constitute the actual copyright regulation of the sector covered by the agreement in question. As such, they epitomize user generated law.

4.2 Heterogeneous Demands

Statutory copyright includes a number of provisions (especially limitations on exclusive rights) which attempt to balance different needs and interests in various sectors and contexts. Apart from this, copyright law

---

[14] See Thomas Riis and Jens Schovsbo, 'Extended Collective Licenses and the Nordic Experience: It's a Hybrid but Is It a Volvo or a Lemon?' (2010) 33 *Colum. J. L. & Arts* 471.

does not provide much flexibility. An examination of the existing ECLs suggests that heterogeneous demands do exist for copyright regulation regarding mass use of works. A number of parameters may affect the content of a collective agreement such as the kind of use works are put to, the economic value of the use, and the nature of the user. For instance, the agreement granting a large commercial cable operator cable retransmission rights regulates a relation that is very different from the one where a public school is granted the right to use old examination papers for teaching purposes. Some of the narrow and specific ECLs based on the general ECL rule in the Danish Copyright Act do not even include a real obligation of payment but are simply put in place to clear copyright and make things work in the absence of any substantial economic value.

ECLs can be applied only to the use of copyrightable works within "a specified field"[15] or "delimited field",[16] which probably means that it is not possible to subject a broad and substantial part of copyright to an ECL. This statutory limitation on the scope of ECLs can be said to support the flexibility which is necessary for meeting the heterogeneous demands of users.

The dynamic at work is not singular: ECLs provide flexibility when it comes to different types of usage; yet ECLs do standardize conditions when it comes to the individual right holders. This does not differ from other forms of collective management of copyrights by means of blanket licences. A uniform pricing structure is inherent in a blanket licence, which means that licensing terms and pricing are identical for all works. This implies that in fact the most popular works subsidize the least popular works.[17] The owners of the rights to the most popular works are expected to find that the provisions of the collective agreement are not

---

[15] E.g. Danish Copyright Act, section 50(2).

[16] E.g. Swedish Copyright Act, section 42h, and Norwegian Copyright Act section 36(2).

[17] This feature of blanket licences led Cohen Jehoram to conclude that CMOs are the "great equalizers among rightowners": Herman Cohen Jehoram, 'The Future of Copyright Collecting Societies' (2001) 23 *E.I.P.R.* 134, p. 136. See also Christian Handke and Ruth Towse, 'Economics of Copyright Collecting Societies' (2007) 38 *I.I.C.* 937, p. 945; Martin Kretschmer, 'The Failure of Property Rules in Collective Administration: Rethinking Copyright Societies as Regulatory Instruments' (2002) 24 *E.I.P.R.* 126, p. 134; and Roger Wallis, Charles Baden-Fuller, Martin Kretschmer and Michael George Klimis, 'Contested Collective Administration of Intellectual Property Rights in Music. The Challenges to the Principles of Reciprocity and Solidarity' (1999) 14(1) *Eur. J. Comm.* 5, p. 15.

the optimal ones and hence would demand another regulatory model. The possibility of opting out would not put the right holder in a better position because in most circumstances opting out is only a theoretical and not a practical possibility (since collective management is the only practical means of exercising the rights). It is an inherent feature of all kinds of collective agreements that the provisions of the agreement must be determined on the basis of the aggregated interest of all the parties covered by the agreement. This implies that the collective agreement is not the optimal solution for all right holders but simply the best possible one for most.[18]

4.3 Expectation of Benefits

ECLs presuppose collective management of copyright (and, as noted previously, collective management of copyrights exploits economies of scope and scale in the exercise of copyrights by reducing transaction costs). The distinct feature of ECLs is that the collective management scheme is extended to unrepresented right holders.

The extension effect implies that more rights are able to be managed via this process than under collective management alone. For the right holders this means that a higher price can be claimed for the copyright licence. Conversely, the collected remuneration has to be shared between more right holders. Since the traditional function of CMOs is considered a natural monopoly, the CMO will enjoy benefits from economies by the increase in the scale of its operation.[19] For the user of the copyrightable works the extension effect reduces the legal risks since the user is shielded from claims initiated by unrepresented right holders.

The extent to which expectations are met depends on the performance of the CMOs. The monopoly character of CMOs entails a risk that they may misuse their market power to impose excessive prices on users or unreasonable costs on members. These concerns may to some extent be dealt with under competition law.[20] Yet since such monopolization risks are systemic to the CMOs (and because competition law provides only for a blunt and slow-working system for dispute resolution) an element of

[18] The complex issue concerning whose interests the CMO is representing is further dealt with below in relation to "asymmetric information".

[19] E.g. Thomas Riis, 'Collecting Societies, Competition, and the Services Directive' (2011) 6(7) *Journal of Intellectual Property Law & Policy* 482, p. 484.

[20] E.g. Jens Schovsbo, 'The Necessity to Collectivize Copyright – And Dangers Thereof', in Jan Rosén (ed.) *Individualism and Collectiveness in Intellectual Property Law* (Edward Elgar, 2012), p. 166.

control would normally also be internalized in the Copyright Acts to provide *inter alia* for *ex ante* authorization of CMOs or *ex post* dispute resolution models.[21] The need for such control is particularly pertinent for right holders who are not members of the CMO and as such do not have control (direct or indirect) over matters such as the distribution plan.

4.4 Asymmetric Information

ECLs outperform compulsory licensing in terms of solving the problem of asymmetric information possessed by the legislator/judiciary and the parties affected by the law. Compulsory licensing combined with collective management of copyrights will in theory provide an optimal solution in clearing copyrights. However, the legislator or the judiciary will have to determine the provisions of the licence and the size of the licence fee, and in practice will not possess adequate information to solve these tasks in an optimal way. When an ECL is used, the process of determining licence provisions and the licence fee is a negotiation between the parties. Since the negotiation is free, a concluded collective agreement will be considered beneficial to both parties.

In a collective agreement it is not possible for the CMO to accommodate the specific needs and interests of the individual right holders. The CMO negotiates and enters into agreements on behalf of *all* right holders. In that function it is essential to determine whose interests the CMO represents. The organization must be representative of authors of a certain type of work. In Denmark and Norway, representativity is ensured by requiring that the organization comprises of "a substantial number of authors of a certain type of works which are used in" Denmark/Norway.[22] In a Norwegian decision from 2011 the so-called Cable Dispute Tribunal (*Kabeltvistnemda*) found that "a substantial amount of right holders" implies a representativity rate at approximately 50%.[23] The Norwegian legislator has, however, recently emphasized that it was never the intention to require that a CMO must represent a majority (or

---

[21] E.g. Danish Copyright Act, sections 50 and 51 (English language version available at http://kum.dk/servicemenu/english/services/legislation/ (accessed 20 January 2016)). On the EU-level some element of control will also be required by Directive 2014/26/EU of the European Parliament and of the Council of 26 February 2014 on collective management of copyright and related rights and multi-territorial licensing of rights in musical works for online use in the internal market.

[22] Danish Copyright Act, section 50(1).

[23] Cable Dispute Tribunal's decision of 28 June 2011.

something near a majority) of right holders of a certain type of work used in Norway.[24] Rather, the requirement of "a substantial amount of rights holders" is relative and flexible and implies a discretionary assessment where various factors must be taken into consideration.[25] In Sweden and Finland the organization must represent a majority of right holders of a certain type of work used in these nations.

In theory a foreign organization can manage ECL schemes; but for all practical purposes the organizations which enter into ECL agreements are *national* organizations. One may ask whether a national organization is suitable to represent the interests of foreign right holders,[26] including deceased foreign right holders who are numerous when it comes to orphan works. Different interests and preferences exist between cultures, and the copyright-based markets can differ significantly from one country to another.[27] For ECLs this may also have implications for their ability to "represent" right holders, which may in turn challenge their authorization to rely on the extension effect. In this way, the ECL model contains a "self-destruction" mechanism which should in principle secure that the ECL is only workable in situations where the CMO is in fact in a position to possess information about the right holders' interests. This model might make good sense from an ideological perspective and it may also suit national settings involving the works of national authors; but it may also make the use of ECLs very difficult (impossible even) in situations where representativity is difficult to obtain. Notable, here, would be cases where foreign rights holders are in the majority.

In spite of these possible limitations affecting organizations' representativity, there are no apparent reasons to doubt that a freely negotiated agreement between a CMO and a user will be based on much more adequate information than a decision made by the legislator or the

---

24 See the commentaries to the proposal for a General ECL in Norway, Prop 69 L (2014–2015) 28.

25 Ibid., 29. See also Ole-Andreas Rognstad, 'Avtalelisens som nordisk løsningsmodell'(2012) 82 *Nordiskt Immateriellt Rättsskydd* 620, p. 627.

26 For some elaboration on this issue, see Gunnar Karnell, 'Outsiders' Rights: A Dilemma for Collective Administration of Authors' Rights in a Present and Enlarged European Community' (1991) 13 *E.I.P.R.* 431, p. 435.

27 In this vein, see Daniel Gervais, *Application of an Extended Collective Licensing Regime in Canada: Principles and Issues Related to Implementation, Study Prepared for the Department of Canadian Heritage 40* (June 2003), p. 19; who claims that in the Nordic countries, royalties are more often than not redistributed in accordance with a collective spirit and objective, through a method to which the right holders in any given category, or their associations, have agreed.

judiciary. It follows that asymmetric information is essential for the emergence of ECLs.

4.5 The Role of Lead Users

Historically speaking, collective management of copyrights is a process which has clearly relied upon lead users. As noted, this was evident from the outset when a number of prominent and popular French authors worried about how to collect fees for the performance of their works and *inter alia* formed organizations for that purpose. These authors share the same characteristics as lead users in von Hippel's theory on user innovation in the sense that they demonstrate a high level of innovative activity because they are the parties who expect to gain most from the new regulatory model.

While the concept of the lead user has great explanatory power in relation to the emergence of collective management of copyrights, the same cannot be said concerning the extension effect. The extension effect cannot be directly attributed to users. Rather, it has arisen from the combined efforts of a visionary law professor, from a culture of practices involving *inter alia* a high level of trust and a tradition for collective labour organizations, and from compromise-seeking governments. Yet indirectly there may be some involvement of users regarding the extension effect. Whereas in the first phase legislators relied on existing CMOs and tied ECLs to those, in the later phases they have sought to encourage the development of *new* CMOs in order to expand the range of the ECL model and thus of the extension effect. This development has reached its climax with the new "general" ECL rule which enables users to propose the use of an ECL in areas which can be defined in a sufficiently clear way and where a CMO is available. In this way, a complicated system based on feedback loops from the level of legislation to the level of self-governance has emerged. Here, the legislator constantly facilitates the enrolment of new "lead" users (see, also, section 6 below on the proactive use of ECLs).

5. DISSEMINATION

It is an essential part of an ECL's rationale that all rights to a certain form of use of copyrightable works can be cleared in one place – a one-stop-shop solution. Hence, users within the designated territory cannot copy the ECL because the whole of the territory is already covered.

Dissemination of an ECL can take place in multiple ways. First, it can be copied in other territories (which in practice would be equivalent to other jurisdictions). Second, it can be copied with the purpose of covering other forms of use. Third, it can be copied for other types of IPR (e.g. patents).

For patents, the ECL model might offer inspiration which is applicable to situations where access to certain technologies is necessary for a multitude of users (e.g. a standard *de jure* or *de facto*, or other upstream technologies). In such circumstances, patent holders may form communities – such as "patent pools" – to regulate access to the technology. Such communities are only competent to grant access to patents on a collective basis if the patent holders have transferred the right to do so to the pool. If one were to copy the ECL model to such an environment, the extension effect would imply that users would not only have access to the use of patents which have been transferred to the pool but also to patents which have not been transferred. Access to the use of such patents would have to be delimited to cover only "certain specific areas" (*ad modum* the "general" ECL rule). There are no examples of such uses. Some patent systems operate a system of "licences of right" in which patent holders may indicate their preparedness to grant licences in the patent register.[28] This practice may point in the direction of an ECL-like effect by allowing for some sort of *ex ante* access right. Yet for an extension effect to be introduced, the patent legislation would need to provide specific authorization. It is doubtful that the international patent law framework would allow for such a system, and consideration of the issue would depend on a reading of the three-step-test in TRIPS, Article 30. The mere fact that ECLs are permissible under the corresponding test in copyright law cannot by itself be taken to imply that the position in patent law would be the same.

External, comparable forms of disseminating legal innovation cannot be used unaltered for ECLs. The dissemination of ECLs must be modified to acknowledge that ECLs cannot be copied by the user alone. In addition, the legislator needs to copy the statutory provision that extends the binding effect of the collective agreement to unrepresented right holders, which is an essential feature of the ECL.

---

[28] E.g. Regulation (EU) No. 1257/2012 of the European Parliament and of the Council of 17 December 2012 implementing enhanced cooperation in the area of the creation of unitary patent protection, Art. 8.

5.1 Dissemination to Other Jurisdictions

While the ECL system is of Nordic origin, the model has attracted attention elsewhere. In the European Union, the ECL has long been accepted as being compatible with EU law. Pursuant to Article 3(2) of the Satellite and Cable Directive 1993,[29] Member States "may provide that a collective agreement between a collecting society and a broadcasting organization concerning a given category of works may be extended to right holders of the same category who are not represented by the collecting society". Moreover, recital 18 of the Infosoc Directive 2001[30] states that the Directive "is without prejudice to the arrangements in the Member States concerning the management of rights such as extended collective licences". In principle, this implies that ECLs may be provided for irrespective of the "exhaustive" list of exceptions and limitations permitted under the Directive. It is no secret that the Nordic countries were the driving forces behind these provisions and statements, and the fact that the ECL model has been tolerated by the EU legislator is not tantamount to the model being disseminated to the EU. Amid the discussions about mass digitization and orphan works in the EU in the early 2010s, the ECL model was proffered as a possible option. However, in its impact assessment on the cross-border online access to orphan works (2011), the EU Commission took significant steps toward rejecting ECLs as a solution on an EU level.[31] In this connection, under the Orphan Works Directive, the ECL was accepted as a national solution[32] (without the model being adopted as a way of dealing with orphan works on an EU-wide level).

Hence, while the ECL model has not been disseminated to the EU as such, it has been (or is likely to be) imported by certain Member States. In the United Kingdom, a general ECL scheme was introduced in 2014, following the 2013 revision of the Copyright, Designs and Patents Act 1988, which provided the basis for such a scheme.[33] Under these

---

29 Council Directive 93/83/EEC of 27 September 1993.

30 Directive 2001/29/EC of 22 May 2001.

31 COM (2011) 289 final, pp. 27–9.

32 Directive 2012/28/EU, recital 24: "This Directive is without prejudice to the arrangements in the Member States concerning the management of rights such as extended collective licences". See also Art. 1(5) of the Directive, which confirms that the Directive "does not interfere with any arrangements concerning the management of rights at national level".

33 Regulation No. 2014/2588 of 11 September 2014, in force 1 October 2014, available at http://www.legislation.gov.uk/uksi/2014/2588/pdfs/uksi_

regulations, the operation of an ECL scheme requires authorization from the Secretary of State responsible, and this authorization must specify the permitted use and the types of relevant work to which it applies.[34] The representation of the relevant licensing body in the type of relevant works must be "significant" and provisions must be made for opt out arrangements designed to protect the interests of right holders. In these ways, the ECL scheme under UK law resembles the Nordic general ECL model. The introduction of an ECL scheme has also been discussed in the Netherlands where the Institute of Information Law at the University of Amsterdam has delivered a report on ECLs as a solution to be used in the process of mass digitization. This report was commissioned by the Dutch ministries, and was based on a detailed analysis of the Nordic ECL rules.[35] Outside Europe, Malawi has introduced an ECL scheme to be used for certain educational purposes, while an ECL system has been proposed in China in connection with the use of musical and audio visual works for karaoke bars. Moreover, the ECL model has been a subject of prolonged interest and consideration in Canada (without being implemented in Canadian legislation as yet). Recently, too, the US Copyright Office has recommended legislation establishing an ECL option initially taking the form of a limited pilot programme for mass digitization in the US.[36]

5.2 Dissemination to Other Forms of Uses

The Nordic experience illustrates the expansion that is possible regarding ECL modes of exploitation. As noted above, the ECL model was initially launched as a solution to rights clearance problems in the broadcasting sector in the early 1960s once the medium of television had emerged. Since then, almost every bill for a revision of the Nordic Copyright Acts has contained provisions on new ECLs, from photocopying for educational purposes in the 1970s to mass digitization in libraries and archives in the 2000s. The development has culminated in the introduction of a general ECL designed to meet any demand for use of

---

20142588_en.pdf (accessed 20 January 2016). Cf. Copyright, Designs and Patents Act, sections 116B–116D.

[34] Regulation 2014/2588, sections 4(1), (2).

[35] Available at http://www.ivir.nl/publicaties/download/1471 (accessed 20 January 2016).

[36] See the report *Orphan Works and Mass Digitization*, June 2015, available at http://copyright.gov/orphan/reports/orphan-works2015.pdf (accessed 20 January 2016).

copyrighted works in new technological environments where individual right clearance is not likely to occur.

6. ADOPTION

In terms of their legal evolution, ECLs emerged in a distinct sequence. First came the organizations, then came the agreements, and only then came the "law" (in the form of the Copyright Act). From this perspective, an ECL can clearly be said to be adopted: a privately produced regulatory model is by means of statute elevated to cover all copyright clearances in a specific field, including rights owned by persons not party to the agreement.

Prima facie, the scenario described here resembles a *reactive* process where legislators have left a legal vacuum into which user generated law developed spontaneously. Subsequently, the user generated law was integrated into State-enacted law by the statutory provision on the extension effect. At the time when the first ECLs were adopted in 1960–61, some collective agreements designed to clear rights for broadcasting did exist, but the agreements fell far short of covering all the relevant rights. Comprehensive infringements took place and the right holders and the users of copyrightable works were not able to find a solution to that problem. The statutory ECL provision provided the solution. In this way, the user generated law was corrected by the legislator who actually broadened the autonomy space by expanding the scope of application of the collective agreements.

Once positive experiences had amassed regarding the functioning of ECLs, the process of adopting more statutory ECL provisions shifted from being reactive to *proactive*. This is most clearly illustrated by the adoption of the "general" ECL rule in section 50(2) of the Danish Copyright Act, section 42h of the Swedish Copyright Act, and section 36(2) of the Norwegian Copyright Act. In contrast to the other ECL rules, the general ECL rule was not adopted to solve a specific, existent problem. Instead, the function of the general ECL rule is to provide a legal framework for solving future problems of right clearance in cases of mass use of copyrightable works. The legislator has thus anticipated future needs for legal regulation to deal with mass uses of copyrightable works which remain unknown at this point.

The adoption of the general ECL rules has instituted the ECL model as a fall-back position throughout most of the areas covered by copyright law. This development clearly signals the enormous success of the ECL model in Nordic copyright law. There might also be signs, however, that the pendulum may have reached its extreme position and is beginning to swing back. In some of the areas covered by the ECL where access has been granted to use material on the internet, authorized access has been combined with user limitations dictating that only users with a national IP address may gain access. This provision arises because the relevant ECL has only cleared the necessary rights for use within the domestic territory. One example is the Norwegian site bokhylla.no, which offers access to more than 50,000 book titles digitized by the Norwegian National Library from its book collection on the basis of an agreement with the Norwegian right holders' organization Kopinor and the ECL for library uses. The site is only accessible for users with a Norwegian IP address. The extent to which such technological protection measures (TPMs) are practically effective and legally viable remains to be seen. The mere fact, however, that the ECL needs to be combined with TPMs (which is just another layer of user generated regulation) points to a general vulnerability of the ECL model regarding uses on the internet (i.e. uses which cannot be generally linked to the specified territory). It is tremendously difficult for the ECL model to provide for an international solution to trans-border uses because of the requirement of representativity. It is a simple fact that the use of copyright protected works is shifting towards online access and for this reason the traditional grounds covered by ECLs (notably broadcasts and photocopying) are being steadily eroded. It will be very difficult (impossible?) to apply and enforce ECLs in areas where no CMOs are in place which provide a practical and very substantial limitation on the prospective use of ECLs.

7. PERSPECTIVES AND IMPLICATIONS

The ECL system has served Nordic copyright well for the past 50 years and has helped make copyright "work" through periods of dramatic technological and legal changes. From photocopying in schools, to cable transmission, to the digitization of the archives of the public broadcasting organizations, to the use of orphan works, ECLs have been part of the solution. The attractiveness of the ECL has been that it offers the advantages of compulsory licensing while at the same time respecting the individual basis of copyright law. User involvement has been central to the success.

Collective rights administration is challenged by what can broadly be labelled "internationalization" and "individualization". The traditional CMOs (which are linked to specific territories and function under national laws) are having a hard time because works are increasingly being used online across physical borders in what the EU politicians would like to see as a "single market" for services.[37] The second challenge is brought about by the fact that users of protected works may gain access through individual contracts established directly with right holders or through membership agreements with new commercial providers such as Spotify or Netflix. Thus, substantial questions exist now as to whether the ECL model will continue to provide an attractive and efficient mechanism. These questions will only grow in the light of the upcoming challenges, in particular the issue of whether the element of user involvement provides the ECL model with an advantage or a disadvantage.

The ability of the CMOs to represent right holders is absolutely central to the ECL model. Ideologically, this is what distinguishes it from a compulsory licence model. Legally, the extension effect hinges on it. If a CMO ceases to be able to represent right holders, it simply becomes impotent and cannot negotiate contracts with users regarding non-members. Yet the ability of CMOs to represent is being steadily eroded by the two factors indicated above. *Internationalization* is making it harder for national CMOs to represent the right holders whose works are actually being used. This development may to some extent be delayed by measures such as relying on TPMs to restrict access from outsiders; but clearly such endeavours will not be able to hold back the tide. The process of *individualization* is also problematic. Politically, the acceptance of collective models for rights administration has always been considered a "second best" approach (with the best model being individual agreements). Until now, individual licensing has not been feasible for many situations involving mass use. This is changing; and the push towards individual models will no doubt continue. Today, music and films are available through online services. Tomorrow, it will be books. In such an environment, where users will increasingly have an alternative to collective rights administration, the willingness of the legislator to support collective licensing might soon evaporate. Furthermore, like the artists of the 1860s, today's *lead users* – high profile authors and composers – will not sit idly by if they find that the present collective structures do not provide them with the benefits they are able to secure for themselves individually.

The "double crunch" from internationalization and individualization will put all collective rights management models under pressure. It is a

---

[37] E.g. *A Digital Single Market Strategy for Europe*, COM(2015) 192 final, Brussels, 6 May 2015.

fundamental challenge to the system that the ability to represent cannot be instituted by legislation. An influential user's decision to join a CMO may become increasingly contingent and uncertain, yet the long-term ability of this CMO to deliver under the ECL very much depends on right holders joining. Hence, the whole structure is very vulnerable to changes in user behaviour.

User behaviour is also vital to the effective governance of CMOs. The Nordic CMOs acting under the ECL have been remarkably effective in the sense that hardly any conflict has arisen during the many years the system has been operating. Seen from a political point of view, the ability of the CMOs to "make copyright work" has played a major part in the success of the model. The period from the 1960s until now has been characterized by a constant expansion of copyright's legal and economic reach. The rewards have been constantly growing. This fact may partly explain why the Nordic experiences with the ECL have been so apparently harmonious: there have been relatively few problems to fight about. In the future, this will change for the reasons explained above. We expect that the user involvement will make it difficult for a CMO to adapt to negative changes. First, the right holders may "vote with their feet" and effectively erode the legitimacy of the CMO (and in turn its ability to rely on the extension effect). Second, the smooth functioning of the CMO depends on the willingness of the members to behave loyally and accept compromises for the sake of the common good. Altering revenue streams from one type of use (say photocopying) to another (say online) may therefore create tensions when new distribution keys have to be decided upon. Since users are (by definition) involved because they expect to secure some benefit for themselves, any organizational inability to constantly optimize *their* benefits could be problematic. Finally, shifts in the established patterns for revenue and distribution would also accentuate difficulties faced by any institution, not least user-driven ones: viz. the problem of controlling the biases and vested interests of incumbent users vis-à-vis new users; and controlling biases harboured by the institutions themselves vis-à-vis their members? For users, the issue of nationality has been hinted at above and will no doubt become more acute. Yet we should not overlook the self-interested stake an organization may have in preserving the market conditions (i.e. market failures) on which their business model is based. CMOs would, for instance, find it hard to actively promote individual licensing models at the expense of collective ones, or cross-border licensing at the expense of national licensing, despite the general interest in such models.

The anticipated challenges CMOs must face stemming from internationalization and individualization may indicate that user-driven models are generally vulnerable to changes affecting the underlying assumptions upon which they were founded (i.e. that individual licensing is not possible). The foundational user-driven solution may also be vulnerable (based, as it has been, on organizations which represent *the* users). These problems would seem to be accentuated in the ECL system, where the legislator has been so actively involved and where the "jewel in the crown" – i.e. the extension effect – can only be provided by legislation. Until now, the ECL system has been a happy marriage which has brought together the best of both worlds: the dynamics of user involvement based on individual decisions and the effectiveness of the *erga omnes* effect flowing from legislation. What has probably been overlooked thus far is that the combination has also combined some of the weaknesses. The challenges of internationalization and individualization affect the representativity of the CMOs, and a decrease in the degree of representativity harms the ability of the CMOs to conclude efficient collective agreements in a market setting and also harms the legitimacy of the operations of the CMOs. Securing the ability of the CMOs to represent users is beyond the competences of the legislator.

8. CONCLUSION

CMOs and ECLs provide prime examples of user generated law in action. The CMO system "emerged" in eighteenth-century Paris on the initiative of visionary lead users when new uses of their works led to a breakdown of the statutory model based on individual rights management. Later, legislation through the ECL system "adopted" the user-driven model and used legislation to reinforce it with the "extension effect" that enables organizations to make binding contracts with users (also concerning right holders who are not members).

The expectation of benefits is an important element for right holders when they decide on the mode of rights management. The underlying factors that determine whether the expectations of users are best met by collective rights administration or by individual administration are not constant. Growing opportunities to contract individually may be turning the tide against the collective models. Due to the requirement of representativity, the ECL system "self-destructs" if right holders opt out of the organizations or if users shift to using material that is not easily representable by a CMO. This is taking place already and the tendency is likely to increase.

The ECL model has been "disseminated" within the Nordic copyright systems and exported to other jurisdictions. However, the scope for further dissemination of ECLs in Scandinavia is arguably exhausted and the prospects for dissemination in other jurisdictions are likely to be limited due to the lack of certain preconditions for the establishment of an ECL system: namely, a high level of trust and a tradition for collective organization.

Technology creates new forms of usage and provides new means for rights clearance. In order to make copyright work, new answers to an abiding question must be found in the coming years: what benefits might CMOs offer to users in the modern world? It may transpire that the strength of the past (in the form of users' involvement) turns out to be an Achilles heel for the system as we know it. The viability of the requirement of representativity is being eroded in the light of trans-border uses of works, and it remains to be seen whether new, trans-border user communities will evolve.

4. Emerging models for cross-border online licensing

Sebastian Felix Schwemer

1. INTRODUCTION

Since the early 2000s when players outside the traditional music ecosystem started to commercialise new forms of digital distribution, the consumption of creative content has rapidly shifted over to Internet-based services. In response to consumers' demand for modern and more convenient forms of consuming entertainment – all enabled by faster Internet connections – digital service providers like Spotify, YouTube or SoundCloud have made interactive on-demand streaming the main form of music consumption via the Internet.[1] In Denmark, a recent assessment showed that streaming accounted for as much as 58.5% of all revenues from recorded music, and in Norway the figure was 77%.[2]

Concurrently, the traditional picture of national exploitation of copyright has changed. The licensing of novel uses of copyright-protected materials from right holders and their organisations has been described as anything but smooth. It appears that traditional licensing mechanisms and arrangements have not always been able to facilitate right-clearance in the changed environment. In the previous chapter, various aspects of the collective management of copyright were examined, including the traditional rationale of reducing transaction costs of collective management

[1] YouTube was founded in 2005; Spotify dates back to 2006; Deezer, Grooveshark and SoundCloud launched in 2007. In 2012, the European Commission counted more than 300 music streaming services available in the EU.

[2] The numbers refer to 2014 (Denmark) and the first half of 2014 (Norway) respectively. See http://www.ifpi.dk/?q=content/fortsat-v%C3%A6kst-i-dansk-musik; http://www.ifpi.no/flere-nyheter/item/67-halvarsstatistikk-2014 (accessed 20 January 2016).

organisations (CMOs).[3] In the digital world, some of these economic rationales for collective administration have been questioned.[4]

New licensing arrangements and entities have emerged: sometimes influenced or accompanied by regulatory action and sometimes not. In the EU, restrictions that prevent multi-territorial licensing (which means the licensing of music that covers more than one jurisdictional territory at a time) are a focal point for policymakers and scholars.[5] The European legislator has been observing the area for at least 20 years.[6] In this period, various institutional actors (such as different Directorate Generals within the European Commission) have taken action. Recently, the facilitation of licences even spearheaded the EU Commission's Digital Agenda as "Action 1" where the cross-border licensing dimension attracted the legislator's special attention and culminated in the adoption of Directive 2014/26/EU on collective management of copyright and

---

[3] A collecting society (now commonly referred to as a "collective management organisation" within the EU) is defined in Art. 3 lit (a) of Directive 2014/26/EU as an organisation which is authorised by law or by way of assignment, license or any other contractual arrangement to manage copyright or rights related to copyright on behalf of more than one right holder, for the collective benefit of those right holders, as its sole or main purpose, and which fulfils one or both of the following criteria: (i) it is owned or controlled by its members; (ii) it is organised on a not-for-profit basis. Given the different shades between the national CMOs, the Directive does not refer to the level of solidarity or regulation as characteristics.

[4] See e.g. Josef Drexl, 'Competition in the Field of Collective Management: Preferring "Creative" Competition to Allocative Efficiency in European Copyright Law', in Paul Torremans (ed.), *Copyright Law, Handbook of Contemporary Research* (Edward Elgar, 2007), p. 261; or Ariel Katz, 'The Potential Demise of Another Natural Monopoly: New Technologies and the Administration of Performance Rights' (2006) 2(2) *Journal of Competition Law and Economics* 245.

[5] Lucie Guilbault, 'The Draft Collective Management Directive', in Irini Stamatoudi and Paul Torremans (eds), *EU Copyright Law: A Commentary* (Edward Elgar, 2014), p. 698, e.g., notes that a significant portion of royalties derives from non-domestic repertoire, which makes the facilitation of multi-territorial licences an important issue. The increasing demand for cross-border access and licensing solutions for different content types has also been one topic of the EU Commission Copyright Consultation 2014.

[6] See e.g. European Commission, Green Paper, *Copyright and Related Rights in the Information Society*, COM(95) 382 final, 71 (19 July 1995).

related rights and multi-territorial licensing of rights in musical works for online use in the internal market (hereinafter "CRM Directive").[7]

According to the user generated law framework, "law that accommodates the needs of the knowledge society" is characterised by (1) flexible norms (2) with cross-border scope and (3) which are industry- and subject-specific. This chapter revisits the developments in the field with regard to licensing arrangements and tests whether the user generated law methodology can construe the emerging legal regulatory (based on contracts and laws) and non-regulatory models (based on technology and social norms). The history of these cross-border licensing models can to a large extent be seen as interplay between regulatory activity and private mechanisms. This is also the area of interplay that this chapter will focus upon.

First, the chapter examines the emergence of cross-border licensing models for online use, revisiting the distinct phases of model contracts, multi-territorial mono-repertoire licensing entities, licensing hubs, and the most recent forms of licensing and related regulatory activities. In its second part, the chapter analyses how well these developments accord with the user generated law methodology. Does the example of online licensing pass all phases of the theoretical model? Why have the licensing arrangements been created in the first place? Do determinants from the methodological model have an influence on the emergence of the specific user generated law? The chapter concludes with some broader observations on the applicability of the user generated law model.

2. EMERGING LICENSING MODELS – STOCKTAKING AND OUTLOOK

2.1 Model Contracts as User Generated Law – Competition Concerns and Soft Law

Traditionally, mass uses of copyright protected works have been confined to the territory of specific countries. Right holders assign the management of their rights to the respective national collective management

[7] Directive 2014/26/EU consists of two major parts: the first part establishes a governance and transparency framework for all collective management organisations. The second part establishes a set of rules specifically for multi-territorial licensing of music for online use by author CMOs.

organisation (CMO).[8] In order to offer licences for a wider repertoire covering global (non-domestic) repertoire, CMOs have entered into a complex network of so-called reciprocal representation agreements (RRAs) with each other.[9] Hereby, along with its own national repertoire, a CMO obtains the right to license the repertoire of the CMOs with which it has a bilateral arrangement. As such, the traditional arrangement has revolved around national monopoly one-stop-shops which have licensed the entire world music repertoire for use in the respective domestic territories.[10]

Back in the 1970s, the European Commission did not have concerns regarding CMOs' practices "of restricting their activities to delimitated administration territories and of concluding representation agreements to national one-stop-shop".[11] In the early 2000s, the CMOs' umbrella organisations developed two standard agreements which amended pre-existing agreements.[12] These model contracts aimed at enabling licensees to obtain a licence for online exploitation of the worldwide repertoire from their national CMO. This time, however, soon after the two standard agreements were reached, the Directorate General Competition of the European Commission (DG COMP) expressed competition concerns regarding a customer allocation clause contained in both agreements –

---

[8] See e.g. A. Capobianco, 'Licencing of Music Rights: Media Convergence, Technological Developments and EC Competition Law' (2004) *E.I.P.R.* 113, 114; Thomas Riis, 'Collecting Societies, Competition, and the Services Directive' (2011) 6 *Journal of Intellectual Property Law & Practice* 482; Violaine Dahin, 'The Future of Legal Online Music Services in the European Union: A Review of the EU Commission's Recent Initiatives in Cross-Border Copyright Management' (2010) 32(5) *E.I.P.R.* 223; or Tilman Lüder, 'The First Experience with EU-Wide Online Music Licensing' (2007) *GRUR Int.* 649.

[9] This remains the norm. See e.g. Directive 2014/26/EU, recital 40. See also: Dahin, note 8 above, p. 223; and Lucie Guilbault and Stef van Gompel, 'Collective Management in the European Union', in Daniel Gervais (ed.), *Collective Management of Copyright and Related Rights* (Kluwer Law International, 2010), p. 135.

[10] Peter Gyertyánfy, 'Collective Management of Music Rights in Europe After the CISAC Decision' (2010) *I.I.C.* 60.

[11] Ibid., p. 69, pointing towards the first GEMA decision of 2 June 1971.

[12] These were: the Santiago Agreement covering the rights of online public performance (by the author societies' umbrella organisation, CISAC); and the Barcelona Agreement covering digital reproduction (issued by the mechanical collecting societies' umbrella organisation, BIEM).

despite its support for the underlying one-stop-shop principle.[13] The agreements have not been renewed and concluded respectively. In proceedings related to the Online Music Recommendation (see below), stakeholders pointed towards the difficulty of reconciling the digital ubiquitous nature of the Internet with traditional RRAs which did not foresee that CMOs would grant licences beyond their home territory.[14]

The CISAC proceedings dealt with model law and the systematic delineation of territory, too.[15] In reviewing a process which dated back to a complaint in 2000, the DG COMP assessed RRAs between 24 European author-CMOs based on a CISAC model contract.[16] In its decision from 2008, the Commission took the standpoint that a series of aspects, including membership and territorial restrictions incorporated in the RRAs concluded between the CMOs, constituted infringements of competition rules under Article 101 TFEU.[17] The defendant CMOs were obliged to strictly bilaterally renegotiate their representation agreements.[18] Almost all CMOs appealed the decision, and in 2013 the General Court partially annulled the DG COMP's decision, yet only in respect of the question of whether the CMOs had engaged in concerted action – not in respect of membership and exclusivity clauses.[19]

Beyond its assessments concerning competition law, the European Commission has also sought to scrutinise multi-territorial licensing from a Single Market perspective. In 2004, having observed the collective management of copyright for several years, a Communication was issued

---

[13] European Commission, Notification of cooperation agreements (Case COMP/C-2/38.377 – BIEM Barcelona Agreements) (2002/C 132/10) and European Commission, Notice published pursuant to Article 27(4) of Council Regulation (EC) No. 1/2003 in Cases COMP/ C2/39152 – BUMA and COMP/ C2/39151 SABAM (Santiago Agreement – COMP/C2/38126) (2005/C 200/05). See European Commission, Press Release IP/04/586 of 3 May 2004.

[14] Lüder, note 8 above, p. 655.

[15] For a comprehensive overview on CJEU case law on representation agreements prior to 2008, see Gyertyánfy, note 10 above, p. 67f.

[16] In 2000, RTL filed a complaint against the German CMO GEMA because it had requested a pan-European multi-repertoire licence which had been rejected by GEMA on the grounds that it only held multi-repertoire for Germany. In 2003, Music Choice Europe (MCE) filed a complaint against the umbrella organisation, CISAC, claiming that the model standard contract was a concerted practice to avoid competition between CMOs.

[17] Cf. Commission Decision of 16 July 2008 Case COMP/C-2/38.698 – CISAC, [2008] OJ C 323/12.

[18] See Gyertyánfy, note 10 above, p. 73.

[19] Case T-442/08 *CISAC v European Commission*.

stating that "more common ground on several features of collective management is required" in order to achieve the Single Market.[20] The Commission opted for a soft law instrument, and in May 2005 published its Recommendation 2005/737/EC on collective cross-border management of copyright and related rights for legitimate online music services. Aiming to introduce competition both up- and downstream, it advocated the introduction of multi-territorial licences and stipulated that right holders should have the right to assign the management of their online rights necessary to operate online music services to a CMO of their choice, irrespective of the residence or the nationality of either the CMO or the right holder (Article 3).[21]

Drexl (2007) notes that in utilising this model the Recommendation opted for a "totally new system of direct licensing without relying on reciprocal representation agreements"[22] instead of recommending a system similar to the IFPI/Simulcasting model for RRAs.[23] Academics and various stakeholders have criticised the Commission's approach and the consequences it had regarding the licensing practice.[24]

---

[20] Cf. European Commission, *Communication from the Commission to the Council, the European Parliament and the European Economic and Social Committee, The Management of Copyright and Related Rights in the Internal Market*, COM(2004) 261 final, 19 (16 April 2004).

[21] Lüder, note 8 above, p. 656. See also Sebastian Felix Schwemer, 'The Licensing of Online Music Streaming Services in Europe', in Richard Watt (ed.), *Handbook of the Economics of Copyright: A Guide for Students and Teachers* (Edward Elgar, 2014), p. 152.

[22] Drexl, note 4 above, p. 280.

[23] The situation for simulcasting or webcasting (i.e. non-interactive broadcasting of musical works via the Internet) is somewhat special and outside the scope of this chapter. It is, however, noteworthy that the fear of competition by means of price dumping was not shared. RRAs regarding the licensing of the related rights of phonogram producers did not contain an economic residence clause thus enabling competition between CMOs; the European Commission thus granted an antitrust exemption (European Commission, Decision of 8 October 2002 relating to a proceeding under Article 81 of the EC Treaty and Article 53 of the EEA Agreement (Case COMP/C2/38.14 – IFPI "Simulcasting") (2003/300/EC)).

[24] For instance, Drexl, note 4 above, argues that the Recommendation focuses on output and price in terms of a static competition model "without taking into account the purpose of copyright to promote creativity and cultural diversity".

2.2 Emergence of Multi-Territorial Mono-Repertoire Direct Licensing

At the beginning of 2006, the licensing landscape began to change fundamentally when a major music publisher withdrew its mechanical rights for the online use of its Anglo-American repertoire from the respective national CMOs.[25] Instead, it enshrined its rights in customised licensing entities that use a direct licence model for a single repertoire on a multi-territorial basis.[26]

The other major publishers and several independent publishers followed suit with similar models which appointed their rights to new licensing entities or CMOs as exclusive or non-exclusive agents. Interestingly, the newly formed entities were in several instances formed as subsidiaries of major European CMOs. Guilbault and van Gompel (2010) point out that this process may have been negotiated at the expense of smaller CMOs.[27] Most importantly, these developments meant a further fragmentation of repertoire.[28] As a result, national CMOs could no longer grant licences for the entire global repertoire. Instead, a licensee was required to obtain licences both from the national CMO and via the mono-repertoire licensing arrangements.[29]

Yet the phenomenon of multi-territorial licensing remains inextricably intertwined with mono-territorial licensing (i.e. licensing for only one

---

[25] CELAS (Central European Licensing and Administration Services) was a licensing agency jointly owned by the German and British CMOs GEMA and PRS for Music. CELAS provided a one-stop-shop for the repertoire of EMI Music Publishing for online exploitation. In 2014, Sony/ATV Music Publishing, PRS for Music and GEMA launched a new joint venture called SOLAR – a one-stop-shop for the Sony/ATV and EMI music publishing licensing catalogue. This followed the acquisition of EMI Music Publishing by Sony in 2012. SOLAR replaced the CELAS and PAECOL licensing systems. For a more detailed overview, see Schwemer, note 21 above, pp. 154–5.

[26] Giuseppe Mazziotti, 'New Licensing Models for Online Music Services in the European Union: From Collective to Customized Management' (2011) Columbia Public Law Research Paper No. 11-269, uses the term 'customized' collective rights management. V. Dehin, 'The Future of Legal Online Music Services in the European Union: A Review of the EU Commission's Recent Initiatives in Cross-Border Copyright Management' (2010) 32(5) *European Intellectual Property Review* 220, p. 228 refers to it as the "new rights managers model".

[27] Cf. Guilbault and van Gompel, note 9 above, p. 161.

[28] See e.g. Riis, note 8 above, p. 482.

[29] In 2012, the European Commission estimated that approximately 30 licences are needed in order to clear author rights for a pan-European service.

country).[30] Musical works often have several authors and may be published by more than one publisher.[31] These split copyrights mean that it is sometimes not sufficient to clear rights with only one right holder in order to cover a single song (see also recital 37 of Directive 2014/26/EU). Ultimately, from the online service providers' and consumers' perspective, the aggregation of a global repertoire is the major concern, as the European Parliament's Committee on Legal Affairs points out.[32] The fragmentation of rights, right holders and repertoires is at the core of high transaction costs.[33]

The development of these novel direct licensing arrangements must be seen in the context of the two actions taken by the EU Commission which sought to foster multi-territorial licensing of music rights for the Internet: the CISAC proceedings and Recommendation 2005/737/EC.[34] The European legislator reflects in recital 39 of Directive 2014/26/EU that the Recommendation has not been sufficient to encourage the widespread multi-territorial licensing or to address the specific demands.[35] Guibault (2014) concludes that the "majority of scholarly commentators, policymakers and stakeholders agree that the intention behind the Recommendation of fostering competition between individual collective management organisations has created chaos rather than anything else".[36]

It is interesting to note that the European legislator has chosen not to apply the rules of the CRM Directive to mono-repertoire licensing entities. If such entities represent only a single right holder, they fall outside the scope of the definitions of Article 3 lit. m of Directive 2014/26/EU.

---

30 See also Schwemer, note 21 above.

31 Gyertyánfy, note 10 above, p. 65.

32 Guilbault, note 5 above, p. 770, citing Working Document COM(2012)0372-C7-9183/2012 – 2012/0180(COD) (4 March 2013).

33 KEA European Affairs, *Licensing Music Works and Transaction Costs in Europe*, Final study (September 2012), p. 51.

34 Gyertyánfy, note 10 above, refers to Munich District Court LG München No. 7 O 4139/08 of 25 June 2009 – *MyVideo v Celas* at 11.

35 While a Recommendation is a soft law tool, it is taken into account by the CJEU when interpreting the acquis communitaire.

36 Guilbault, note 5 above, p. 763. Gyertyánfy, note 10 above, p. 85, for example, states that the "Commission successfully demolished an essential element of collective management – in exchange for very few competition law advantages".

2.3 Licensing Hubs Formed by Author CMOs

More recently, new influences have appeared in the online music licensing ecosystem: several collective management organisations have joined forces and formed so-called "licensing hubs" with the aim of providing a one-stop-solution for acquiring licences for online use of music.

These licensing hubs differ from the mono-repertoire multi-territorial direct licensing entities (see section 2.2 above) in terms of the repertoire they license: a licensee can acquire a multi-territorial licence for the joint repertoire of all the CMOs taking part in the respective hub model (multi-territorial, multi-repertoire).

The emergence of these hubs began as early as 2007, when the Spanish, French and Italian author-CMOs (SGAE, SACEM and SIAE respectively) announced their joint one-stop-shop licensing platform Armonia. While officially formed as a European Economic Interest Grouping (EEIG) in 2013, this hub actually licensed its first deal in November 2012.[37] Several other CMOs joined the hub, which currently covers repertoires of SACEM (France and Luxembourg), SGAE (Spain), SIAE (Italy), SPA (Portugal), SABAM (Belgium), Artisjus (Hungary), SUISA (Switzerland) and a bulk of Anglo-American and Latin-American works.[38] The German, Swedish and British societies GEMA, STIM and PRS for Music have announced a similar initiative, which has recently been approved by the European Commission in an investigation under the EU Merger Regulation.[39] Since 2009, the Nordic and Baltic States have had a cooperation model in place which allows users to obtain a licence covering mechanical reproduction and performance rights for online exploitations from a single source for the respective territories. In this set-up, Nordisk Copyright Bureau (NCB), which is owned by the Nordic author-CMOs, acts as a single entry point for the licensee but does not hold the respective rights.

This trend towards licensing hubs of CMOs can partially be seen in the context of the licensing regime that Directive 2014/26/EU proposes with the aim of facilitating the re-aggregation of rights for online use. In the

---

[37] Schwemer, note 21 above, p. 159.

[38] See Armonia press release, available at http://www.armoniaonline.eu/release/SUISAjoinsEN.pdf (accessed 20 January 2016).

[39] See http://www.musicweek.com/news/read/prs-partners-with-gema-and-stim-for-combined-licensing-hub/055064 (accessed 20 January 2016). European Commission, Press Release IP/15/5204 of 16 June 2015 in Case M.6800 – PRSfM/STIM/GEMA/JV.

preparatory work for the Directive, the European legislator opted for a model referred to as the European Licensing Passport. While the notion of a passport model was dropped in the final Directive, the legislator kept the basic idea, now enshrined in Articles 24 and 30 of Directive 2014/26/EU. Entities, which must fulfil certain minimum requirements, are expected to aggregate repertoire for multi-territory licensing. Local uses, on the other hand, would still be licensed by the national collective management organisation. As I have pointed out earlier, the European Commission expects that by encouraging the voluntary aggregation of music repertoire, the number of licences a user needs to obtain in order to operate a multi-territorial service shall be reduced.[40]

Thus, the legislator has further narrowed the autonomy space in which CMOs operate. The CRM Directive must be implemented by the Member States by April 2016. The re-aggregation is mainly based on voluntary actions by CMOs and it is still too early to predict whether the licensing hub model will be more broadly used and lead to the predicted market consolidation.

2.4 Towards New Players and (Even More) Direct Licensing?

As noted, the market for online licensing is under transition. There have been several recent controversies, where right holders either have chosen not to license their content catalogue for online exploitation by music streaming services or have pulled their catalogue. Besides the question of whether streaming constitutes a substitute for other forms of consumptions,[41] royalty rates have been a key concern. Right holders have expressed their discontent with the negotiations led by the CMOs to which they have transferred their rights for exploitation. In a context characterised by increased transparency and technical means (namely backend software and reporting standards), academics, right holders and users pose the question as to whether traditional collective management organisations are the most efficient means of licensing content.[42]

---

[40] European Commission, Impact Assessment 2012, 163. Recital 24 of the proposed Directive. Schwemer, note 21 above, p. 157.

[41] For an economic analysis, see Godefroy Dang Nguyen, Sylvain Dejean and François Moreau, 'Are Streaming and Other Music Consumption Modes Substitutes or Complements?' (2012), available at http://ssrn.com/abstract=2025071 (accessed 20 January 2016).

[42] For a discussion of the traditional rationales for collective management in the digital era, see Katz, note 4 above.

In the United States, a new player called Global Music Rights (GMR)[43] is aiming to take on music publishing incumbents for performance rights. Through direct licensing of selected popular songwriters, the licensor aims to negotiate higher royalties than the counterparts BMI and ASCAP. This leverage exists, for example, because GMR can refuse permissions regarding its songs, while the incumbents are highly regulated and need to offer blanket licences.[44] While this specific example has to be seen in the context of the US ecosystem, it seems reasonable to consider whether similar developments would be possible in Europe.

The CRM Directive opens up for direct licensing in respect to multi-territorial licensing under certain conditions in order to prevent a national repertoire lock-in. Article 31 of Directive 2014/26/EU regulates that right holders can withdraw their online rights in musical works from traditional CMOs so as to grant multi-territorial licences for their online rights in musical works themselves or through any other party they authorise or through any collective management organisation complying with the provisions of the Directive. Right holders do not have to withdraw those rights from their CMO for the purpose of mono-territorial licensing. Guibault (2014) notes the critique expressed by the CMOs umbrella organisation GESAC, which argues that the direct licensing possibility in Article 31 contradicts the principle of exclusivity in the assignments of rights in favour of the initial CMO.[45]

In Article 3 lit (b) the legislator also introduced the new notion of "independent management entities".[46] The main difference between

---

43 More information, see http://globalmusicrights.com (accessed 21 January 2016).

44 See http://www.nytimes.com/2014/10/30/business/media/new-venture-seeks-higher-royalties-for-songwriters.html (accessed 21 January 2016).

45 Guilbault, note 5 above, p. 775 with more references.

46 Article 3 lit (b) defines "independent management entity" as any organisation which is authorised by law or by way of assignment, licence or any other contractual arrangement to manage copyright or rights related to copyright on behalf of more than one right holder, for the collective benefit of those right holders, as its sole or main purpose, and which is: (i) neither owned nor controlled, directly or indirectly, wholly or in part by right holders; and (ii) organised on a for-profit basis. In recital 15 to Directive 2014/26/EU, those are described as commercial entities *inter alia* because they are not owned or controlled by right holders. However, to the extent such independent management entities carry out the same activities as collective management organisations, they should be obliged to provide certain information to the right holders they represent, collective management organisations, users and the public.

collective management organisations and an independent management entity lies in the ownership or control structure; the latter is neither owned nor controlled by right holders and is organised on a for-profit basis. So far, there is some ambiguity as to what such entities are and it remains a matter of speculation as to whether the European legislator had such developments in mind.[47]

It remains to be seen how Member States will choose to implement the definition and the rule in Article 31, which is directed towards situations where a CMO does not grant or offer to grant multi-territorial licences or does not allow another CMO to represent those rights for such purpose by April 2017.

2.5 The Operational Picture

In the context of cross-border licensing, the user generated law framework may need to consider the relevance not only of initial licensing and renegotiation but also the operations of such services. Many challenges in relation to online music are not directly related to licensing but reside in the operational processes such as documentation and reporting from service providers about played tracks and the payment of royalties from the respective organisations to their right holders.[48] There have been several initiatives to tackle some of these operational challenges. The Global Repertoire Database, for example, was an industry initiative started in 2008 with the goal of creating a joint database covering ownership and control of musical works. The Swedish CMO has started the International Copyright Exchange (ICE). In 2012, Network of Music Partners (NMP) was founded which centres its activities on the administrative processes of invoicing for use of music and distributing royalties. NMP is jointly owned by NCB and PRS for Music. NMP handles the administrative back-office *inter alia* for the Nordic-Baltic online markets and the pan-European central licensing of the EMI catalogues. Front-office activities such as licensing and member services remain with the parent companies (NCB and PRS for Music). The services by NMP and ICE are also used by other European CMOs, for example the Dutch

[47] Given the reference to "collective benefit" in the definition of an independent management entity, the feature that right holders have no control over the management entity the provision appears somewhat contradictory.

[48] The European Commission, for example, mentions the outsourcing of back-office functions in the accompanying memo to its proposal for the CRM Directive (MEMO/12/545 at point 15). See also my prior research in Schwemer, note 21 above.

society Buma/Stemra.[49] In addition, several standards such as DDEX, CCID or ISNI have been developed for tasks such as reporting and invoicing.

3. ASSESSMENT: THE ONLINE MUSIC-LICENSING ECOSYSTEM AS AN EXAMPLE OF USER GENERATED LAW

The previous section illustrates that multiple intertwined developments and arrangements for the licensing of music online have occurred and that they must be seen in their distinct historical context. This section analyses how well these developments accord with the user generated law framework. Does the example of online licensing pass all phases of the theoretical model? Why have the licensing arrangements been created in the first place? Do all determinants from the methodological model have an influence on the emergence of the specific user generated law?

There are multiple entry points to the process of evaluating the legal innovations created by users. First, model contracts (as in the case of the Barcelona and Santiago Agreements or CISAC terms) could be seen as examples where users create a layer of private regulation. A second starting point is the emergence of multi-territorial mono-repertoire licensing entities, which can be observed since 2006. Third, the more recent development of licensing hubs formed by CMOs seems worthy of further scrutiny. In addition, other current developments such as a potential move towards more direct licensing or legal arrangements outside of licensing (e.g. regarding operations) could be relevantly construed under the framework. The focus of this chapter will be on the first three examples.

3.1 Autonomy Spaces and Interdependencies Between the Licensing Models

The developments around cross-border licensing models are characterised by an interplay between private arrangements and regulatory activity. This interaction is between self-organisation, on one side, and soft law measures (such as Green Papers), Recommendations and recent legislative measures, as well as competition proceedings, on the other side. Such interactions are an important consideration when applying the user

---

[49] See press release at https://www.ncb.dk/05/news/2014-12-03-nmp-buma-ice-press-release.pdf (accessed 21 January 2016).

generated law framework to these licensing models. This dynamic can partly be understood according to what is termed autonomy spaces in user generated law methodology. Autonomy spaces refer to State-enacted law that defines a space within which persons or organisations may act autonomously.[50]

Collective management organisations are regulated to a varying degree across European countries and set up in a range of ways. In some cases, for example, national collecting societies are *de facto* monopolies and in other cases *de jure* monopolies.[51] The degree of regulation can also vary: the German CMOs, for instance, were traditionally highly regulated, while the French CMOs were intermediately regulated, and the British CMOs lightly regulated.[52] Thus, European CMOs traditionally had different spaces within which to operate.

In addition, there might also be a certain interplay between the different licensing models. Have the Barcelona and Santiago standard agreements served as inspiration for later models or prepared conditions for them? Is the licensing hub idea implemented in the current multi-territorial licensing models? Or are all arrangements more or less independent developments, created without reference to other or earlier models? Given the complexity of the developments in a field that is not static but constantly developing, it is difficult to obtain a clear picture; but it is safe to say that there have been at least some interdependencies. While further exploring these questions does not fall within the scope of this chapter, it is important to acknowledge that the correlations between the different licensing models can point towards the dissemination criterion of the user generated law model. If a licensing model has been copied or served as inspiration for later constructions, the original model has been disseminated and thus further processed within the model framework.

Figure 4.1, below, displays a simplified overview of the evolution of the licensing arrangements which have been described in the first part of this chapter. The traditional landscape consisted of national CMOs, which – via reciprocal representation agreements (RRAs) based on model

---

[50] See Riis, Chapter 1 of this book.

[51] In Italy or Austria, for example, CMOs are regulated as legal monopolies. See e.g. G. M. Riccio and G. Codiglione, 'Copyright Collecting Societies, Monopolistic Positions and Competition in the EU Single Market' (2014) 7 *Masaryk U.J.L. Tech.* 287.

[52] An early overview of how CMOs in several countries have been regulated is given by Stanley Besen and Sheila Nataraj Kirby, *Compensating Creators of Intellectual Property, Collectives That Collect* (RAND Corporation, 1989).

contracts – were able to grant mono-territorial, multi-repertoire licences. In light of the CISAC decision and the Recommendation of 2005, new customised licensing entities which license multi-territorial on a mono-repertoire basis have emerged as additional licensors. Directive 2014/26/EU codifies some of the developments and promotes *inter alia* a regime of licensing hubs in which CMOs join forces to license on a multi-territorial and multi-repertoire basis, potentially leading to the re-aggregation of rights. Besides this, the Directive differentiates between CMOs and so-called independent management entities (IMEs) which are organised on a for-profit basis and are neither owned nor controlled, directly or indirectly, wholly or in part, by right holders. It is important to note that the different licensing arrangements have not necessarily replaced each other but rather added additional licensing layers over time.

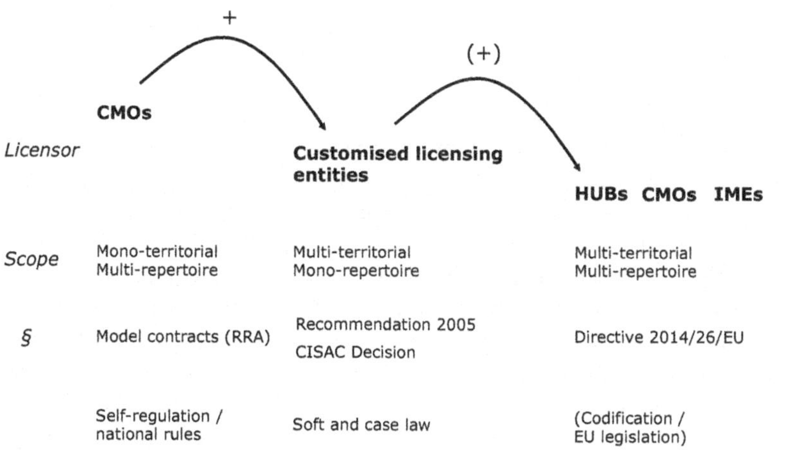

Figure 4.1 Evolution of licensing arrangements

3.2 The Emergence of Cross-Border Models

The first phase of user generated law is the emergence phase, which is deemed to rely on four determinants: (1) heterogeneous demands for legal solutions, (2) expectation of benefits, (3) asymmetric information and (4) the existence of one or more lead users. Can those four determinants construe the emergence of private regulatory models within this sub-space of intellectual property rights?

(1) Heterogeneous demand

The first determinant for the emergence of user generated law is held to be the heterogeneous demand for legal solutions. Though not contained in the original model by von Hippel, the cross-border dimension is proffered as a crucial element within the user generated law framework.[53] The Internet's borderless technological nature enables users to access content from all over the world. Online licensing is inherently more of a cross-border undertaking than traditional offline licensing. This is also where the heterogeneity lies. Existing licensing models, it appears, have not been able to deal with cross-border licensing in the digital context.

As I have noted in the findings of earlier research:

> music-streaming services usually approach their markets on a territorial and not on a pan-European level. The decision to enter a local market is influenced by a combination of several elements: one key consideration constitutes the ability to get the respective rights at a cost efficient level. A second key consideration concerns the general economic situation and the general legal context of the respective local market.[54]

(2) Expectation of benefits

Private regulatory models are supposedly only created if users can expect benefits from them (i.e. the models generate value by being used). This condition is fulfilled if the parties (right holders and licensees) benefit from the licensing models. We can differentiate between regulatory models that do not require an institutional set-up (e.g. pure contractual agreements) and models that do (e.g. copyright collective management organisations that require an organisation to collect remuneration).[55] The greater the set-up costs involved, the greater the expected benefits must be in order for a private regulatory model to be deployed. KEA Affairs (2012) identifies in its report on online music licensing that the fragmentation of rights, right holders and repertoires is at the core of high transaction costs in Europe.[56] On this issue, the European legislator formulates the aspiration of the CRM Directive to facilitate new online services and thereby enhance consumer choice and lead to a reduction in transaction costs which should be passed on to consumers.[57] When imposing legislation on the space, the Commission expresses its expectation that music publishers would consider "re-entrusting part of their

[53] Riis, Chapter 1 of this book.
[54] Schwemer, note 21 above, p. 150.
[55] Riis, Chapter 1 of this book.
[56] KEA Affairs, note 33 above, p. 51.
[57] Directive 2014/26/EU, recital 44.

rights to collecting societies that comply with passport requirements and fulfil certain conditions of good governance".[58] The mere existence of the multi-territorial licensing arrangements suggests that either the parties enjoy benefits or that the legislator has forced these models.[59]

(3) Asymmetric information

Compared to legislating multi-territorial licensing, private arrangements are argued to be better at addressing the problematic asymmetry of information possessed by the legislator and the parties affected by the law. The ensuing argumentation and narrative adhere closely to the discussion in the previous chapter on "Collective Agreements for the Clearance of Copyrights – The Case of Collective Management and Extended Collective Licences", with minor adjustments. In practice, the legislator will regularly lack the requisite information for solving the task in an optimal way. A freely organised multi-territorial licensing regime between the different parties will be based on much more adequate information than a decision made by the legislator. In this way, asymmetric information is an essential dynamic in the emergence of cross-border licensing models. In regard to such cross-border licensing, the legislator has partly regulated the field with the CRM Directive. This has implications for the adoption of the legal innovations and will be discussed in the section devoted to that part of the model.

(4) The existence of one or more lead users

The existence of individual or multiple lead users is the final element that is said to foster the formation of user generated law. Initially, it is important to identify the "users" in the CMO/new licensing entities model. Users in user generated law are not only the persons subjected to but also affected by the law. A reasonable starting point when identifying "users" is to look towards the relationship between licensors and licensees. In downstream licensing this would be the relation of collective management organisations to online music service providers. Here, service providers acquire a licence for the respective repertoire from a CMO. A second horizontal licensing relation can be found between the CMOs where organisations via reciprocal representation agreements

---

[58] See European Commission, Impact Assessment 2005, 162. CELAS, for example, concluded sub-agency agreements with collecting societies such as KODA (DK), STIM (SE) and TEOSO (FI).

[59] It is an open question as to whether the users benefit as well, considering the monopoly power of right holders.

enable each other to offer licences for other CMOs' repertoires in their respective territories.

When looking at the horizontal relation between collective management organisations, industry umbrella organisations have played a crucial role in developing model contracts and facilitating best practices. As noted in the previous section, the organisations CISAC and BIEM have developed several model contracts for their member organisations. While information on the exact development of these model contracts is scarce, one can assume that the umbrella organisations have acted in a fashion that matches the definition of a lead user. However, one caveat in regard to the model is related to motivation: Schovsbo (2010) emphasises the importance of acknowledging that CMOs, like all other institutions, "have a vested interest in maintaining a system which is dependent on their services".[60]

In the downstream relation it is more difficult to draw a clear picture. One can assume that online music service providers (and possibly right holders themselves) have pushed CMOs to offer the requested licences.[61] Yet there is no clear evidence available that this would have led to the development of private regulation. Scrutiny of the commercial motivations of those involved suggests that service providers initially had little interest in multi-territorial licensing models since they approached markets for commercial reasons on a country-by-country basis.

In relation to the emergence of direct licensing (i.e. multi-territorial mono-repertoire licensors like CELAS) the General Court argued in the *CISAC* case that:

> the abandonment of the exclusivity clause made possible certain developments in the market, namely the grant of the first direct licenses, which are necessary if an eventual move beyond the national territorial limitations is to be envisaged.[62]

The Court continued that:

> [t]he spread of direct licensing required, in particular, that a demand for such licences develop on the part of major users which – instead of turning to the

---

[60] See Jens Schovsbo, 'The Necessity to Collectivize Copyright – And Dangers Thereof' (30 June 2010), available at http://ssrn.com/abstract=1632753 or http://dx.doi.org/10.2139/ssrn.1632753 (accessed 21 January 2016), p. 9.

[61] Cf. also note 66 below.

[62] Case T-442/08 *CISAC v European Commission*, recital 125.

collecting societies of all the countries in which they operate – would prefer to acquire direct licences, valid worldwide, over the repertoires which interest them.[63]

The foundation of CELAS was announced in early 2006, making it the first mover in the field. Anecdotal evidence shows that the major (US American) repertoire right holders behind the novel licensing entities and arrangement had a preference for this set-up.[64] On the other hand, smaller right holders such as those dealing with niche repertoire might not necessarily gain the same benefits from this set-up.[65] The large incumbents acted in a fashion described as lead users within the user generated framework.

When looking at licensing hubs, the initiating CMOs, such as the founding societies of Armonia, have taken a lead user role. In a different field (visual arts) a comparable one-stop-shop by the respective CMOs has been offered by OnLineArt SCRL since 2002. While the European legislator makes reference to this model in some of its documents, it is unclear to what extent the solution for online music licensing has been inspired by this set-up. The Nordic-Baltic one-stop-storefront solution offered by NCB also exhibits similarities. In this context, the CRM Directive appears as codification parallel to the developments of the market (also discussed in section 3.4 below under “Adoption Phase”). The Directive has to be implemented by the Member States by April 2016, so in a way the CMOs are early in adopting this model; but one could argue that the latest developments are at least partially imposed by the regulative context. This is also supported by the fact that in its Recommendation of 2005 the European Commission was envisioning the pooling of repertoire into a major online licensing platform.[66]

In summary, it is evident that this process has relied on the engagement of different lead users with different levels of involvement. CMOs feature as users, along with the community consisting of right holders and other relevant stakeholders in the industry. Yet right holders themselves have also engaged in the process in ways which resemble the lead user paradigm.

---

63 Ibid., recital 127.

64 See e.g. Gyertyánfy, note 10 above, p. 59.

65 Compare Lüder, note 8 above, p. 657.

66 Notably, on the matter of authors, composers and publishers pooling into one platform: see Lüder, note 8 above, p. 656.

3.3 Diffusion Phase

Once new licensing arrangements emerge, communities form around the legal innovation. This is the second phase of the user generated law framework. The framework does not offer further refinement of the community definition, which can be understood in both a broad and a narrow sense.

Model contracts developed by umbrella organisations have been used by CMOs as a basis for their bilateral reciprocal agreements.[67] In regard to multi-territorial mono-repertoire licensing, entities like CELAS, all other major publishers, and several independent publishers have followed suit and adopted similar models. In the case of licensing hubs, several other collective management organisations have joined Armonia. Thus, it appears that all of the described licensing arrangements have formed more or less broad communities around them.

3.4 Adoption Phase

The user generated law methodology foresees two forms for the adoption phase of legal innovations, which both take their starting point in the legislator: private regulatory models evolve either as new layers of law based on State-enacted law or as sui generis legal systems. Again, it is useful to differentiate between the arrangements as legal innovations: model contracts, multi-territorial mono-repertoire licensing entities, and licensing hubs.

As seen in section 3.1, there is a distinct interplay between private initiatives and regulatory activity in the sphere of online music licensing. A lack of satisfactory legal innovation (in this context referring to a solution for cross-border licensing of online music) led the legislator to come up with a non-binding instrument, namely the Recommendation of 2005, in order to achieve its policy goals. Almost one decade later, the legislator has regulated part of the playing field. The CRM Directive aims towards the establishment of hubs for the licensing of online music by author CMOs. In this context it is interesting to note that the European legislator has chosen not to apply the rules of the CRM Directive to the mono-repertoire licensing entities.[68] In the working documents accompanying the Directive there is no evidence that would offer further insight into the legislator's reasoning. This might point towards the fact that the European Commission has been satisfied with the developments in the

[67] See e.g. Lüder, note 8 above, p. 654.

[68] See discussion above under section 2.2.

space. As seen above, the development of initiatives such as Armonia dates back to before the entry into force of the Directive but after the Recommendation. Regarding the codification of this specific licensing form, it appears that the legislator does not adopt the legal innovations but rather takes action in order to define the playing field for licensing – the autonomy space – given the lack of satisfactory solutions provided by the actors.

Competition authorities have also been actively involved in stirring up the licensing arrangements. This ultimately meant that the lead users (umbrella organisations) and its community (CMOs) did not pursue their legal innovation further (reciprocal representation agreements based on model contracts containing customer allocation clauses) culminating in the CISAC proceedings. The intervention of DG COMP does not imply a failing of the user generated law, but suggests rather that the model has been partly adopted and the respective autonomy space corrected. Other initiatives to facilitate industry solutions represent a further grey-zone regarding the legislator's engagement.[69] All told, it seems that the case of multi-territorial licences is not easily put into the existing categories and that more levels of adoption might arise from this complexity.

4. CONCLUDING REMARKS

For over a decade, stakeholders have been busy adapting the traditional licensing arrangements for online music licensing from the territorial tradition of copyright to the cross-border and multi-territorial reality of a knowledge society. In the user generated law framework, "law that accommodates the needs of the knowledge society" is characterised by (1) flexible norms, (2) with cross-border scope and (3) which are industry- and subject-specific. It appears that the developments in cross-border licensing of music rights are in many ways a prototype of those characteristics. The licensing solutions are highly industry- and subject-specific: namely addressing the situational need for interactive on-demand streaming, thus permitting users to actively choose the musical works and the time of consumption, and thereby reflecting the heterogeneity in demand for legal solutions. The cross-border element has also been crucial in the development of legal solutions, reflecting the global dimension of the content and its distribution via the Internet.

---

[69] For example the Licences for Europe stakeholder dialogue (2014); see https://ec.europa.eu/licences-for-europe-dialogue/en/content/about-site (accessed 3 February 2016).

Finally, the question arises as to whether the norms are flexible, reflecting the complexity and the fast pace of development. One could argue that because of the highly specific subject matter related to a technological and market phenomenon (i.e. streaming of music), these new developments are not sufficiently covered to qualify as flexible. Understanding flexibility within this sub-space, it appears that the norms are sufficiently adaptive. In the case of music licensing, it is striking that in different facets the European legislator has played an important role: an interplay that is challenging to construe within the user generated law framework.

The developments in the licensing landscape must be seen in the multi-faceted context of enabling the Digital Single Market across all European Member States; fostering innovation of new digital service providers in Europe; addressing competition concerns towards the collective management of rights; and dealing with the legacy of the traditional territorial nature of copyright administration and exploitation. The regulatory framework and new ways of exploitation affect the formation of private mechanisms of clearance of copyrights. Only time will reveal whether the current licensing arrangements are fit for purpose and able to facilitate future (and already existing) services like SoundCloud, where mashups and remixes are a major part of the content.

Music is often described as a harbinger for other forms of entertainment goods, and the trend towards on-demand access can be seen in the number of consumers now watching films and TV productions via services like Netflix, or accessing books via commercial players like Oyster in the US or Mofibo in Denmark or the Bokhylla (Norwegian for "bookshelf") project by the Norwegian national library. These industry verticals face similar market challenges, but may have gone through different developments (or indeed some common trends) concerning their licensing models. By also applying the user generated law model to those verticals, the paradigm will be tested further, which may in turn give rise to important policy implications.

5. Open source licences

Henrik Udsen

This chapter analyses the extent to which open source licences accord with and thereby support the model of user generated law which was outlined in Chapter 1. Initially, we will address the legal protection afforded to computer programs under statutory copyright law. Hereafter, we will scrutinize the concept of open source licences. Finally, we will examine the relationship between open source licences and the notions of "emergence", "diffusion" and "adoption" in the user generated law model.

1. THE LEGAL PROTECTION OF COMPUTER PROGRAMS

In order to understand the nature of open source licences it is necessary to understand the legal starting point for protection of computer programs. In the 1950s and early 1960s computer programs were integrated parts of the computers used. As computer programs became separated from the hardware (and third party suppliers started developing programs during the late 1960s and 1970s) questions arose initially as to whether computer programs should be legally protected. These soon gave way to questions about *how* such programs would be protected. It was the general perception that programs needed some kind of legal protection in order to ensure the necessary incentive for companies to invest in the development of computer programs.

A number of different models for legal protection were discussed, including *sui generis* protection of computer programs.[1] However, since the need for a protection model was considered an urgent matter by the software industry, legislators around the world decided to protect computer programs by copyright: a solution which had the advantage of the

[1] In 1978, published in WIPO's draft "Model Provisions on the Protection of Computer Programs".

copyright system already being in place and to a large extent internationally harmonized through the Berne Convention.[2] In 1980, the US Copyright Act was amended to explicitly state that computer programs could be protected as copyright protected works. In the mid-1980s, the first European countries started to change their Copyright Acts in order to specify that computer programs were protected under copyright. These national developments were followed by an EU directive on the legal protection of computer programs (Directive 1991/250),[3] hereinafter referred to as "the Software Directive".

The Software Directive states that the Member States shall protect computer programs, by copyright, as literary works. The author of a program has the exclusive rights to copy, translate and alter the program and make it available to the public. However, the Directive includes a number of exceptions to these exclusive rights. Only to the extent that such exceptions apply are the users entitled to copy, alter and distribute the programs. According to Article 5(1) the user may copy the program when this is "necessary for the use of the computer program by the lawful acquirer in accordance with its intended purpose, including for error correction". According to Article 5(2) the user may make backup copies of the program necessary for the use of the program. By Article 5(3) the user may make copies in order to study the program and its underlying ideas. Under Article 6, it is permissible to make copies of a program and translate it from machine code to source code (decompilation) when this is necessary for achieving the interoperability of an independently created computer program with other programs when certain conditions are met.

In order to understand open source licences we must understand the rights which are *not* granted to the users under copyright law:

- Users are not entitled to copy the program except when this is necessary to use the program for its intended purposes, for backup purposes, or to study the program.
- Users are not entitled to alter the program except when this is necessary to use the program for its intended purposes (which will very seldom be the case).

---

2 Berne Convention on the Protection of Literary and Artistic Works with effect from December 1887, and today ratified by more than 160 countries.

3 The Directive was replaced by Directive 2009/24/EU, though without any material changes to the scope of protection.

- Users are not entitled to translate the program from machine code to source code except when this is necessary to achieve interoperability between two programs (and certain conditions are met).
- Users are not entitled to distribute the program to others except when making a redistribution of the user's own copy, in which case the user may no longer use the program.

This copyright regulation is the point of departure for software developers and users when considering contractual regulation of the rights to computer programs.

In a "classic" proprietary software licence the user:

- Is granted a limited right to use the program.
- Is not entitled to make amendments or error corrections to the program.
- Is not provided with access to the source code.

Thus, in general, the classic proprietary software licence does not fundamentally provide the user with other rights than those following from statutory copyright law. Open source licences, on the other hand, provide users with much broader rights as described below.

2. OPEN SOURCE LICENCES

2.1 History and Philosophy of Open Source Licences

When developing computer programs became an industry in its own right during the 1970s and 1980s, the software industry wanted to protect its investments in the creation of programs. This was achieved by using (early) technical measures and by securing copyright protection for programs in the legal process described above. This development gave more power to the industry and less to the users. In 1983, as a reaction to this, Richard Stallman announced the GNU project – a project which aimed to provide users with an operating system that would be free to use, modify and redistribute. In 1985, Stallman founded the Free Software Foundation (FSF),[4] an organization dedicated to working for the idea of free software and to being the anchor of the GNU project. Stallman's philosophy was laid down in the Free Software Definition,

---

[4] See fsf.org.

which is maintained by FSF. The Free Software Definition starts out by defining the term "free software":

> "Free software" means software that respects users' freedom and community. Roughly, it means that the users have the freedom to run, copy, distribute, study, change and improve the software. Thus, "free software" is a matter of liberty, not price. To understand the concept, you should think of "free" as in "free speech," not as in "free beer".

The definition continues by proposing the four essential freedoms of free software:

> A program is free software if the program's users have the four essential freedoms:
>
> - The freedom to run the program as you wish, for any purpose (freedom 0).
> - The freedom to study how the program works, and change it so it does your computing as you wish (freedom 1). Access to the source code is a precondition for this.
> - The freedom to redistribute copies so you can help your neighbor (freedom 2).
> - The freedom to distribute copies of your modified versions to others (freedom 3). By doing this you can give the whole community a chance to benefit from your changes. Access to the source code is a precondition for this.

In 1989, Stallman wrote the first version of the GNU General Public License (GPL) for use with the programs developed as part of the GNU project. The licence provided users with the four freedoms cited above but also required that any modification made by any user to the program should be licensed under the GPL. Through this requirement Stallman made sure that not only the original program but also all modifications would continue to be free software under the above definition. The requirement is known as "copyleft" (see section 2.2 below).

During the 1990s, the free software movement became increasingly popular and the free software model was also considered usable by the commercial software industry (demonstrated *inter alia* by the fact that the Netscape Communications Corporation released its popular Netscape Communication software suite as free software). However, the social activism approach and the free software movement's very dogmatic belief in user rights was considered by many to be an obstacle to the model being adopted by the industry.

In 1998, a group which included Jon Hall, Larry Augustin, Eric S. Raymond and Bruce Perens founded the Open Source Initiative (OSI)[5] in order to promote the use of open source software. The commercial software industry was also targeted since the group believed that there would be business potential in the idea of sharing software developments. It was a deliberate choice to use the term "open source software" instead of "free software" in order to distance the concept from the social activism approach evinced by the free software movement. The OSI has made its own open source definition with 10 requirements:

1. Free Redistribution

> The license shall not restrict any party from selling or giving away the software as a component of an aggregate software distribution containing programs from several different sources. The license shall not require a royalty or other fee for such sale.

2. Source Code

> The program must include source code, and must allow distribution in source code as well as compiled form. Where some form of a product is not distributed with source code, there must be a well-publicized means of obtaining the source code for no more than a reasonable reproduction cost preferably, downloading via the Internet without charge. The source code must be the preferred form in which a programmer would modify the program. Deliberately obfuscated source code is not allowed. Intermediate forms such as the output of a preprocessor or translator are not allowed.

3. Derived Works

> The license must allow modifications and derived works, and must allow them to be distributed under the same terms as the license of the original software.

4. Integrity of the Author's Source Code

> The license may restrict source-code from being distributed in modified form only if the license allows the distribution of "patch files" with the source code for the purpose of modifying the program at build time. The license must explicitly permit distribution of software built from modified source code. The license may require derived works to carry a different name or version number from the original software.

5. No Discrimination against Persons or Groups

> The license must not discriminate against any person or group of persons.

---

[5] See opensource.org.

> 6. No Discrimination against Fields of Endeavor
>
> The license must not restrict anyone from making use of the program in a specific field of endeavor. For example, it may not restrict the program from being used in a business, or from being used for genetic research.
>
> 7. Distribution of License
>
> The rights attached to the program must apply to all to whom the program is redistributed without the need for execution of an additional license by those parties.
>
> 8. License Must Not Be Specific to a Product
>
> The rights attached to the program must not depend on the program's being part of a particular software distribution. If the program is extracted from that distribution and used or distributed within the terms of the program's license, all parties to whom the program is redistributed should have the same rights as those that are granted in conjunction with the original software distribution.
>
> 9. License Must Not Restrict Other Software
>
> The license must not place restrictions on other software that is distributed along with the licensed software. For example, the license must not insist that all other programs distributed on the same medium must be open-source software.
>
> 10. License Must Be Technology-Neutral
>
> No provision of the license may be predicated on any individual technology or style of interface.

When comparing FSF's free software definition with OSI's open source definition it is evident that they are not in conflict with each other. Most of the software deemed "free software" under the FSF definition will also be "open source software" under the OSI definition and vice versa. The differences between the FSF's and OSI's approaches are largely philosophical. As such, the FSF and the free software movement focus on users' rights. The social activism approach of FSF is illustrated by this wording from the Free Software Definition:

> We campaign for these freedoms because everyone deserves them. With these freedoms, the users (both individually and collectively) control the program and what it does for them. When users don't control the program, we call it a "nonfree" or "proprietary" program. The nonfree program controls the users, and the developer controls the program; this makes the program an instrument of unjust power.

The OSI and the open source movement have a more pragmatic approach which exhibits a greater focus on the ability to share software developments in ways which best fit the developers and the users. However, these philosophical differences have not resulted in many practical differences. As we have noted, most free software will also be open source software and vice versa. Similarly, there are no large differences between free software licences and open source licences with the one exception of the copyleft clause which is a part of the GPL and the philosophy of Richard Stallman and the FSF but which is not a requirement under the OSI open source definition.

2.2 Copyleft

As noted above, "copyleft" refers to a clause in an open source licence requiring all modifications to the software to be licensed under the same licence as the original program. In this way it will not be possible to make modifications to an open source program and then license the modified version of the program under a closed/proprietary licence. Richard Stallman described the concept of copyleft in his GNU manifesto from 1985:

> GNU is not in the public domain. Everyone will be permitted to modify and redistribute GNU, but no distributor will be allowed to restrict its further redistribution. That is to say, proprietary modifications will not be allowed. I want to make sure that all versions of GNU remain free.

The GPL contains a copyleft clause which in turn means that not only modified versions of the open source program but also proprietary software that is built together with open source software may be "caught" by the open source licence requiring the software developer to make the source code of the proprietary software available to the users. In all likelihood, this has been (and remains) the single most important factor behind resistance to open source software, especially from the software industry.

The OSI's open source definition does not require that open source software is licensed under copyleft clauses; it leaves this instead for the software developer to decide. On the other hand, the definition does not prevent the use of copyleft clauses. The licences approved by the OSI as complying with the open source definition include both licences with copyleft clauses and licences without copyleft clauses (so-called "permissive licences"). The OSI's open source definition does, however, require that the licence must not place restrictions on other software solely on the grounds that is distributed along with the open software. For instance, the licence must not insist that all other programs distributed on the same medium must be open source software (see requirement 9 of the definition).

2.3 Open Source Licences and the Practical Use of Open Source Software

2.3.1 Main characteristics of an open source licence

Although there are differences between the various open source licences, they are all based on the same key principles which are very different from the principles of the "classic" proprietary software licence.

As already stated in a proprietary software licence the user:

- Is granted a limited right to use the program.
- Is not entitled to make amendments or error corrections to the program.
- Is not provided with access to the source code.

In an open source licence the user:

- Is granted a broad right to copy the program.
- Is entitled to make amendments and error corrections to the program.
- Is provided with access to the source code.

The open source licence thereby provides the user with much broader rights than those stemming from statutory copyright law and makes it possible for the user, both legally and practically, to make their own corrections and amendments to the program and further develop the program.

It is worth recalling that the open source licence may be with or without a copyleft clause, which is the most fundamental distinction between the open source licences.

2.3.2 Different open source licences

The term "open source" is not trademark protected (or otherwise legally protected) and everybody may therefore use the term "open source" for his or her own licence. However, both FSF and OSI maintain lists of licences that comply with the free software definition and open source definition respectively.[6] Around 70 licences have in this way been approved by OSI.

The most frequently used open source licence is the GPL published by FSF. The latest (third) version is from 2007. One third of all open source software is licenced under GPL v. 2 and 3. Other popular open source licences are the MIT licence and the Apache licence. Neither of these two licences includes copyleft clauses (in contrast to the GPL). A number of software companies, including Microsoft, Apple and IBM, have published their own open source licences.[7] In 2009, the European Commission published the European Union Public Licence (EUPL); however, it has not been widely used. One of the aims of the EUPL was to create an open source licence that took European Union law into account and used some of the European copyright terms. Yet the market needs for such a licence have apparently been limited.

2.3.3 The practical use of open source software

The increase in use of open source software has been dramatic over the last 10 to 15 years. Today, many of the most widely used computer programs are wholly or partly based on open source software. Examples include the Linux operating system, the Firefox browser and the Android operating system for mobile devices. All large software developers, including Apple, Microsoft and IBM, are currently using open source software. Gartner has predicted that by 2016, the vast majority of mainstream IT organizations will use elements of open source software in mission-critical IT solutions.[8] In other words, open source software and open source licences are an integrated and increasingly important part of the software industry.

2.4 The Interplay Between Open Source Licences and Copyright Legislation

Proprietary licences are based on the legal copyrights granted to the developer of a program. According to statutory copyright law, users are (with some exceptions) only entitled to copy, alter and distribute the

---

[6] See http://www.gnu.org/licenses/license-list.html and http://opensource.org/licenses (accessed 3 February 2016).

[7] A list of the top 20 open source licences can be found at https://www.blackducksoftware.com/resources/data/top-20-open-source-licenses (accessed 21 January 2016).

[8] See https://www.gartner.com/doc/2822619/widespread-use-opensource-software-demands (accessed 21 January 2016).

program with approval (licence) from the developer of the program. The initial philosophy of the free software movement maintained that copyright law too strongly favoured the developers as opposed to the users. The open source licence provides users with many more rights than what follows from copyright law. For this reason, free and open source software has been seen as a rejection of copyright. However, this is not the case. On the contrary, open source licences also rest on the copyright provided to the author of the open source program. Although an open source licence provides users with many rights, it also establishes user requirements which demand compliance, including information requirements (and for some licences copyleft clauses). If a user does not comply with these requirements the licence is invalid, and the user can no longer claim the rights provided under the licence. Consequently, the user cannot copy, modify or distribute the program without infringing the copyright of the developer of the program. It is thus the underlying copyright that makes it possible for the developer to lay down requirements in the open source licence.

Briefly stated: an open source licence strikes a different balance between developer and user than the one established by statutory copyright law. Ultimately, though, it is copyright law which makes it possible for the developer to enforce this balance. In this way, an open source licence to some extent both rejects and embraces statutory copyright law.

2.5 The Legal Status of Open Source Licences – Contractual Relationship?

There has been intensive debate about whether open source licences establish a contractual relationship between the developer and the user. It has been argued that the open source licence is a "bare licence" containing a one-sided permission by the licensor to do something with the program that would not otherwise be allowed. Others have argued that the open source licence places mutual obligations on the parties involved since the licensee accepts certain obligations by using the program which makes the licence a contract.[9]

Answers may differ from country to country, but the prevailing view seems to be that at least in civil law countries the open source licence is

[9] For further references see Luke McDonagh, 'Copyright, contract, and FOSS', in Noam Shemtov and Ian Walden (eds), *Free and Open Source Software* (Oxford University Press, 2013), section 3.7.

considered a contract. Thus, case law from both Germany and France has given contractual validity to an open source licence.[10]

3. OPEN SOURCE LICENCES AND THE USER GENERATED LAW MODEL

3.1 Emergence

As expounded in Chapter 1, user generated law can be expected to emerge when there are heterogeneous demands for law; when expectations of benefit exist; when asymmetric information is a factor; and when lead users exist and exert influence. Licence contracts in general are tools for flexibility in the supply of legal regulatory models. The fact that some software developers shifted from proprietary to open models for distribution and development of software reflects a need for a broader variety in licence contracts. However, the open source licences actually used are highly standardized, arguably much more standardized than proprietary licence contracts. Hence, heterogeneous demands for law cannot be considered an important contributing factor for the emergence of open source licences.

Each of the remaining user generated legal conditions for emergence is considered in relation to open source licences in the following sections.

3.1.1 Expectation of benefits

The user generated law model begins with the premise that potential innovators can expect an economic benefit (profit) from the new regulatory model. As noted earlier, the concept of open source licences was originally established as a counter reaction to commercial proprietary software licences. Neither the initial initiative by Richard Stallman and the FSF nor the later initiative by OSI and its founders had the purpose of making a profit on the new licensing model; these initiatives sought, rather, to establish open and free sharing of improvements of software amongst the community at large. Since the purpose was clearly altruistic, no expectation of economic benefit by the original innovators existed. This is also emphasized by the fact that such open source licences can be used for free. Both FSF and OSI are non-profit organizations covering their costs by donations made by volunteers.

---

10 See ibid., p. 99.

However, if one broadens the understanding of the notion "expectation of benefits" to include non-economic benefits such as an increase in an innovator's reputation,[11] it seems likely that there exists an expectation of benefits in relation to open source licences. The more an open source licence is used the more the innovator's reputation is increased. This is demonstrated by the way in which GPL's author Richard Stallman has become a famous and highly respected person both within open source communities and beyond them (in spite of the fact that not all agree with his social activism approach). This is not the same as saying that Stallman or other open source pioneers were chiefly driven by a wish to gain reputation and acknowledgement. It may very well be that the prime motivator was the desire to do something good for the community and for society at large. Nonetheless, an expectation of benefit may be considered present even if the desire to create benefits for society at large is an innovator's prime motivation. In this respect, the open source licence model demonstrates the need to consider whether and how the activities of NGOs and other non-commercial persons and parties can fit in with the notion of "expectation of benefit".

Additionally, we have referred to the fact that commercial software companies are also licensing their software under open source licences today. This use is with an expectation of economic benefits. However, these software companies are not the user generated law model's "innovators" of this new legal form (open source licences), but simply the model's "users". The expectation of benefit by these companies is therefore not a factor which can explain the emergence of the open source licence model.

The expectation of benefit criterion includes a presumption that the costs of establishing the prospective legal model do not outweigh the benefits. When the benefits are of an economic nature this assessment is (in theory) a simple comparison between the expected costs and the expected revenue. The assessment is of a more complex nature when the benefits are of a non-economic nature. In spite of this, it is still a precondition that benefits trump costs. Since costs cannot be covered by revenue in non-commercial scenarios, the emergence of new legal models innovated by NGOs or other non-profit organizations requires volunteers to donate time and/or money. This is also the case in the open source community where the work of the open source NGOs still depends on volunteers and on donations by users, together with others wanting to support the movement and the philosophies behind it.

---

[11] Cf. Chapter 1 of this book.

3.1.2 Asymmetric information

In the user generated law model the notion of "asymmetric information" means that the legislator has a lesser knowledge of users' exact needs. Namely, the users (and especially the lead actors, referenced again in section 3.1.3 below) have more information of a higher quality regarding their community's legal needs. They are also better informed about how these needs may be accommodated within a legal model.

This must, to a large extent, be considered true with regard to open source licences. Traditionally, users have not had a strong voice when it comes to copyright regulation and balancing the rights of right holders with the rights of users. The main reason for this is that the users have not been as well-resourced or effectively organized as the right holders. Hence, it is fair to say that the lobbying power of the right holders has been much stronger than that of the users' organizations. A likely effect of this imbalance in lobbying power is that legislators have not been fully aware of the needs of the users.

Evidence of this can also be seen in the movement towards stronger user rights in copyright law that has emerged during the last few years. This movement is partly caused by the rise of users wielding more power than they did previously. Google is an example of a powerful user (although in other situations also a right holder) that has been lobbying for more user rights in copyright law. This movement has managed to create political awareness of (some) users' needs in a way that was not seen before the rise of users with such power.

3.1.3 Lead actors

We recall from Chapter 1 that the term "lead actor" is more suited for the user generated law model than the term "lead users" used in von Hippel's theory on user innovation. A lead actor is an organization, community or intermediary who sets the scene and is perceived as directly or indirectly representing user interests and is often not motivated by an expectation of obtaining benefits from the creation of legal innovation.

In terms of open source licences the FSF must be considered a lead actor. This non-profit organization was established in 1985 by Richard Stallman in order to promote the philosophy of free software. As part of its activities the organization developed the GNU operating system and drafted the GNU General Public License (GPL) to cover the use of the GNU operating system. The GPL is currently the most widely used open source licence globally. The FSF has the classic characteristics of a lead actor: the organization and its founder Richard Stallman identified a need before others did; it created a legal innovation (the GPL) in order to accommodate existing needs; and it is broadly acknowledged by a majority of open source communities (although not necessarily all of them) as indirectly representing user interests.

Since the first version of the GPL was drafted, many other open source licences have been drafted by other organizations and companies. Most of these licences cannot be considered legal innovations compared to the GPL as they are based on the same licence model as the GPL. In order for a new open source licence to be considered innovative in itself it must include conceptual changes compared to the existing model.

Such a change occurred when open source licences emerged which left out the copyleft term of the GPL. As explained in section 2 above, this development was partly a response to the resistance that had amassed concerning the copyleft term, which many users considered too restrictive and not in compliance with many users' needs. This movement was to a large extent driven by OSI and its founders who in the user generated law model must also be considered lead actors. The emergence of open source licences without the copyleft term is an example of users becoming additional lead actors by making further innovative developments to the existing model based on an identification of additional/different user needs.[12]

3.2 Diffusion

Section 3.1 above contends that open source licences provide an example of a new user generated legal model and the process of emergence. The next step in the user generated law model is the diffusion of legal innovation. The open source licence model is diffused to a very large extent. This is demonstrated by a few key figures (further specified in section 2.3 above). Today, there are more than 70 open source licences, most of which are accepted under the open source definition of the OSI. Most of the large software companies currently use open source licences and a number of them have published their own open source licence.

The open source model has been diffused extensively enough to ensure that it is used beyond its own area (software). This is exemplified by Creative Commons licences which are based on and inspired by the open source licence model. This process has made the same model available to works well beyond the software category. The notion of "openness" has

[12] Licences granting the users a right to copy, modify and distribute the program without a copyleft clause did exist prior to the OSI initiative and may also be identified prior to the GPL. However, it was the OSI initiative that can be said to have established open source licences, including licences without copyleft, as a more general phenomenon.

spread out to many other areas, such as patent law where "open innovation" is an emerging concept.[13]

The massive diffusion of the open source licence model may be explained by the fact that open source licences have been made available for free. Additionally, the lead actors concerned managed to build up strong communities supporting the philosophies behind the model. Through the community network, support of the open source licence model was made widespread and resulted in further support, which culminated with the model becoming known and accepted outside the core open source communities.

3.3 Adoption

The last phase of the user generated law model is the adoption phase. As we have established, legal innovations can be deemed "adopted" if: (1) the legislator and the court accept the model and do not find grounds for legal corrections; (2) the legal innovation is adopted as statutory rules or the court applies the legal innovation as the default rule.

The open source model has not found its way into statutory law; nor have there been any judgments by courts expanding the user rights under copyright law with reference to the open source philosophy. In this sense there has been no adoption of the open source licence model. However, neither legislators nor the courts have found reasons for correcting the autonomy spaces for the open source licence model. As outlined in section 2.5 above, the existing case law seems to accept open source licences as valid and enforceable contracts. Hence, open source licences have been adopted as a well-functioning user generated regulatory model that governs a substantial part of contracting in the software sector.

4. CONCLUDING REMARKS

Open source licences are illustrative of the process in which new licence models are established because existing models and regulations do not cover specific user needs. The user generated law model is well-suited for construing this process through its emergence, diffusion and adoption phases.

---

[13] See Andrew Katz, 'Open Everything', in Noam Shemtov and Ian Walden (eds), *Free and Open Source Software* (Oxford University Press, 2013) 439.

Looking at the current market situation it seems likely that open source licences will be even more widespread in the years to come. An indicator of this likelihood is the European Commission's Open Source Strategy 2014–2017 according to which the commission will support the adoption and use of open source software. However, open source licences cannot be expected to replace proprietary licences; they will remain a supplementary process.

6. IP coordination models: revealing some of the "magic" behind patent pools and clearinghouses?

Esther van Zimmeren[1]

1. INTRODUCTION

In our global, heavily networked knowledge-based society the exchange, sharing and utilization of knowledge is increasingly important for promoting innovation. Within this context, patents may act as a barrier but also as a tool to enable the exchange and utilization of the underlying knowledge. Proponents of open innovation[2] consider patents as more

[1] The author thanks the participants at the workshop and the conference on User-Generated Law organized by the University of Copenhagen on April 6–7, 2014 for their kind feedback on this paper. Moreover, Mr. L. Horn and Ms. K. Neuman (MPEG LA) have provided important insights into the operation of MPEG LA, the MPEG-2 pool and Librassay, which have been used to illustrate the application of the user generated law model to patent pools and clearinghouses.

[2] "Open innovation" is a concept that was first "coined" by Henry Chesbrough in 2003 and is now commonly used by academics, policymakers and companies to indicate that "firms can and should use external ideas as well as internal ideas, and internal and external paths to market, as the firms look to advance their technology". The central idea behind open innovation is that, in a world of widely distributed knowledge, companies cannot afford to rely entirely on their own research, but should instead buy or license IP from other companies. In addition, internal inventions not being used in a firm's business should be taken outside the company. See Henry Chesbrough, 'The Era of Open Innovation' (2003) 44 *MIT Sloan Man. Rev.* 35; Henry Chesbrough, *Open Business Models: How to Thrive in the New Innovation Landscape* (Harvard Business School Press, 2006); Henry Chesbrough, *Open Innovation: The New Imperative for Creating and Profiting from Technology* (Harvard Business School Press, 2006); Henry Chesbrough, Wim Vanhaverbeke and Joel West, *Open Innovation: Researching a New Paradigm* (Oxford University Press, 2008); and

than mere means for excluding others from using an organization's ideas and technologies; patents are rather expected to play a key role as a means for transferring ideas and technologies from one entity to another. The growing need to facilitate the exploitation of patents has led to the rise of a "patent marketplace"[3] where a variety of new entities focusing on patent-related transactions are emerging. Some specialized IP firms seek to monetize patents (e.g. Intellectual Ventures), or create strategic patent portfolios for licensing purposes (e.g. MPEG LA). Other companies offer an online marketplace where patents and ideas can be traded (e.g. NineSigma), or establish a co-operative venture that buys and licenses patents to its members for defensive purposes (e.g. RPX).[4]

Patent pools and clearinghouses[5] operate in this evolving patent marketplace and are nowadays widely recognized as useful intellectual property (IP) coordination and exchange mechanisms for situations where a particular technology is burdened with a large number of fragmented IP rights.[6] They are designed to offer a one-stop-shop to patented technologies for licensees while generating reasonable royalties for patent owners. For instance, various patent pools have been established in parallel with standardization efforts, offering access to the essential technology, which is part of the standard and has been patented, under so-called FRAND terms (fair, reasonable and non-discriminatory conditions), to enable firms to develop compatible and inter-operable products and services.

Henry Chesbrough, Wim Vanhaverbeke and Joel West, *New Frontiers in Open Innovation* (Oxford University Press, 2014).

[3] Tomoya Yanagisawa and Dominique Guellec, 'The Emerging Patent Marketplace' (OECD Science, Technology and Industry Working Papers, 2009/09, OECD Publishing).

[4] Ibid.

[5] For a more detailed definition and an explanation of these models, see sections 4 and 5 of this chapter.

[6] For instance Jeanne Clark et al., *Patent Pools: A Solution to the Problem of Access in Biotechnology Patents* (USPTO, 2000); Carl Shapiro, 'Navigating the Patent Thicket: Cross Licenses, Patent Pools, and Standard Setting' (2001) 1 *Innovation Policy and the Economy* 119; and Organisation for Economic Co-operation and Development (OECD), 'Guidelines for the Licensing of Genetic Inventions' (OECD, 2006), available at http://www.oecd.org/sti/biotech/36198812.pdf (accessed January 21, 2016).

Despite the fact that there is abundant economic analysis regarding the design and functioning of patent pools[7] and clearinghouses,[8] no clear, single recipe for a successful pool or clearinghouse has been provided. For instance, different views appear to exist on the "optimal" design and the desired governance structures.[9] Due to concerns about the anti-competitive effects of pools, competition authorities have provided guidance and imposed some restrictions on the design of patent pools.[10] Even though there is still some scope for differentiation as to the particular features of the pool, in practice many pools follow the model of the MPEG-2 pool, the pioneer model, which has paved the way for the modern patent pools. The set-up of clearinghouse models has not yet been curtailed in a similar way, and hence a wide variety of potential patent clearinghouse models can be distinguished.[11]

---

[7] The most influential economic papers in this respect are those of Josh Lerner and Jean Tirole: Josh Lerner and Jean Tirole, 'Efficient Patent Pools' (2004) 94 *The American Economic Review* 691 and Josh Lerner, Marcin Strojwas and Jean Tirole, 'The Design of Patent Pools: The Determinants of Licensing Rules' (2007) 38 *The RAND Journal of Economics* 610.

[8] In fact, most economic literature is focused on patent pools. However, Reiko Aoki and Aaron Schiff published various working papers on clearinghouses specifically, but their main findings are combined in one published study: Reiko Aoki and Aaron Schiff, 'Promoting Access to Intellectual Property: Patent Pools, Copyright Collectives and Clearinghouses' (2008) 38 *R&D Management* 198.

[9] For instance Shapiro, note 6 above; Robert P. Merges, 'Institutions for Intellectual Property Transactions: The Case of Patent Pools', in Rochelle Dreyfuss, Dianne Zimmerman and Harry First (eds), *Expanding the Boundaries of Intellectual Property: Innovation Policy for the Knowledge Society* (Oxford University Press, 2001), pp. 123–66; Lerner and Tirole, note 7 above; Lerner, Strojwas and Tirole, note 7 above; and Steffen Brenner, 'Optimal Formation Rules for Patent Pools' (2009) 40 *Economic Theory* 373.

[10] See US Department of Justice (USDOJ) and US Federal Trade Commission (USFTC), *Antitrust Guidelines for the Licensing of Intellectual Property* (Washington, DC, 1995) and USDOJ and USFTC, *Antitrust Enforcement and Intellectual Property Rights: Promoting Innovation and Competition* (Washington, DC, 2007); Japan Fair Trade Commission (JFTC), *Guidelines on Standardization and Patent Pool Arrangements* (Tokyo, 2005); and European Commission, *Communication from the Commission – Guidelines on the application of Article 101 of the Treaty on the Functioning of the European Union to technology transfer agreements* (Brussels, 2014, *OJEU* C89/03), section 4.4 on "technology pools".

[11] In Esther van Zimmeren et al., 'A Clearing House for Diagnostic Testing: The Solution to Ensure Access to and Use of Patented Genetic Inventions?' (2006) 84 *Bulletin of the World Health Organization* 352, a distinction is made

Therefore, notwithstanding the available literature on pools and clearinghouses, fresh insights can be produced by employing novel theories or interdisciplinary approaches to try to decipher the "magic formula" for setting up a successful pool or clearinghouse model. For instance, in a recently published interdisciplinary (legal-philosophical) paper, Benjamin Six et al. employ a critical account of social capital theory and suggest that trust is crucial to generating collaboration with collective action institutions, such as pools and clearinghouses.[12] The present chapter is another attempt to add to the literature regarding pools and clearinghouses, by applying the model of user generated law to these institutions.

The model of "user generated law"[13] deals with the evolution of private regulatory models as "new layers of law based on State-enacted law, or as sui generis legal systems".[14] It is based on the premise that law which accommodates the needs of a knowledge-based society is characterized by its flexible norms (reflecting the complexity and fast pace of (technical) developments), its cross-border scope (in line with the global dimension of today's knowledge society), and its industry-specific and subject-specific nature (due to the heterogeneity in demands for legal solutions).[15] Patent pools and clearinghouses can be regarded as private regulatory models "par excellence", as typically they are initiated by patent owners seeking an efficient one-stop-mechanism for patent licensing.[16] Pools and clearinghouses are relatively flexible models that can be

between information clearinghouses, technology exchange clearinghouses, open access clearinghouses, standard licences clearinghouses and royalty collection clearinghouses. Cf. Aoki and Schiff, note 8 above.

12 Benjamin Six et al., 'Trust and Social Capital in the Design and Evolution of Institutions for Collective Action' (2015) 9 *International Journal of the Commons* 151, available at http://www.thecommonsjournal.org/index.php/ijc/article/view/435 (accessed January 21, 2016).

13 See Chapter 1 of this book.

14 Ibid.

15 Ibid.

16 I note, however, that patent pools have also been set up with government involvement in the past. The Manufacturers Aircraft Association or the "US aircraft patent pool" was actually even imposed/recommended by the US government. See Harry T. Dykman, 'Patent Licensing within The Manufacturer's Aircraft Association (MAA)' (1964) 46 *J. Pat. Off. Soc'y* 646. For a very critical analysis of this pool, see Ron D. Katznelson and John Howells, 'The Myth of the Early Aviation Patent Hold-Up – How a U.S. Government Monopsony Commandeered Pioneer Airplane Patents' (2015) 24 *Industrial and Corporate Change* 1.

designed according to the heterogeneous needs of stakeholders.[17] Therefore, these models generally relate quite specifically to a particular industry or sector (e.g. Librassay for personalized medicine and health care), or technology standard (e.g. MPEG-2 pool). Despite the territorial nature of patent rights, pools and clearinghouses tend to collect relevant patent families and not just patents related to a particular territory. Thus, they offer a cross-border, global solution as required by the market.

Notwithstanding the typically "private" nature of patent pools and clearinghouses, lately several IP coordination mechanisms have been set up through the initiative and/or with the involvement of public international organizations. Examples of such hybrid "public/private" IP coordination mechanisms are the Medicines Patent Pool (MPP) and WIPO Re:Search.[18] As this chapter focuses on private regulatory models in testing the user generated law model, it will not extensively deal with these examples but will concentrate on the specific characteristics of privately initiated patent pools and clearinghouses.

Section 2 of this chapter will raise a number of "ex ante" questions that are vital for determining whether the establishment of a pool or clearinghouse would be feasible. Next, the main features of the user generated law model which are relevant for the current analysis will be listed (section 3). This particular list of features will be used as the conceptual framework for analysing the operation of patent pools (section

---

[17] For instance, a distinction can be made between pools administered by an independent licensing administrator (e.g. various pools managed by MPEG LA) and pools managed by one of the patent owners (e.g. various pools operated by Philips, e.g. DVD-pool). As long as the models comply with the limits set by the law, in particular competition law, and offer certain institutional safeguards, the initiators are free to determine the detailed arrangements.

[18] The MPP was established and funded as a separate legal entity in 2009 by UNITAID. The MPP negotiates licences with patent holders to key HIV medicines, making them available to generic companies and other manufacturers to produce low cost HIV treatments for use in developing countries. In 2011, our second example, WIPO Re:Search, was formed through the efforts of several major pharmaceutical companies, the World Intellectual Property Organization (WIPO) and BIO Ventures for Global Health. WIPO Re:Search has a broader scope than the MPP. It provides access to IP for pharmaceutical compounds, technologies, know-how and data available for research and development for neglected tropical diseases, tuberculosis and malaria. For more information, see Six et al., note 12 above; Esther van Zimmeren, 'Towards a New Patent Paradigm for the Biomedical Sector? Facilitating Access, Open Innovation and Social Responsibility in Patent Law in the US, Europe and Japan' (Ph.D. thesis, University of Leuven, 2011); and Esther van Zimmeren et al., 'Patent Pools and Clearinghouses in the Life Sciences' (2011) 29 *Trends in Biotechnology* 569.

4) and clearinghouses (section 5). To illustrate the actual operation of the models, two case studies will be utilized in sections 4 and 5. As a case study for the patent pool model, I will refer to the MPEG-2 pool, which was the first pioneer patent pool within the standardization context and has been used as a model by various later pool projects. The clearinghouse model covers a wide variety of potential institutional designs and may fulfil different purposes ranging from the mere provision of information services to IP consultation and match-making to acting as a collective manager of patent rights. The latter is comparable to the objectives of copyright collecting societies.[19] In practice this more "advanced" type of patent clearinghouse is relatively uncommon. We will use the Librassay "licensing supermarket" (the health care related "sibling" of the MPEG-2 pool) to illustrate the lessons learnt from the user generated law analysis. Librassay was initiated by MPEG LA, the administrator of the MPEG-2 pool, and it thus offers an interesting example for examining why certain sectors may be more suitable for the establishment of a clearinghouse type of model rather than a pool model. A comparison between pools and clearinghouses through the "lens" of the user generated law model is carried out in section 6. The chapter then offers a number of concluding remarks on the user generated law model in section 7.

2. "EX ANTE" QUESTIONS

Before analysing the user generated law model and its application to pools and clearinghouses, I would like to highlight two questions that need to be taken into account when examining IP coordination mechanisms. First, does a verifiable demand exist for establishing an IP coordination mode in a certain sector or for a certain technology? Second, assuming that this specified demand exists, which actor is best positioned to respond to that need and take the required initiatives towards (the stimulation of) establishing a pool or clearinghouse?

To explain the relevance of the first question, I underline that the establishment of patent coordination mechanisms is a long and challenging process which requires a strong engagement from the stakeholders.

---

[19] For a comparison of copyright collecting societies see Esther van Zimmeren, 'Clearinghouse Mechanisms in Genetic Diagnostics: A Conceptual Framework', in Geertrui Van Overwalle (ed.), *Gene Patents and Collaborative Licensing Models: Patent Pools, Clearinghouses, Open Source Models and Liability Regimes* (Cambridge University Press, 2009) 63.

These mechanisms emerge particularly in areas where patent rights are highly fragmented and both patent owners and users recognize the importance of a one-stop-shop access. Responding to hype about the existence of so-called "patent thickets" or a "tragedy of the anti-commons" is hence unwise.[20] These metaphors have become popular terms, but are often not sufficiently defined. Empirical data showing the existence of such thickets is often lacking, inconclusive or reflects the complex regulatory context of the alleged thicket rather than the actual causal link between the thicket and access problems in a certain sector or industry.[21]

Various authors have emphasized this metaphorical conception of thickets, writing of "a tangled, twisted mass of intellectual property rights, which criss-cross the established walkways of commerce" and where progress requires "numerous contracts with multiple, independent right holders".[22] Shapiro speaks of "a dense web of overlapping intellectual property rights that a company must hack its way through in order to actually commercialize new technology".[23] I consider a patent thicket as a situation where organizations encounter (1) *many overlapping* and *essential* patents (2) held by *many patent owners* in the area where they are doing research, are developing products or carrying out services. In my opinion, patent thickets and anticommons problems are "close cousins".[24] The distinction between patent thickets and anticommons problems primarily lies in the patent scope. If property rights are broad and patents owned by multiple owners overlap,[25] the problem is that of patent thickets. These overlapping rights can be owned by a relatively

---

[20] Cf. Timothy Caulfield at al., 'Evidence and Anecdotes: An Analysis of Human Gene Patenting Controversies' (2006) 24 *Nat. Biotechnol.* 1091.

[21] See e.g. Robert Cook-Deegan et al., 'Impact of Gene Patents and Licensing Practices on Access to Genetic Testing for Inherited Susceptibility to Cancer: Comparing Breast and Ovarian Cancers with Colon Cancers' (2010) 12 *Genet. Med.*, Suppl. S15-38; and Isabelle Huys et al., 'Legal Uncertainty in the Area of Genetic Diagnostic Testing' (2010) 27 *Nat. Biotechnol.* 903.

[22] Robert P. Merges, 'Contracting Into Liability Rules: Intellectual Property Rights and Collective Rights Organizations' (1996) 84 *Calif. Law Rev.* 1293.

[23] Shapiro, note 6 above, p. 120.

[24] Dan L. Burk and Mark A. Lemley, *The Patent Crisis and How the Courts Can Solve It* (Chicago University Press, 2009), p. 78.

[25] This might have been the intention of the patent office, for instance in case an improvement fits within the scope of an earlier claim in a selection patent or second medical use claim. Or the overlap might be due to a failure of the patent office to identify prior art.

limited number of companies with large portfolios.[26] If property rights are too narrow and divided among many patent owners, the problem is that of an anticommons. The emergence of one or the other may vary across industries and technologies. Therefore, in the remainder of this chapter I will mostly use the more descriptive term "fragmentation", rather than employ these two commonly applied metaphors.

Although the aforementioned definitions suggest the presence of a large number of patents, I would like to highlight that "large number" may be relative. In certain technology fields, a relatively small number of fragmented patent rights may be sufficient to prompt a conclusion that there is a problem of fragmentation. The related costs involved in locating licensing partners ("search costs"), in negotiating licensing conditions ("bargaining costs") and in enforcing the licensing agreement ("enforcements costs") – all told, the transaction costs – together with the potential of royalty stacking, may impede second comers from engaging in related research or entering the market. So even in cases of limited fragmentation – depending on the type of technology and the cost structure of the market – existing patent rights may already create an "undue burden" for a certain entity.[27] This undue burden becomes eminent if the patent covers "essential" products or processes, meaning that researchers or companies need access to the patented invention in order to operate successfully in a certain field. In such cases, the actual number of relevant fragmented patent rights will be less relevant and the establishment of a small pool or niche clearinghouse could be appropriate anyway.

Fragmentation generally occurs in fields with complex products, production or research processes or in areas where many organizations compete in R&D in the same area.[28] In such sectors, innovation is often cumulative: each invention builds on many previous findings, which increases the risk of overlapping patents. This is also the case, for instance, within the context of standardization. It has further been

---

[26] Burk and Lemley, note 24 above, p. 78.

[27] By "undue burden" I mean that these "rights are a substantial obstacle on the organization's path to research, product development and/or the provision of (clinical testing) services". See Esther van Zimmeren, Sven Vanneste and Geertrui Van Overwalle, *Patent Licensing in Medical Biotechnology* (Acco, 2011).

[28] Sadao Nagaoka and Yoichiro Nishimura, *An Empirical Assessment of the Effects of Patent Thickets* (SPRU 40th Anniversary Conference – The Future of Science, Technology and Innovation Policy, September 11–13, 2006, University of Sussex, SPRU-Science & Technology Policy Research).

suggested that in the biomedical sector, in particular in genetics, the risk of fragmentation would disrupt innovation because in this field substitutes for genetic inventions are often lacking and competitors will therefore often not be able to invent around those patents. Various scholars[29] and policymakers[30] as well as national and international advisory organs, such as the OECD,[31] the US Secretary's Advisory Committee on Genetics, Health, and Society (USSACGHS),[32] the Human

---

[29] See e.g. Eric Noehrenberg, 'Implications of Patent Pools on Innovation Regarding Antiretrovirals' (2010) 4 *Open AIDS J.* 67; G. Van Overwalle, 'Turning Patent Swords into Shares' (2010) 30 *Science* 1630; van Zimmeren, note 19 above; Birgit Verbeure, 'Patent Pooling for Gene-Based Diagnostic Testing: Conceptual Framework', in G. Van Overwalle (ed), *Gene Patents and Collaborative Licensing Models – Patent Pools, Clearinghouses, Open Source Models and Liability Regimes* (Cambridge University Press, 2009) 3; Birgit Verbeure et al., 'Patent Pools and Diagnostic Testing' (2006) 24 *Trends in Biotechnol.* 115; Geertrui Van Overwalle et al., 'Models for Facilitating Access to Patents on Genetic Inventions' (2006) 7 *Nat. Rev. Genet.* 143; Dianne Nicol and Janet Hope, 'Cooperative Strategies for Facilitating Use of Patented Inventions in Biotechnology' (2006) 24 *Law in Context* 85; Ted J. Ebersole, Marvin C. Guthrie and Jorge A. Goldstein, 'Patent Pools and Standard Setting in Diagnostic Genetics' (2005) 23 *Nat. Biotechnol.* 937; Anatole F. Krattiger, 'Financing the Bioindustry and Facilitating Biotechnology Transfer' (2004) *IP Strategy Today*, No. 8-2004; and Frank Grassler and Mary A. Capria, 'Patent Pooling: Uncorking a Technology Transfer Bottleneck and Creating Value in the Biomedical Research Field' (2003) 9 *J. Comm. Biotechnol.* 111.

[30] See e.g. Australian Senate-Community Affairs References Committee, *Gene Patents* (Commonwealth of Australia, November 26, 2010) available at http://www.aph.gov.au/Senate/committee/clac_ctte/gene_patents_43/report/report.pdf (accessed January 21, 2016); WHO-Expert Working Group on Research and Development Financing, *Research and Development: Coordination and Financing* (WHO, 2010), available at http://www.who.int/phi/documents/RD FinancingwithISBN.pdf (accessed January 21, 2016); WHO-Intergovernmental Working Group on Public Health, Innovation, and Intellectual Property, *Report of the Intergovernmental Working Group on Public Health, Innovation, and Intellectual Property* (WHO, Sixty-first World Health Assembly, 2008) A61.9, available at http://apps.who.int/iris/bitstream/10665/23425/1/A61_9-en.pdf (accessed February 3, 2016).

[31] OECD (2006) and OECD (2002), *Genetic Inventions, Intellectual Property Rights and Licensing Practices – Evidence and Policies*, Paris, OECD, available at http://www.oecd.org/dataoecd/42/21/2491084.pdf (accessed January 21, 2016).

[32] US Secretary's Advisory Committee on Genetics, Health, and Society (USSACGHS), *Revised Draft Report on Gene Patents and Licensing Practices and Their Impact on Patient Access to Genetic Tests* (Office of Science Policy – National Institutes of Health – Office of Biotechnology Activities, February 5,

Genome Organization (HUGO),[33] the Australian Law Reform Commission (ALRC)[34] and the European Society for Human Genetics (ESHG)[35] have recognized the role patent pools and other collaborative licensing efforts could play in dealing with fragmented patent rights in the biomedical sector, notably in genetic testing.[36] Lately, patent pools have also been mentioned specifically as an interesting option in the area of stem cell research[37] and vaccines.[38] Even the United States Patent and Trademark Office (USPTO), normally only involved in the issuance of patents rather than the post-grant phase of the "life" of a patent, considered the promotion of patent pools in biotechnology sufficiently important to publish a White Paper on the topic.[39] However, empirical

---

2010), available at http://oba.od.nih.gov/oba/SACGHS/SACGHS%20Patents%20Report%20Approved%202-5-20010.pdf (accessed January 21, 2016).

[33] Human Genome Organization (HUGO), *Statement on the Scope of Gene Patents, Research Exemption and Licensing of Patented Gene Sequences for Diagnostics* (HUGO IP Committee, 2003), available at (2003) 14(3–4) *Journal International de Bioéthique* 201.

[34] Australian Law Reform Commission (ALRC), *Genes and Ingenuity: Gene Patenting and Human Health* (Australian Law Reform Commission, 2004) Final Report ALRC 99, available at http://www.alrc.gov.au/publications/report-99 (accessed February 3, 2016).

[35] Ségolène Aymé et al., 'Patenting and Licensing in Genetic Testing – Recommendations of the European Society of Human Genetics' (2008) 16 *Eur. J. Hum. Genet.*, Suppl. 1 S3–9.

[36] According to van Zimmeren, Vanneste and Van Overwalle, note 27 above, pools are perceived as a valuable solution in an even broader variety of fields, including drug discovery, pharmaceuticals, diagnostics and genetic testing, especially for patents on gene sequences, processes and methods.

[37] Gulam Bahadur and Michael Morrison, 'Patenting Human Pluripotent Cells: Balancing Commercial, Academic and Ethical Interests' (2010) 25 *Human Reproduction* 14, p. 19; and Karl Bergman and Gregory D. Graff, 'The Global Stem Cell Patent Landscape: Implications for Efficient Technology Transfer and Commercial Development' (2007) 25 *Nat. Biotechnol.* 419.

[38] See e.g. Hillary Greene, 'Patent Pooling Behind the Veil of Uncertainty: Antitrust, Competition Policy, and the Vaccine Industry' (2010) 90 *Bost. U. L. Rev.* 1397.

[39] J. Clark et al., *Patent Pools: A Solution to the Problem of Access in Biotechnology Patents?* (USPTO, December 5, 2000), available at http://www.uspto.gov/web/offices/pac/dapp/opla/patentpool.pdf (accessed January 21, 2016). At the moment of the publication of the report, Q. Todd Dickinson, the Under Secretary of Commerce for Intellectual Property and Director of the USPTO, clarified why they thought it was vital to point the biotechnology industry to the possibility to set up pools: "Biotechnology, an increasingly important industry to the American economy, is heavily dependent on patent

studies have shown that some of the concerns have not materialized.[40] Moreover, the decisions of the US Supreme Court in the *Mayo* and *Myriad* cases[41] have resulted in a limitation of patent-eligible subject matter in the United States, and this has relieved a lot of the fears in the field as far as the United States is concerned.

In addition to the challenges involved in exploring the actual demand for an IP coordination mechanism, the particular nature of such models needs to be recognized in terms of the requirement for a firm commitment by the stakeholders. Pools and clearinghouses are so-called "two-sided markets",[42] intermediaries or platforms where two sets of agents, patent owners and licensees, interact. Getting "*both sides*" on board is fundamental for the development and success of each platform. The actual engagement of both sides will also affect the design of the platform and the functioning of the platform, for instance in terms of its licensing and pricing strategies. Therefore, the heterogeneous interests of patent owners and licensees will be determinant for the actual emergence and (successful) operation of pools and clearinghouses. Dynamics *within* the group of patent owners and the group of licensees will most likely involve

---

protection to maintain viability. While most biotechnology companies are *responsible* corporate citizens, offering *reasonable* access to their patented inventions, one concern about broad patenting in biotechnology, especially regarding genomic inventions, is the ease and cost of licensing multiple patents. ... Patent pools can allow *reasonable* access to patented genomic inventions, thereby promoting research and development while also promoting competition through patenting" (emphasis added) USPTO, *USPTO issues White Paper on Patent Pooling*, Press Release, No. 01-06, January 19, 2001, available at http://www.uspto.gov/news/pr/2001/01-06.jsp (accessed January 21, 2016).

40 See e.g. US National Research Council of the National Academies-Committee on Intellectual Property Rights in Genomic and Protein Research and Innovation, *Reaping the Benefits of Genomic and Proteomic Research: Intellectual Property Rights, Innovation, and Public Health* (The National Academies Press, 2006); John P. Walsh, Ashish Arora and Wesley M. Cohen, 'Effects of Research Tool Patents and Licensing on Biomedical Innovation', in Wesley M. Cohen and Stephen A. Merrill (eds), *Patents in the Knowledge-based Economy* (The National Academies Press, 2005) 285 and Caulfield et al., note 20 above.

41 US Supreme Court, *Mayo Collaborative Services dba Mayo Medical Laboratories and May Clinic Rochester v. Prometheus Laboratories, Inc.*, 132 S.Ct. 1289 (2012) and US Supreme Court, *Association for Molecular Pathology et al. v. Myriad Genetics, Inc. and Directors of the University of Utah Research Foundation*, 569 U.S. (2013). See also section 5 below within the context of Librassay.

42 Jean Tirole and Jean-Charles Rochet, 'Platform Competition in Two-Sided Markets' (2003) 1 *Journal of the European Economic Association* 990.

divergent interests as well. For instance, if a certain field has patents which are distributed amongst small research-only companies, vertically integrated research and manufacturing companies, as well as universities, considerations for determining whether to participate in a pool or clearinghouse will be very different.

Assuming that a demand for an IP coordination mechanism is identified, the second "ex ante" question focuses on the actor most appropriate to take initiatives towards creating a pool or clearinghouse. One may wonder whether (without imposing a top-down public pool or clearinghouse model) it may be opportune for a regulator to construct a fertile ground for developing such models by creating certain incentive structures. Or would it better to let the market decide freely, leaving optimal space for a pure bottom-up initiative by the stakeholders, patent owners and users? Alternatively, the research community in a certain sector may be another key player that could drive such an initiative, because a call from the community would likely reflect the perspective of both patent owners and users. Or individual researchers may take the lead in setting up a private regulatory model, as has happened with the Creative Commons initiative with Lawrence Lessig as the main "architect". In some cases, an intermediary with experience in administering pool or clearinghouses may volunteer and try to attract patent owners with a call for patents followed by the set-up of a licensing programme (i.e. MPEG-2 pool and Librassay). Lastly, funding institutions may further ground the establishment of pools or clearinghouse models by providing formal (i.e. IP policy), informal (i.e. information) and financial supporting measures. In some cases all or several actors may get involved.

The user generated law model provides some interesting lessons, especially in terms of the involvement and role of the regulator in setting the boundaries of the "autonomy space", the role of so-called "lead actors" at the "emergence phase" of the private regulatory model, and the "reputational effects" of the involvement of a veteran patent pool administrator. These concepts (and some others) will be described in greater detail in section 3 and will be applied to pools and clearinghouses in sections 4 to 6.

3. MAIN FEATURES OF THE USER GENERATED LAW MODEL

The user generated law model is explained in more detail in Chapter 1 of this book. It starts from the assumption that the "circumstances and the actors involved in the development of legal innovations to a high degree resemble the development of product and service innovations". If we grant that the "production processes" of legal innovations and product and service innovation can indeed be compared, the insights of Eric von Hippel's theory on user innovation[43] may provide a better understanding of how user generated law develops (i.e. private regulatory models). Riis claims that the model could indeed "contribute to the creation of a better law" and could be "used to identify the best legal institutional conditions for the promotion of user generated law".[44] Certainly, the time lag and inflexibility of statutory law and case law, on the one hand, and the notion of IP law as a balancing mechanism, on the other hand, have been the subject of debate and a number of new non-legislative, private regulatory models have emerged. Typically, the top-down IP statutory law does not work as intended (meaning that fragmentation of patent rights results in high transaction costs and royalty stacking). In such instances, private arrangements redefine the legal position and change the balance between the opposite interests inherent in IP law (i.e. the economic incentives for the creation of new knowledge harboured by creators/IP owners versus the broader access to the new knowledge desired by users/licensees).

For user innovations, the following three phases can be identified: emergence (section 3.1), diffusion (section 3.2) and adoption (section 3.3). Emergence refers to the phase of creating a private regulatory model and getting stakeholders to embrace this model. Diffusion means that the model is "copied" and employed by others. Adoption implies that the model is acknowledged by the legislator or other producers of State-enacted law as a workable alternative regulatory model. In the next sections, the main features of these three phases are briefly discussed. (For a fuller explication of the model, see Chapter 1 of this book.)

3.1 Emergence

It is anticipated that private regulatory models will emerge more regularly in certain legal and societal sectors, while other sectors will have less use for these models (or indeed none at all). It follows that specific areas of the law will be most affected and altered by such models. There are different determinants that influence why private actors expect private regulatory models to perform better than State-enacted law. The user generated law model reveals five determinants: the scope of the

---

[43] Eric von Hippel, *The Sources of Innovation* (Oxford University Press, 1988); and Eric von Hippel, *Democratizing Innovation* (MIT Press, 2005).

[44] Riis, Chapter 1 of this book.

autonomy space (section 3.1.1), heterogeneous demands of the stakeholders (section 3.1.2), the expectation of benefits (section 3.1.3), the existence of asymmetric information (section 3.1.4) and the role of lead actors (section 3.1.5).[45]

3.1.1 Autonomy space

State-enacted law defines a space within which actors operate autonomously, which Riis refers to as the "autonomy space". In some parts of State-enacted law, public policy considerations are dominant and private actors only have very limited freedom to establish private regulatory models (*narrow autonomy space*). In other parts of State-enacted law, public policy considerations play a minor role which gives a large degree of freedom to establish private regulatory models (*wide autonomy space*). User generated law emerges in these autonomy spaces.[46]

The State-enacted law that determines the scope of the autonomy space can be either "proactive" or "reactive". Where a proactive process is used, the legislator anticipates a future need of regulation and adopts law that defines the autonomy space *before* an actual need of law has emerged. In a reactive process, user generated law develops spontaneously in the area where a legal gap exists. After the emergence of the user generated law (and in some cases after/during the diffusion phase) two scenarios are possible. First, the user generated law may be considered in conflict with the needs of society at large and the legislator may decide to limit the autonomy space. Second, the user generated law may be regarded as compatible with societal interests and the legislator may decide not to intervene in the private practice or even to institutionalize it into State-enacted law. In these two situations, the user generated law is said to be adopted.[47] Therefore, the scope of the autonomy space not only affects the first "infant phase" of the "life" of the private regulatory model concerned, but also the next two phases towards a more "mature" user generated law model.

---

[45] Ibid. I note that the scope of the autonomy space is not explicitly categorized by Riis as a determinant of the phase of emergence, but rather as a separate issue. This is probably explained by the fact that the scope of the autonomy space also influences the later phases (diffusion and adoption). Nonetheless, I decided to include it as a determinant under the emergence phase as it seems most prominent and decisive in this phase for the success of the private regulatory model (see e.g. Librassay model).

[46] Riis, Chapter 1 of this book.

[47] Ibid.

However, in reality the boundaries of autonomy spaces are diffuse and dynamic. The legislator may decide to intervene by adjusting the scope of the autonomy space. Such adjustments may be directly related to the user generated law model or they may indirectly affect the emergence, diffusion and adoption of the model. Riis notes that this dynamic interaction between user generated law and State-enacted law is not reflected in the theory on user innovation.[48] Nonetheless, the example of the Librassay model in Chapter 5 will clearly show the potential impact of a limitation of the autonomy space on the emergence of a clearinghouse model.

3.1.2 Heterogeneous demands

The large number of different business models, user communities, transactions and the development of a patent marketplace (see section 1 above) in the knowledge economy shows the heterogeneity of stakeholder interests. However, State-enacted law that creates autonomy spaces is primarily based on public policy considerations which are determined by the needs of society at large rather than the needs of those stakeholders. This could be referred to as a kind of "few sizes fit all approach". Since stakeholders' needs are heterogeneous, this approach will leave many of them dissatisfied with the status of State-enacted law. When market participants do not find a solution that is workable within the provided autonomy space, they are likely to "invent around" the legal framework by modifying existing legal arrangements or developing legal innovations that respond to their own needs.[49]

3.1.3 Expectation of benefits

The creation of private regulatory models generally involves substantial fixed costs, especially when a given model requires an institutional set-up (e.g. copyright collecting societies, patent pools and patent clearinghouses). In addition, the actual design of the model and the availability of a large variety of licensing options (i.e. different standard contracts offered by the pool or clearinghouse) also have a cost for IP owners, licensees and the institutionalized private regulatory model itself. The presence of many options implies a considerable level of complexity. Thus, it will typically take some time for stakeholders to get a good understanding of the different options, consider each choice, perhaps seek legal advice, and balance the pros and cons of each of them.

---

[48] Ibid.

[49] Ibid.

Depending on the number of options, it is possible that it is more efficient for patent owners or users to actually ignore the private regulatory model and negotiate individual licence contracts with the relevant patent owners specifically tailored to the needs of the licensee. It is unlikely that any standard licence, regardless of the exact number of available variations, would offer a similar level of specificity.

Stakeholders will seek to ensure that the costs involved in the establishment and use of the model can be recouped. This can, for instance, occur by reducing risks (as risks represent costs). The more a model capable of reducing risk levels is used, the more value it generates. In addition, in some cases legal innovations can generate benefits of a non-economic nature that are sufficiently high to foster the private regulatory model. The more an innovation is used by peers or in a certain community, the more the initiator's reputation is increased. Moreover, fixed costs may also be recouped by the private regulatory model, as it may offer a service that the stakeholders cannot offer independently such as a one-stop-shop model that coordinates and provides access to rights owned by different patent owners. Patent owners will get a reasonable return on their R&D investments. If (some of those) patent owners also have an interest in gaining access to (part of) the pooled assets, they will have a "double", "two-sided" interest in collaborating with the private regulatory model. On the other hand, users of the patent rights that do not own any relevant rights themselves may benefit from working with the model by clearing their freedom to operate in a certain field or with respect to a certain technology and by preventing royalty stacking. Therefore, irrespective of the sort of benefits user generated law may create for owners and users, we can assume that a new regulatory model will only be created if it is expected to be sufficiently used.[50]

3.1.4 Asymmetric information

Information on the needs for legal intervention within autonomy spaces is generally unequally distributed between the legislator and stakeholders. Moreover, such needs tend to be very heterogeneous. Satisfying these heterogeneous demands is very complex. Normally, stakeholders will be able to deal with these complexities in a more efficient way; but stakeholders will be inclined to optimize their own needs and preferences. Asymmetric information may also be present when the legislator is overwhelmed by the amount of available information and is not able to distinguish between more and less relevant information. This may happen

---

[50] Ibid.

with respect to private regulatory models due to lobbying in the legislative process or in the wake of scientific or media hypes. Lobbyists usually provide "coloured" information which promotes a specific perspective on the issues concerned. This may lead to an information overload that obscures rather than clarifies the facts and sheds no light on the need for intervention.[51] Alternatively, highly regarded experts within a certain community may express particular concerns that do not have a thorough basis in empirical data. If such concerns are taken up in relevant scientific literature, and potentially also by the popular media, an unsubstantiated hype may be created. In some cases, private regulatory models may be proposed without actual evidence of a problem. Legislators and other types of (international) public and private organizations may be inclined to interfere by calling for or becoming involved in the initiation of such a model. This should be prevented at all times by requiring thorough empirical evidence before investing in the establishment of a private regulatory model.

3.1.5 Lead actors

According to von Hippel's user innovation model, successful innovations often start up as user innovations and are subsequently adopted by manufacturers who commercialize them. In this process, lead users can provide very useful information to manufacturers that they would not otherwise have. Lead users demonstrate a higher level of innovative activities because they expect to gain the most from a new product or service.[52] Riis proposes to replace the concept of "lead users" with "lead actors" within the context of user generated law.[53] The term "lead actors" is more precise and comprises not only individual users, but also communities and intermediaries who set the scene and are perceived as directly or indirectly representing user interests. Contrary to the concept of "lead users" in the theory on user innovation, lead actors are not necessarily motivated by an expectation of obtaining direct benefits from the creation of a legal innovation. For instance, non-profit organizations such as Creative Commons, which develop certain model contracts, are driven by their focus on the wide dissemination of the contracts (and ultimately information) rather than by their expectations concerning direct benefits.[54] Thus, depending on the private, public or hybrid nature of a certain patent pool or clearinghouse, the initiators of such models

---

51 Ibid.

52 Von Hippel, note 43 above, s. 108; and Riis, Chapter 1 of this book.

53 Riis, Chapter 1 of this book.

54 Ibid.

may or may not be motivated by direct benefits. Such benefits may be financial or otherwise.

3.2 Diffusion

Legal innovations may spread by marketing such models using social media in ways which are similar to the diffusion of innovative products and services. As a consequence, a community may be formed around the legal innovation that supports the use of the private regulatory model and/or actively participates in the diffusion and operation of the model. The actual extent of diffusion is closely related to the costs of establishing the model but may also be affected by other factors such as "reputational effects" and "network effects".[55]

3.2.1 Reputational effects

A private regulatory model that is being used and actively promoted by part of the community concerned will possibly generate positive reputational effects that reduce the uncertainties for new users and, therefore, lead to even wider diffusion. For instance, the patent pool model with which various administrators have experimented is likely to reassure new market participants that no unexpected serious legal risks will occur and that the model operates smoothly.

Within the context of reputational effects, the name of the private regulatory model functions like a trademark and may develop into a strong brand (potentially associated with certain values, e.g. Creative Commons, GNU General Public License) which leads to the further dissemination of the model. The association with a certain private regulatory model is a means to signal that the user of the model is part of a broader community that supports the model and backs the values concerned.

3.2.2 Network effects

Network effects exist when one user of a product positively affects other people's perception of the product's value. When network effects are present, the value of a model increases with the number of other persons using the same model. In section 2, I explained that patent pools and clearinghouses are two-sided markets. Network effects are extremely important for such two-sided markets. With "two-sided network effects", the platform's value to any given user largely depends on the number of

[55] Ibid.

users on the network's other side.[56] The value of the model increases when the pool or clearinghouse matches the demands from both sides.

3.3 Adoption

According to Riis, the private regulatory model can be "adopted" in two ways. First, the legislator and other producers of State-enacted law acknowledge the model, decide that it works well and that no legal corrections are necessary. Second, the model may be incorporated into State-enacted law either by including it in statutory rules or by courts applying the model as the default rule. However, the act of "adopting" a certain model is not an "either-or decision" (fully accepted (adopted) or fully rejected (non-adopted)).[57] In most cases, the key features of the private regulatory model will be adopted with some minor tweaks in order to adapt the model and enable use beyond the particular experimental scope. As a result, the scope of the autonomy space will be adjusted.

4. PATENT POOLS[58]

The term "patent pool" has acquired different meanings. For some, the term may simply refer to a loose collection of patents held by several patent owners. However, I propose a narrower, legal definition that better aligns with the view of pools as a private regulatory model. According to that definition, patent pools are complex legal arrangements consisting of different sets of agreements aimed at clearing a multitude of patents held by multiple patent owners. The establishment of a pool generally requires (at least) two types of agreements: first, a multiparty agreement[59] between two or more patent owners to license one or more of their patents to one another; second, a standard package (sub)licence for third parties willing to pay the royalties associated (third party licence). The

---

[56] Tirole and Rochet, note 42 above, pp. 990–1029.

[57] Riis, Chapter 1 of this book.

[58] This section is closely based on part of the analysis in Chapter 12 of my Ph.D. thesis: see van Zimmeren, 'Towards a New Patent Paradigm for the Biomedical Sector? Facilitating Access, Open Innovation and Social Responsibility in Patent Law in the US, Europe and Japan' (Leuven, May 2011, unpublished manuscript available at the Library of the KU Leuven).

[59] In some cases the multiparty agreement is replaced by a set of separate bilateral agreements between each individual contributor and the pool/pool administrator.

emergence of pools is not a new phenomenon, as pools were not uncommon in the United States at the end of the nineteenth century. However, in the 1990s these models revived when stakeholders involved in standardization sought an effective, flexible solution for facilitating access to patents covered by the standard. Nowadays, a considerable number of pools related to a standard exist.

Patent owners benefit from the pool model by gaining an income from their patents without going through an individual licensing process which would require more time and resources. A patent pool may also provide an opportunity for patent owners to expand their market by encouraging the spread of the technology concerned. On the other hand, licensees value the pool model as it allows them to easily obtain most, if not all, of the licences required to practice the technology covered by the pool with a single licensing transaction ("one-stop-shop").[60] Moreover, licensing through the pool will normally be cheaper than obtaining them separately from each patent owner, as the pool is aimed at preventing royalty stacking and is obliged to offer licensing conditions under fair, reasonable and non-discriminatory terms (so-called FRAND-terms).

The business or management model of the pool will differ according to the number of patent owners involved, the complexity of the technology and the nature of the initiator of the pool. Third-party licensing may occur directly by one of the patent owners of the pool – appointed by the owners amongst themselves – to the licensees.[61] Alternatively, third-party licences may be administered indirectly through a separate joint venture or independent licensing agent.[62] The first model is most appropriate for pools with a relatively limited number of participating patent owners. However, in pools where one of the patent owners manages the pool, it is vital that there are some safeguards with respect to its independence and so-called "Chinese walls" to preserve the confidentiality of sensitive business information. Such small groups of (usually larger) patent owners

---

[60] Often one or more patent owners decide not to participate in the pool, or several pools related to the same technology and managed by different administrators may exist in parallel.

[61] See e.g. USDOJ, *Business Review Letter DVD-Toshiba* (Washington, DC, 1999), available at http://www.usdoj.gov/atr/public/busreview/2485.pdf; and USDOJ, *Business Review Letter DVD-Philips* (Washington, DC, 1998), available at http://www.usdoj.gov/atr/public/busreview/2121.htm (accessed January 21, 2016).

[62] See e.g. USDOJ, *Business Review Letter MPEG-2* (Washington, DC, 1997), available at http://www.justice.gov/atr/public/busreview/215742.htm (accessed January 21, 2016).

that start licensing out under a common scheme managed by one of the partners often present themselves as "joint licensing schemes" rather than patent pools. Most of these joint licensing schemes, nonetheless, follow the rules set by the competition authorities for pools and are open to patent owners interested in joining and licensees willing to license the technology. Examples of such joint licensing schemes are the package licences offered by Philips.

Large pools would place too heavy an administrative burden on the managing partner. Therefore, the administration of large pools will generally be delegated to an independent third party, either specifically set up for the management of the pool or pre-existing. The standard-driven pools that have been set up since the 1990s tend to follow this model. Since then, this model has been diffused widely and several independent agents have emerged that are managing several pools (e.g. MPEG Licensing Authority (MPEG LA),[63] ViaLicensing Corporation, SISVEL, 3G licensing, the Open Patent Alliance and ULDAGE, though their approaches towards pool management and the number of pools that they are administering at the same time may differ). The pools managed by a separate licensing entity are run very professionally, starting with open calls for essential patents. The independent agent employs patent attorneys who evaluate the patents filed in response to the call to verify whether the patents are indeed essential. The administrator sets the royalty rates for the pool and the other licensing conditions in close dialogue with the patent owners. Patent owners transfer certain rights concerning their patents to the administrator, which licenses those rights, collects the royalties, distributes them to a pre-agreed scheme, and monitors patent enforcement.

In the 1990s, the first patent pool to emerge in the standardization context was the MPEG-2 pool. During the standardization process, companies concluded that there were too many overlapping patent rights involved in the MPEG-2 standard (a digital compression technology used in many different products and services, including DVD, cable, satellite and broadcast television, telecommunications and digital video applications). Therefore, an alternative solution had to be found to deal with

---

[63] MPEG LA strongly emphasizes that it operates truly independently and impartially: it regards both patent owners and licensees as its customers and is aimed at "balancing reasonable access for users with reasonable return to patent owners". L. Horn, 'Case 1. The MPEG LA Licensing Model. What Problem Does It Solve in Biopharma and Genetics?', in G. Van Overwalle (ed.), *Gene Patents and Collaborative Licensing Models: Patent Pools, Clearinghouses, Open Source Models and Liability Regimes* (Cambridge University Press, 2009) 33, p. 36.

all these patent rights, which would otherwise block the manufacture and development of technology around the standard. The competition law implications of the MPEG-2 pool model were cleared by the US Department of Justice (USDOJ) by way of a so-called "business review letter"[64] in 1997.[65] The European Commission, which issued a comfort letter to MPEG LA in 1998,[66] and the Japanese Fair Trade Commission, duly aligned their guidelines regarding patent pools[67] with the conditions set out in this business review letter and later ones.[68]

A separate licensing administrator (MPEG LA)[69] was set up to administer these rights. The pool offers worldwide, non-exclusive, non-discriminatory and reasonable licensing of essential patents. An independent expert determines which patents are essential to compliance with the MPEG-2 standard. The pool allocates a portion of the licensing fee to each member of the pool, according to a pre-set formula. MPEG LA is authorized to audit licensees, but will not transmit any sensitive business information to others. Over time, the MPEG-2 patent licence portfolio has grown from the original eight patent owners and 100

---

[64] The business review procedure allows the USDOJ to review proposed business conduct and state whether it forgoes the initiation of antitrust proceedings should the proposed conduct be carried out. Regulations describing the procedure were issued at 28 C.F.R. §50.6. The US Federal Trade Commission has a similar advisory procedure, see 16 C.F.R. §§1.1–1.4.

[65] USDOJ, note 62 above. Cf. US Department of Justice and US Federal Trade Commission, *Antitrust Guidelines for the Licensing of Intellectual Property* (Washington, DC, 1995) and US Department of Justice and US Federal Trade Commission, *Antitrust Enforcement and Intellectual Property Rights: Promoting Innovation and Competition* (Washington, DC, 2007).

[66] European Commission, Comfort Letter December 1998, Case No. IV/C.3/36.849. See also European Commission, 'Commission approves a patent licensing programme to implement the MPEG-2 standard', Press Release, IP/98/1155, Brussels, December 18, 1998, available at http://europa.eu/rapid/press-release_IP-98-1155_en.htm?locale=en (accessed January 21, 2016).

[67] European Commission, *Communication from the Commission – Guidelines on the application of Article 101 of the Treaty on the Functioning of the European Union to technology transfer agreements* (Brussels 2014, *OJEU* C89/03), section 4.4 on "technology pools"; and Japan Fair Trade Commission, *Guidelines on Standardization and Patent Pool Arrangements* (Tokyo, 2005).

[68] See for instance USDOJ (1998) and USDOJ (1999), note 61 above; and USDOJ, *Business Review Letter 3G PPP* (Washington, DC, 2002), available at http://www.usdoj.gov/atr/public/busreview/200455.pdf (accessed January 16, 2016).

[69] See http://www.mpegla.com/main/default.aspx (accessed February 3, 2016).

essential patents to include more than 1,000 essential patents owned by 27 patent owners and 1,924 licensees.[70] The successful MPEG model has benefitted from significant network and reputational effects and has been widely diffused. The conditions originally set out in the USDOJ business review letter have become the template for many later pools and have influenced the delineation of the autonomy space. Although several other patent administrators have entered the patent marketplace, MPEG LA appears to have acted as the lead actor in experimenting with the patent pool model and generating trust in the marketplace amongst the stakeholders. It is currently administering ten active licensing programmes. Moreover, MPEG LA is experimenting with new business models aimed at balancing the generation of reasonable licensing revenue with affordable access beyond the area of consumer electronics and telecommunications, for instance in biotechnology and energy.[71] Librassay, which will be described in section 5 below concerning clearinghouses, is one of these experiments. In addition, MPEG LA is examining opportunities to combine its licensing programmes with a more tailored technology transfer services component.[72]

5. CLEARINGHOUSES[73]

The term clearinghouse is derived from banking institutions and refers to the mechanism by which cheques and bills are exchanged amongst member banks in order to transfer only the net balances in cash. Nowadays the concept has acquired a much broader meaning. Within the context of patent law, a clearinghouse can be depicted as a private regulatory model operating as an intermediary platform aimed at bringing together a variety of owners and users of goods, services and information in order to lower transaction costs.[74] In the market for technology, patent clearinghouses act in the manner of an independent broker: facilitating exchanges between patent owners and users of technology.

---

[70] L. Horn, 'Overview – New York BIO Conference' (Presentation at New York BIO Conference, May 5, 2015), received from the author, slide 6.

[71] Ibid., slide 4.

[72] Ibid.

[73] This section is closely based on part of the analysis in Chapter 13 of my Ph.D. thesis, see van Zimmeren, note 18 above.

[74] Krattiger, note 29 above, p. 20.

Based on the various functions a clearinghouse may fulfil, five types of patent clearinghouses have been distinguished in the literature.[75] The first two models merely provide access to (protected) information. This can be relatively basic descriptive information related to technology, patents, patent claims, etc. (*information clearinghouse*). A *technology exchange clearinghouse* combines this information with a service which lists technologies available through licensing to allow technology users to initiate negotiations for a licence. Hence, these clearinghouses do not guarantee the authorized use of the patented inventions and still require bilateral licensing negotiations between patent owners and users. The remaining three clearinghouse models, more advanced in scope, aim at catering for both access to and (standardized) use of the inventions. Access and use can be offered by a clearinghouse on a royalty-free, open access basis (*open access clearinghouse*), or via standard licences (*standard licences clearinghouse* and *royalty collection clearinghouse*). A *royalty collection clearinghouse* undertakes to act as a platform able to offer the widest variety of services, such as information exchange, match-making, standard licences, collection and distribution of royalties, monitoring and enforcement, and dispute resolution. This typology has the advantage of being "dynamic". It is dynamic to the extent that in practice – due to the needs of the market – a clearinghouse may develop from one end of the spectrum to the other end: from an information clearinghouse to a more advanced type of clearinghouse. It may be worthwhile to start with the formation of an information clearinghouse for a certain sector, which could later start offering additional services according to the needs of its customers. Initially, it could primarily be a tool to decrease search costs and increase transparency on the patent marketplace. At a later stage, match-making services, licensing support, etc. could be added to further reduce transaction costs.

I will now focus on the patent royalty collection clearinghouse, the most advanced model, which has also been called a "licensing supermarket", where a user can get a licence to all the available technologies needed to legitimately pursue pertinent R&D. A patent owner that appoints a royalty collection clearinghouse increases the visibility of the patents concerned. The clearinghouse will offer a database and market the patented technology. Technology users can easily search the database of the clearinghouse and can contact clearinghouse staff members for more detailed information on patented inventions. The user picks and

---

[75] See e.g. van Zimmeren et al., note 11 above; and Aoki and Schiff, note 8 above. Cf. Krattiger, note 29 above.

chooses all the technologies required and pays at the "cash check". In addition, the clearinghouse can offer fixed standard package licences for a reasonable royalty for certain complementary technologies, but the starting point of the clearinghouse would be flexibility for the users. In case of a high "stacked" royalty rate, the user could request a "discount", which could be granted by the clearinghouse after consultation with the patent owners concerned. The clearinghouse will undertake to collect the royalties and distribute them amongst the patent owners in accordance with the use. The clearinghouse may also offer additional services like monitoring of infringements, enforcement, arbitration and mediation. Economies of scale would lead to a decrease of search costs, negotiation costs and enforcement costs for owners and users. An important prerequisite for the continuity of the patent royalty collection clearinghouse is that there should be a recurring need to transact in patents included in the clearinghouse.[76] Another crucial issue is the need for the clearinghouse to provide a critical mass of high quality and vital patented inventions. Otherwise, the added value of such a private regulatory model would be limited and it would be more interesting for patent owners and users to enter into direct negotiations.

Survey data shows that in Europe a number of organizations in the biomedical sector have experience with clearinghouses as patent owners, in particular universities and research institutes.[77] Their major reason to use the services of clearinghouses is to facilitate licensing out, to generate licensing revenue, and to enable the organization to focus on its core activities. These objectives may be very valuable in light of the promotion of open innovation. Instead of having valuable IP "lying on the shelf", those stakeholders apparently use the services of intermediaries to market their technologies. The survey data also reveals that patent clearinghouses have played only a limited role in safeguarding freedom to operate, which may be due to the fact that existing patent clearinghouse models were not able to collect a critical mass of patented technologies for licensing or that their licensing portfolio became too heterogeneous to fulfil the needs of the users. In any case, the success of the clearinghouse will depend on the extent to which the relevant business and scientific community is willing to embrace the model.

Depending on its objectives, business model and management structure, the clearinghouse can be private or public, for-profit or non-profit. A patent clearinghouse, acting as an independent agent, generally has

---

[76] See also Merges, note 22 above, pp. 1293–386.

[77] Van Zimmeren, Vanneste and Van Overwalle, note 27 above.

objectives independent from those of its customers: the patent owners and technology users.[78] For-profit clearinghouses tend to charge both patent owners and technology users for their services.[79] The scope of the patents covered by a patent clearinghouse is generally broader than the scope of a patent pool, the latter being tailored to a particular standard or end product. In a manner which differs from patent pools, the competition law framework for clearinghouses has not been settled by guidelines and extensive business review letters from competition authorities. The wide variety of intermediaries would probably also make it impossible to make any general statements on the compliance of patent clearinghouse models with competition law.

In September 2012, MPEG LA, the pioneer in administering patent pools, launched Librassay as the first "licensing supermarket" in the biomedical sector.[80] Librassay offers non-exclusive, non-discriminatory licences to developers and suppliers of commercial products and clinical tests for diagnostics and research tools. Reassured by the reputational effects of MPEG LA's successful pool licensing programmes, nine well-respected US institutions decided to participate in Librassay's licensing programme.[81] MPEG LA actively licensed the Librassay patents to several companies for diagnostic tests, life sciences research products, and medical devices.

However, Librassay is currently the "victim" of the risks involved in being a lead actor. In its second year of operation, Librassay experienced the effect of a significant modification of the scope of the autonomy space by the US Supreme Court. In its *Mayo* and *Myriad* decisions,[82] the US Supreme Court considerably limited the patent eligibility of diagnostic methods and isolated nucleic acid sequences. As a consequence,

---

78 Aoki and Schiff, note 8 above, p. 195.

79 Ibid.

80 The analysis regarding Librassay is based on several personal communications during June and July 2015 with Ms. K. Neuman, Executive Director Biotechnology Licensing and Librassay at MPEG LA.

81 Johns Hopkins University, Ludwig Institute for Cancer Research, Memorial Sloan-Kettering Cancer Center, National Institutes of Health, Partners HealthCare, The Board of Trustees of the Leland Stanford Junior University, The Trustees of the University of Pennsylvania, University of California, San Francisco and the Wisconsin Alumni Research Foundation

82 See section 2 above. US Supreme Court, *Association for Molecular Pathology et al. v. Myriad Genetics, Inc. and Directors of the University of Utah Research Foundation*, 569 U.S. (2013) and US Supreme Court, *Mayo Collaborative Services dba Mayo Medical Laboratories and May Clinic Rochester v. Prometheus Laboratories, Inc.*, 132 S.Ct. 1289 (2012).

the patent thickets and stacking issues surrounding multiplex diagnostic tests that may have supported the market need for a one-stop, non-exclusive licence have diminished considerably. When Librassay was launched, the *Mayo* decision had already been issued. Yet, it was assumed that due to Librassay's cost-effective pricing structure, licensees would still opt to include diagnostic method claims within their licensed bundles of gene and other biomarker patents as a way to mitigate infringement risk, even for the potentially vulnerable method claims. When the *Myriad* decision resulted in a further limitation of patent eligibility excluding genomic DNA (gDNA) patents, the main "thicket" of biomarker patents for which Librassay would have facilitated bundled patent licensing disappeared. While the *Myriad* decision did establish that complementary DNA (cDNA) remains patent eligible, according to Librassay's analysis of the needs of the marketplace, only very limited opportunities exist for the licensing of cDNA patents within Librassay's field of use.

The remaining patents in Librassay's portfolio represent very early phase inventions that would require a significant amount of R&D and clinical validation before they could be launched commercially. Licensees often lack the motivation to invest in these activities without an exclusive licence to the underlying patents. Since Librassay is structured to provide non-exclusive licences, it works best when a patent thicket exists covering a single technology or closely related set of technologies that is/are widely used by industry (i.e., market-ready and adopted technologies) for which freedom to operate is desirable and otherwise expensive.

Despite this setback, Librassay is still operational, albeit with more limited opportunities than originally foreseen. It is still actively seeking licensees for the assets in the portfolio and is exploring other areas within the biomedical sector that may be stressed by patent thickets and are in need of a clearinghouse-type solution.

K. Neuman, Executive Director Biotechnology Licensing and Librassay at MPEG LA, strongly believes that the "tragedy of Librassay" is that it came along too late to prevent *Mayo* and *Myriad* from running their course. Had Librassay been in place before (or at least shortly after) the Human Genome Project neared completion in 2000–2001, and had it thus been in a position to demonstrate the value of cutting through patent thickets with a non-exclusive mass-market licensing programme, then perhaps the *Mayo* and *Myriad* cases may never have come to fruition.[83] When Librassay was introduced in 2012, the market listened but the controversy regarding gene patents had hit the ground, attracting the attention of regulators, courts and patent offices and overruling the opportunities for a private regulatory model such as a patent clearinghouse model.

6. COMPARATIVE ANALYSIS

A comparison of the analysis in sections 4 and 5 above reveals some interesting lessons that can be derived from applying the user generated law model to patent pools and clearinghouses, and in particular to the MPEG-2 pool and Librassay clearinghouse. In this section, I highlight the most important findings, which are also presented systematically in Table 6.1 below.

Emergence – Patent law, contract law and competition law leave significant freedom to patent owners and licensees to determine their licensing conditions. The scope of the autonomy space in this area is, therefore, quite wide. This broad scope is generally appreciated by market participants because, due to asymmetric information, legislators will often not be able to respond properly to the heterogeneous demands of the marketplace. In the 1990s, the interests of patent owners forming a pool were relatively homogeneous; more recently it has become increasingly challenging as the profile of the relevant patent owners is more divergent. For patent clearinghouses, heterogeneity is built into its design since it operates as a licensing supermarket.

Public policy consideration may require interventions in the scope of the autonomy space to prevent a restriction of competition, to improve legal certainty, or to support innovation. A legislator or court may limit patent eligibility and, thus, modify the framework conditions within which the private regulatory model is operating (e.g. Librassay). Alternatively, a competition authority can confirm that a certain model complies with competition law principles and provide legal certainty regarding the boundaries of the autonomy space.

[83] Actually, in 2003 MPEG LA had published such a recommendation, but then the marketplace was not ready for it and did not embrace the collective licensing model. See L. Horn, 'Alternative Approaches to IP Management: One-Stop Technology Platform Licensing' (2003) 9 *Journal of Commercial Biotechnology* 119.

MPEG LA began with the management of the MPEG-2 pool and was basically the first independent pool administrator. Later, it launched several other pool licensing programmes related to various standards, leading to ten currently active licensing programmes. MPEG LA is clearly a lead actor in this field. The MPEG-2 pool was followed by several other pools which are significantly smaller and are not managed by an independent intermediary but rather by one of the key patent owners (also constituting joint licensing programmes). Examples are the Philips-pool and Toshiba-pool.[84] Philips is renowned for managing several of such pools and has built an active licensing programme on the pool model, which accounts for an important part of the activities of its IP & Standards division. Philips can, hence, also be regarded as a lead actor in the pooling business.

Administering a patent pool or clearinghouse involves considerable fixed costs. The role of experts involved in patent evaluation and patent licensing requires high investments in terms of human resources and training. Notwithstanding the potential benefits in terms of transaction costs and revenue offered by these one-stop-shops, high-level expertise remains key to generating trust: patents are an important asset and patent owners will only be prepared to release control in cases where a private regulatory model can prove excellence in dealing with these assets. Equally, technology users will only be able to benefit from lower transaction costs, lower royalties and legal certainty in terms of their freedom to operate once a critical mass of patents is entrusted to the pool or clearinghouse for licensing.

Diffusion – Librassay shows the importance of forming a community around legal innovation that will actually support the use of the private regulatory model and actively participate in the operation and diffusion of this model. Although nine key US public research institutions and universities joined the licensing programme, this has proved insufficient for the smooth operation of the model, particularly in view of the limited autonomy space that is left after the interventions by the US Supreme Court. Therefore, in the current circumstances it is unlikely that the clearinghouse model will become widely diffused (in the biomedical sector).

The opposite is true for the patent pool model. In the standardization context, the patent pool model has been embraced by many key stakeholders, many of whom are both patent owner and user of the bundled patents, while others only present as either patent owners or users. The

---

[84] USDOJ (1998) and USDOJ (1999), note 61 above.

MPEG-2 pool offers an excellent illustration of the importance of network effects for pools as two-sided markets. Due to the success and the good reputation of the pool management, the features of the MPEG-2 pool have been copied to many other pooling programmes of MPEG LA and by other licensing administrators in the telecommunications and consumer electronics sector. However, it appears to be much harder to export the pool model to other sectors. Various experts and international organizations suggested patent pools as a way for the biomedical sector to "cut through" existing patent thickets. Yet, in the biomedical sector standards are less agreed upon, and if they do exist they focus on quality rather than on interoperability and compatibility. This was an important reason why Librassay was not framed as a patent pool but as a clearinghouse, a licensing supermarket with more flexibility and heterogeneity. The flexibility and heterogeneity may, however, also render it more difficult to attract a critical mass of key patent owners and users, which is required for the sustainability of the system in view of the costs involved in maintaining a pool or clearinghouse.

Adoption – Regarding the MPEG-2 pool model, competition authorities in the United States, Europe and Japan determined that the model works well and that no significant legal corrections were necessary. The USDOJ's business review letter has acted as an important guideline or "checklist" for many later patent pools and it limited the available autonomy space. It has also influenced competition policy on patent pools in general.[85] For instance, the Philips-pool and Toshiba-pool have also been cleared by USDOJ's business review letters.[86] With respect to the pools, adoption has happened relatively early in the "life" of the current generation of patent pools.[87]

---

[85] E.g. USDOJ, note 65 above and USFTC, note 10 above; JFTC, note 10 above; and European Commission, note 10 above.

[86] USDOJ (1998) and USDOJ (1999), note 61 above.

[87] I note that patent pools have had a more negative reputation amongst competition authorities earlier in the twentieth century. For more information, see for instance Richard J. Gilbert, 'Antitrust for Patent Pools: A Century of Policy Evolution' (2004) *Stan. Tech. L. Rev.* 3.

Table 6.1 User generated law model applied to patent pools and clearinghouses

Stage	Main Features UGL Model	Patent Pools (example MPEG-2 pool)	Clearinghouses (example Librassay)
Emergence	Autonomy space	Patent law, contract law, competition law	Patent law, contract law, competition law
	Heterogeneous demands	Limited, but increasing due to increased variety of stakeholders	Supermarket model – heterogeneity inherent
	Proactive/ Reactive	Reactive (business review letter USDOJ)	Reactive (*Mayo* & *Myriad* cases)
	Expectation of benefits	One-stop-shop Link with standardization	One-stop-shop Substantial fixed costs – role of experts
	Asymmetric information	Raison d'être	Raison d'être
	Lead actors	MPEG LA, Philips	Librassay
Diffusion	Reputational effects	Significant experimentation with patent pool model, see MPEG LA	MPEG LA
	Network effects	Two-sided markets	Two-sided markets
Adaption		Competition law (US business review letters, EU TTG, JFTC Guidelines)	?

7. CONCLUDING REMARKS

The user generated law model is a useful "lens" for examining the extent to which private regulatory law models emerge in a certain field, and the extent to which they are diffused and sometimes even adopted by the legislator. Patent pools and clearinghouses in different sectors have been assessed extensively from both a legal and economic perspective. Yet, the assessment through the lens of the user generated law model situates pools and clearinghouses within a broader trend and emphasizes certain determinants for the success of these models and the relevance of the scope of the autonomy space in this context. The scope of the autonomy space is dynamic. Its scope may directly or indirectly influence the emergence, diffusion and adoption of the model, but it may also be defined by the rules set by a private regulatory model. For patent pools, competition authorities "adopted" the model and aligned the scope of the autonomy space according to the well-tailored boundaries of the MPEG-2 pool. Librassay, on the other hand, is suffering the consequences of decisions by the US Supreme Court which adapted the scope for the autonomy space after Librassay's establishment, thereby thwarting Librassay's business model of a licensing supermarket for genetic diagnostics.

Nonetheless, in certain other fields such as synthetic biology, stakeholders are still interested in applying pools and clearinghouses to facilitate licensing in a fragmented patent landscape.[88] From the present chapter we have learned that at least the following issues would need to be taken into consideration in following such a path. First, it is vital to carry out a careful analysis of the patent landscape to determine the extent to which an undue fragmentation of patent rights may exist: fragmentation which cannot be tackled efficiently by way of bilateral licensing and which contains patented technology that is used repeatedly by a broad community. In short, does a potential demand exist for an alternative approach that might facilitate licensing through a one-stop-shop? Second, one needs to determine to what extent the legal framework is stable or whether it is likely that the applicable patent policy will be reviewed, and, hence, the scope of the autonomy space adapted. Third, the attitude of the relevant community towards private regulatory models such as patent pools and clearinghouses should be examined. What are the values and interests of the relevant stakeholders? Is it likely that they would embrace the establishment of such models in the sector, support them, and ultimately participate as patent owners and/or users? Fourth, since the costs of establishing a pool or clearinghouse model are considerable, it might be better to collaborate with an experienced licensing agent to administer the patent pool or clearinghouse. As such, it is wise to collaborate with lead actors in the field who are able to offer the required support and expertise.

---

[88] Timo Minssen, Berthold Rutz and Esther van Zimmeren, 'Synthetic Biology and Intellectual Property Rights: Six Recommendations – Report from the IP Expert Meeting at the Danish Agency for Science, Technology & Innovation' (2015) 10 *Biotechnol. J.* 236.

Further research focusing on synthetic biology, the current status of its patent landscape and the opportunities for private regulatory models would enable legislators to design a "science-based" autonomy space rather than a "hype-based" autonomy space.

7. More competition-law-FRANDly IPR policies: a solution to SSOs' problems of self-governance?

Olga Kokoulina and Timo Minssen

1. INTRODUCTION

The link between innovation and economic growth has been widely acknowledged. So it comes as no surprise that the promotion of innovation has become a priority of company strategies[1] and government policies.[2] A major regulatory challenge in this paradigm is to craft a well-balanced design of competition law and intellectual property (IP) in a way which allows this Schumpeterian insight concerning innovation economics to be applied consistently. So far it has often been argued that equating intellectual property rights (IPRs) to conventional property rights in the course of antitrust assessment constitutes a proper approach which encourages methodological consistency.[3] However, some examples of ongoing litigation concerned with the exercise of the FRAND-encumbered[4] standard essential patents (SEPs) leave the impression that

---

[1] See, e.g., 'Innovation and Commercialization, 2010: McKinsey Global Survey Results', available at http://www.mckinsey.com/insights/innovation/innovation_and_commercialization_2010_mckinsey_global_survey_results (last visited January 13, 2015).

[2] See, e.g., 'A New Start for Europe: My Agenda for Jobs, Growth, Fairness and Democratic Change', Political Guidelines for the next European Commission, available at http://ec.europa.eu/about/juncker-commission/docs/pg_en.pdf (last visited January 13, 2015).

[3] Joshua D. Wright, Commissioner, FTC, 'Does the FTC Have a New IP Agenda?', Remarks at the 2014 Milton Handler Lecture 'Antitrust in the 21st Century', available at http://www.ftc.gov/system/files/documents/public_statements/288861/140311ipagenda.pdf (last visited January 13, 2015).

[4] FRAND here refers to the commitment given by the holder of a patent declared essential for implementation of the standard. FRAND is generally

competition authorities might be departing from this approach and moving towards more IP-specific antitrust analysis.[5] Furthermore, chief economists of the EU Commission and the Federal Trade Commission (FTC) have recently made some proposals for possible reforms to the IPR policies of standard setting organizations (SSOs).[6] In their article, they strongly emphasize the adverse impact of opportunistic behaviour within standardization since such behaviour can harm consumers and threaten the incentive to innovate. They also assert that SSOs have the responsibility to ensure that this risk is mitigated through an IPR policy that properly addresses this issue. This context gives rise to related claims that many existing SSO policies are not strong or clear enough to achieve this goal.

Reflecting upon this process leads one to a necessary scrutiny of the meaning and effect of the message conveyed to SSOs. In conjunction with this, the employment of the user-generated law methodology might offer germane guidance for assessing the practice and recommendations of competition authorities. Such an approach will contribute to creating a well-informed discussion as to the proper role of antitrust law in shaping and informing originally user-generated internal IP policies of SSOs.

To this end, we devote section 2 to examining the standard setting landscape in the Information and Communications Technology (ICT) sector. Section 3 presents some challenges associated with the IPRs and standards.[7] Section 4 provides a brief overview of the cases initiated by the EU and US competition authorities in the context of standardization. This will serve as the basis for section 5 in which we examine the extent to which the outcomes of antitrust investigations should be incorporated into SSO practice. We summarize our conclusions in section 6.

---

understood as the commitment to license this patent to any third party on fair, reasonable and non-discriminatory terms.

[5] Wright, note 3 above, p. 12.

[6] Kai-Uwe Kuhn, Fiona Scott Morton and Howard Shelanski, 'Standard Setting Organizations Can Help Solve the Standard Essential Patents Licensing Problem', March (2013) 5 *CPI Antitrust Chronicle* (Special Issue), available at https://www.competitionpolicyinternational.com/assets/Free/ScottMortonetalMar-13Special.pdf (last visited January 13, 2015).

[7] For the purposes of our chapter, we limit our discussion to an examination of patents in standard setting. We use IPR and patents interchangeably.

2. THE STANDARD SETTING LANDSCAPE IN THE ICT SECTOR

Section 2.1 introduces some background research on standardization and presents some recent perspectives on the subject. Section 2.2 provides a number of examples of standardization initiatives in the ICT sector with a special focus on technological convergence. Section 2.3 offers an integrated approach to the SSO as a form of self-governance.

2.1 New Research Perspectives on Standardization

Research on standardization emerged in the1980s with the first studies of the roles and types of standards in the information sector.[8] Over the past three decades, economists, lawyers and technology development experts have examined standards strategy, emphasizing the role of technological configuration, the creation of value networks required for standards adoption and the role of IPRs in standardization.[9]

Economic studies have incorporated the insights of game theory, economies of scale and network externalities into the analysis of standardization, thus providing a substantial body of knowledge on the role of economic factors in standards promotion and strategic behaviour. An understanding of such economic issues is also essential for lawyers dealing with standardization matters since it allows a better comprehension of a variety of issues, including the royalty rate level in SEP cases,[10]

---

[8] Paul A. David and Shane Greenstein, 'The Economics of Compatibility Standards: An Introduction to Recent Research' (1990) 1(1–2) *Economics of Innovation and New Technology* 3.

[9] DongBack Seo, *Evolution and Standardization of Mobile Communications Technology* (IGI Global, 2013) 1–15, for an overview of the literature.

[10] See, e.g. discussion of the complements problem by Damien Geradin et al., 'The Complements Problem within Standard Setting: Assessing the Evidence on Royalty Stacking' (2008)14(2) *B.U. J. Sci. & Tech. L.* 144; See Thomas F. Cotter, *Comparative Patent Remedies: A Legal and Economic Analysis* (Oxford University Press, 2013) for a thorough analysis of the patent owner's proper compensation.

specificity of investments in standards[11] and trade-offs in the context of incomplete contracting.[12]

Additionally, though, more and more researchers have recognized the need to account for the complexity of the standardization process beyond the limits of previously conducted economic inquiries. Various recent studies present new perspectives and theoretical models that promote further consideration of the conflicting goals and purposes of standardization's participants.[13] Identification of standardization's users, along with their needs and requirements, offers a more balanced approach which integrates not only the supply but also demand factors.[14]

The 'Social Shaping of Technology' interpretation of technology development has also expanded the taxonomical framework of standardization and enabled researchers to regard standardization as the earliest stage of the technical development process.[15] Nowadays, SSOs set standards in the context of rapid technological growth and shortened

---

[11] See, e.g. F. Scott Kieff and Anne Layne-Farrar, 'Incentive Effects from Different Approaches to Holdup Mitigation Surrounding Patent Remedies and Standard-Setting Organizations' (2013) 9(2) *Journal of Competition Law and Economics* 1091 for an extensive discussion on the types of holdups.

[12] Joshua D. Wright, Commissioner, FTC, 'SSOs, FRAND, and Antitrust: Lessons from the Economics of Incomplete Contracts', Speech delivered at the Inaugural Academic Conference: 'The Commercial Function of Patents in Today's Innovation Economy' held in September 2013 at George Mason University School of Law, available at http://www.ftc.gov/sites/default/files/documents/public_statements/ssos-frand-and-antitrust-lessons-economics-incomplete-contracts/130912cpip.pdf (last visited January 13, 2015).

[13] Good examples of this approach include an Actor Network Theory (ANT) applied to standardization studies by Ian Graham et al., 'The Dynamics of EDI Standards Development' (1995) 7(1) *Technology Analysis & Strategic Management* 3; and a synthesis of ANT with a theory of self-organized complexity employed by DongBak Seo, note 9 above.

[14] This approach is exemplified in research related to the E-business sector by Kai Jakobs, *Information Communication Technology Standardization for E-Business Sectors: Integrating Supply and Demand Factors* (IGI Global, 2009). For a general discussion on the demand-driven innovation, see Eric von Hippel, *The Sources of Innovation* (Oxford University Press, 1994); Shane Greenstein and Timothy F. Bresnahan, 'Technical Progress and Co-Invention in Computing and in the Uses of Computers' (1996) *Brookings Papers on Economic Activity* 7; Andrew McMeekin, Mark Tomlinson, Ken Green and Vivien Walsh, *Innovation by Demand: An Interdisciplinary Approach to the Study of Demand and Its Role in Innovation* (Manchester University Press, 2010).

[15] Kai Jakobs, *Information Communication Technology Standardization for E-Business Sectors: Integrating Supply and Demand Factors* (IGI Global, 2009), p. 32.

technology life cycles. It is quite common that they act in anticipation of new technology, developing standards before products are produced.[16] In effect, this means that SSOs might be considered as a platform for innovation commons. As a user-generated solution, SSOs have introduced a rather high degree of predictability and efficiency for their users. Therefore, the scope of State-enacted regulation and its impact should be assessed with due consideration given to (1) the nature of SSOs as models of self-governance, and (2) the potential that such a form of governance entails for all relevant stakeholders.

To accommodate the aforementioned perspectives on standardization and formulate our approach to SSOs, the next section proceeds with an examination of committee-based standard setting in the ICT sector.

2.2 Standards and Standardization in the ICT Sector

For the purposes of our chapter, we distinguish between two kinds of standards: standards achieved through committee-based, cooperative standardization and single vendor-controlled standards. In the ensuing discussion we will focus on the process of the first type. We propose a broad category of standardization 'committee', using the example of Information and Communications Technologies (ICT). The sector encompasses a great variety of segments that relate to manufacturing or the service industry linked to information processing and data delivery. The trend of emerging convergence of Computing and Telecommunications was first articulated in 1970s[17] and was linked to standard-related developments both in computer and telecommunications industries. Historically, these sectors had quite distinct traditions of standardization.

The lack of common standards and the proliferation of proprietary interfaces in telecommunications constituted a heavy burden for network providers, equipment manufacturers and end-users alike.[18] Consequently, standardization (often induced by the requirement of multi-vendor compatibility) appeared to be fundamental to the establishment of modern telecommunication networks. Growing private demand for deregulation in the industry predefined the key role that coordination platforms and

---

[16] For a discussion on anticipatory standardization see Carl F. Cargill, *Information Technology Standardization: Theory, Process, and Organizations* (Digital Press, 1989).

[17] David Farber and Paul Baran, 'The Convergence of Computing and Telecommunications Systems' (1977) 195 (4283) *Science* 1166.

[18] Mostafa H. Sherif and Duncan K. Sparrell, 'Standards and Innovation in Telecommunications' (1992) 30(7) *IEEE Communications Magazine* 22.

international standardization organizations (in particular, the International Telecommunication Union – ITU) played in the process.[19]

The standardization tradition in the IT sector was quite different from that of telecommunications for a variety of reasons, including differences of perception on technological change, the role of governments, and the way early computer systems operated. Improvement of technology in the IT sector was generally considered to be a competitive first-mover advantage and not to be shared through cooperative standardization.[20] Furthermore, early computer systems operated relatively independently from each other without the necessity for any form of hierarchical private governance or public intervention.[21] There was, therefore, initially no actual pressure to achieve compatibility. Over time, however, the desirability of decentralized access to information reinforced the need for standardization decisions in inter-computer communications. The initiative to provide a framework for information transfer between any two end-systems was soon assumed at the level of international standardization organizations.

Thus, the process of standardization within the IT sector aligned with a transformation of modern computing by assuming different forms of standards competition.[22] As a consequence, the standardization activity at the level of international standardization organizations was soon absorbed into a greater movement towards the 'open systems' paradigm.

The concept of 'open systems' has played a pivotal role for standardization activities in the IT sector at large. Essentially, it has formed the backbone of standardization activities in an increasing segment of technological overlap between the telecommunications and computer industries. One particular facet of such 'openness' has provided a unifying identity and goal for the movement: the opposite of an 'open

---

[19] Such demand was mostly formed by the multinational manufacturing companies and communications users that bore the costs of the artificial monopolies confined to national boundaries. See Hendrik Spruyt, 'The Supply and Demand of Governance in Standard-Setting: Insights from the Past' (2001) 8(3) *Journal of European Public Policy* 371, p. 385.

[20] Martin Weiss and Carl Cargill, 'Consortia in the Standards Development Process' (1992) 43(8) *Journal of the American Society for Information Science* 559.

[21] Ibid.

[22] Joel West and Jason Dedrick, 'Proprietary vs. Open Standards in the Network Era: An Examination of the Linux Phenomenon', in Proceedings of the 34th Annual Hawai'i International Conference on System Sciences, 501–1 (2001), available at http://ieeexplore.ieee.org/xpls/abs_all.jsp?arnumber=926525&tag=1 (last visited January 13, 2015).

system' is not a 'closed', but a 'proprietary' system.[23] The 'open systems' concept describes a special approach to the design of a system where non-proprietary standards define the interaction of its components. Technically, standardization concerned the operating system (OS) and networks – in particular, protocols for the inter-networking. The result of the OS standardization endeavour was a failure of cooperative 'non-proprietary' standard UNIX operating systems[24] and a reassertion of proprietary computing represented by Microsoft Windows and Windows NT. Indirectly, further outcomes of this project included a certain reconsideration of the role of intellectual property, identification of possible constraints to collaboration on the standardization project, and to some extent the emergence of the 'Open Source' movement.

At the same time, the standardization related to the networks within 'open systems' resulted in the complete decline of the model proposed by international standardization bodies (OSI protocols solution).[25] Notwithstanding some technical differences in competing solutions, the discrepancy in roles assigned to the IPR had a significant impact on the standardization outcome – an issue discussed in section 4 of this chapter.

In terms of technology development and standardization, the information technology and telecommunications sectors represent the fields that have the highest overlap and exhibit a trend towards even more convergence in technology development.[26] Furthermore, the idea of IT 'open systems' design and the commercial development of the Internet is predicted to have a significant impact on the way this technology development will progress. Therefore, it is essential to look beyond the narrow confines of international SSOs or regional SSOs (so-called formal SSOs) when conceiving of a primary source and a type of committee-based standardization.[27] The example of standardization provided from

---

[23] Christopher M. Kelty, 'Conceiving Open Systems' (2009) 30(1) *Wash. U. J.L. & Pol'y.* 139, p. 145.

[24] The UNIX standardization attempt did not result in a wide market adoption of the AT&T original standard. The existence of more than 100 often conflicting versions of UNIX standards by the mid-1980s enables one to recognize Microsoft Windows and Windows NT as a winner of the standardization process at the time.

[25] A currently preferred TCP/IP protocols solution has been developed by the Institute of Electrical and Electronic Engineers (IEEE).

[26] Stephan Gauch and Knut Blind, 'Technological Convergence and the Absorptive Capacity of Standardization' (2015) 91 *Technological Forecasting and Social Change* 236.

[27] The reasonableness of such an approach is also supported by the empirical research demonstrating that companies who need to either implement

the ICT sector suggests that a holistic approach to the concept of the SSO is needed. Thus, under the broad concept of the SSO we consider formal standard setting organizations administered at the international, regional or national levels (e.g. ISO, ETSI, ANSI in the United States, DIN in Germany) as well as industry consortia (e.g. OASIS, IETF, W3C, VITA).[28] This approach more accurately reflects the essence of the SSO as an industry-specific and subject-specific user-generated solution. As demonstrated above, the relevant stakeholders exhibit a variety of heterogeneous demands as to the scope and content of the standard setting regulation. The asymmetry of information on their needs was an issue which was well addressed through the emergence of numerous SSOs with different profiles, membership structures and IPR policies. The SSO can be considered the most prominent venue for the realization of these needs.[29] Achieving such wide acceptance can be explained by the stakeholders' expectations of benefits expressed in lowered costs of the property rights exchange. In order to harness the potential of this self-governance solution, an efficient regulatory framework should therefore allow for flexibility to accommodate the diverse needs and interests of the stakeholders and preserve the incentives to join the SSO's model.

Having introduced the notion of standardization committees in the ICT sector through the lenses of user-generated law, we will proceed with conceptualizing our approach to the SSO as a form of self-governance. In doing so, we will try to accommodate some previously overlooked issues of innovation outlined in section 2.1. We will also identify some

---

or set standards pay less attention to the distinction of 'consortium vs. formal SSO' in current professional contexts. Rather, they focus on the details of the processes adopted by SSOs, in particular the IPR policy, see Jakobs, note 15 above, pp. 65–79 (mentioning some business considerations such as company's strategy and business models as important factors). In addition, as was seen in recent legal developments, in certain cases a more flexible approach to SSO categorization is adopted as part of the policy implementation (e.g. the possibility of referencing the ICT technical specifications developed by global ICT forums and consortia in public procurement was recognized at the European level as essential for supporting the Europe 2020 strategy, see Commission Implementing Decision (2014/188/EU) of 3 April 2014 on the identification of ICT technical specifications eligible for referencing in public procurement).

[28] There is some confusion as to precisely what constitutes a 'consortium'. For the purposes of our analysis we follow the concept of a consortium in which competitors cooperate to agree upon standards proposed by Henk J. de Vries, *Standardization – A Business Approach to the Role of National Standardization Organizations* (Springer, 1999).

[29] In contrast to a single-vendor standardization alternative.

challenges SSOs might face and articulate a possible governance model that takes these risks into consideration.

2.3 Nature and Challenges of Standard Setting Organizations

Essentially, SSOs perform a number of different functions. They serve as a 'meeting room' for different stakeholders deciding on technical solutions. At the same time, they are also a platform where participants exchange information, negotiate compromises, publish standards, and set tests and procedures for certifying standards compliance. Depending on an SSO's particular function, SSOs can be variously defined as certifiers that validate proposed technical solutions,[30] forums for the cooperative exchange of some technological information,[31] value-setters of their participants' technologies,[32] and arenas for open innovation.[33] Recognizing this complexity, we will hereafter propose an integrated approach to SSOs that will take into account both demand and supply factors.

In this regard, a model proposed by Timothy Simcoe which treats SSOs as institutions for the collective self-governance of shared technology platforms[34] is of special interest for our discussion.[35] This approach contains the potential for new insights into the content of the

---

[30] Josh Lerner and Jean Tirole, 'A Model of Forum Shopping' (2006) 96(4) *The American Economic Review* 1091.

[31] Paul A. David and Hunter K. Monroe, 'Standards Development Strategies under Incomplete Information: Isn't the "Battle of the Sexes" Really a Revelation Game?' (1994) 2 *MERIT Research Memorandum* 39.

[32] Justus Baron and Tim Pohlmann, 'Who Cooperates in Standards Consortia – Rivals or Complementors?' (2013) 9(4) *Journal of Competition Law and Economics* 905.

[33] Endre Grøtnes, 'Open IT-Based Innovation: Moving Towards Cooperative IT Transfer and Knowledge Diffusion', in G. León et al., *IFIP International Federation for Information Processing*, Vol. 287 (Springer, 2009), pp. 343–59.

[34] In this case, we understand technology platform as a collection of standards describing a reconfigurable base of compatible components on which users build applications in computing after Shane Greenstein and Timothy F. Bresnahan, 'Technical Progress and Co-Invention in Computing and in the Uses of Computers' (1996) *Brookings Papers on Economic Activity* 7; and standards specifying transmission of information and interconnection of transmission equipment in communications after Daniel F. Spulber and Christopher S. Yoo, 'Network Regulation: The Many Faces of Access' (2005)1(4) *Journal of Competition Law and Economics* 648.

[35] Timothy Simcoe, 'Governing the Anticommons: Institutional Design for Standard-Setting Organizations' (2014)14(1) *Innovation Policy and the Economy* 99.

SSO as a user-generated solution. It also provides some examples of the challenges that the SSO faces as a regulatory model.

Employing Simcoe's SSO model as a starting point, we must proceed with some necessary clarifications. From a legal perspective, it is important to first determine the parties involved in such collaboration. Empirical research suggests that firms specializing in the same technological components of the standard are significantly more likely to be joint members of the same consortium.[36] In principle, this means that firms cooperating in SSOs will most likely compete both upstream on the level of technologies, as well as downstream with regard to products and services. In terms of self-governance, such a situation raises a potential risk of over-exclusion from SSO collaboration.

It is also pertinent that information in the form of knowledge and expertise is the main input of such cooperation. In essence, the final product of the SSO standard is information specifying a limited set of solutions to actual or potential matching problems. In other words, the nature of SSOs involves a cooperation of potential/actual rivals on the production of public goods: namely, information. In a deeper context, the tradition of viewing standards as public goods goes back to the 1980s. Kindleberger argued that standards should fall within Samuelson's definition of public goods in that they are available for use by all, and use by any economic actor does not reduce the amount available to others.[37] However, soon after, economic literature on the integrated supply-demand concept of standardization presented another approach to the nature of standards. It was shown that because of adoption and sponsoring costs on the demand side of standard setting, the standard itself actually constitutes non-pure private goods.[38] Such a re-conceptualization has at least three far-reaching implications.

First, the non-rival nature of standards in SSOs means that there is no actual problem of resources becoming depleted and overused.[39] However, due to the presence of the adoption and sponsoring costs, the otherwise

---

[36] Baron and Pohlmann, note 32 above, p. 908.

[37] Charles P. Kindleberger, 'Standards as Public, Collective and Private Goods' (1983) 36(3) *Kyklos* 377.

[38] Cristiano Antonelli, 'Localized Technological Change and the Evolution of Standards as Economic Institutions' (1994) 6(3) *Information Economics and Policy* 195, p. 200.

[39] Problem identified as the tragedy of the commons by Garrett Hardin, 'The Tragedy of the Commons' (1968) 162 (3859) *Science* 1243.

common risk of free-ridership becomes less significant.[40] Second, the way this information is articulated and shared in the course of creating a standard may put the outsiders of SSOs at considerable disadvantage. Therefore, standards are partially excludable. Lastly, standards (as carriers of technical information) are productive in that they make it possible to take advantage of the benefits of technological and network externalities.[41]

In this context, the essence of the cooperation within SSOs is the coordination and dissemination of knowledge and information in a networked economy. Looking at this collaboration from the standpoint of self-governance, it can therefore be concluded that the greatest risk an SSO faces is the potential of over-exclusion. This threat constitutes a special concern in cases of anticipatory standardization: the discouragement of the relevant stakeholders might have an adverse effect not only on the quality of standards, but also on the prospects of innovation at large.

Therefore, the proposed regulatory regime should take into account the potentially detrimental impact of such exclusion. Our adopted approach to the SSO as a collective self-governance of shared technology platforms brings us to the general issue of commons governance. Brett Frischmann, for example, supports the proposition that commons management could be more appropriate for information governance than a 'property' regime.[42] According to his approach, for the purpose of governance one can identify special 'infrastructural' resources that are often best managed by an open access commons model and made subject to certain rules of use, or at least on the model of an open class of users.[43] In principle, the information in the case of SSOs meets the three cumulative criteria of infrastructural resources identified by Frischmann: (1) they are resources that 'may be consumed non-rivalrously for some appreciable range of demand'; (2) they are resources whose demand is primarily as input into downstream productive activities or capital goods; and (3) they are used as input into a wide range of goods and services, including, importantly, downstream public goods and 'social' goods.

---

[40] For a discussion of the difficulties involved in assessing such risk see Martin B. H. Weiss and Ronald T. Toyokuku, 'Free-Ridership in the Standards-Setting Process: The Case of 10BaseT' (1996) 4(4) *Standard View* 205.

[41] Ibid.

[42] Brett M. Frischmann, *Infrastructure: The Social Value of Shared Resources* (Oxford University Press, 2013), p. 61.

[43] Ibid.

It is critical, as Frischmann has argued, to provide for open access to these resources. Importantly, in this context 'open' actually means 'on non-discriminatory terms which do not depend on the users' identity or intended use'. This is a fundamental observation for our discussion on SSO governance. Access to the cooperation within SSOs on a non-discriminatory basis is a crucial prerequisite for successful SSO management. Moreover, in the context of standardization in the ICT sector such a model should also take into consideration the issues of IPR and the matter of ongoing technological convergence. We turn to precisely these questions in our next section.

3. IPR AND STANDARDS

In this section we provide a brief overview of the role of IPRs in standardization activities of the ICT sector. This will help us to identify the challenges that IPR and technological convergence introduce to the way SSOs function (section 3.1). Hereafter, we demonstrate how the general concept of the SSO as a form of self-governance could be translated into IPR policy (section 3.2). Using the examples of disclosure and licensing requirements, we examine whether the current SSOs' self-governance model is capable of accommodating the potential risks of over-exclusion and rent-seeking behaviour (section 3.3).

3.1 Overview of the Role of IPRs in the ICT Sector

As noted earlier, the 'marriage' of IT and Telecommunications brought together two different traditions of standardization. The examples of initiatives such as UNIX, TCP/IP or OSI have demonstrated that IPRs play a significant role in the outcome of standard setting. Even though the UNIX case has been repeatedly used as an example of 'standardization failure',[44] it convincingly demonstrated the centrality of the issue of intellectual property to creation of open systems. The UNIX experience provided a sort of philosophy for the growing movement of Free and Open Source Software (FOSS). As it turns out, FOSS has proved to be a viable and innovative model of organizing software production. Its success in utilizing a specific form of licensing arrangements made some scholars question the necessity of a strong patent system for software

---

[44] Carl F. Cargill, 'Why Standardization Efforts Fail' (2011) 14(1) *The Journal of Electronic Publishing* 31.

platforms.[45] In the light of standardization, this general approach to IPRs has been rendered to the widespread preference for royalty-free licensing among many players in the IT field.[46]

At the same time, the ICT sector is a dynamic marketplace that accommodates a variety of business models, from FOSS developers and implementers to the companies whose primary focus lies in commercialization of software patents. The inter-relationship among these different players might be anything from fierce competition to long-term cooperation.[47] On the one hand, a user-generated solution in the form of the Patent Commons Project[48] seems to confirm a possibility of innovative symbiosis. On the other hand, the proliferation of software patents and their occasional employment in the course of aggressive litigation[49] demonstrate that the idea of fruitful cooperation is not very widely accepted in the industry at large.

The participation of telecom companies in the ICT community introduces an added layer of complexity to this marketplace. In the context of standardization, it can be observed through a significant increase of the number of SEPs in the industry. According to the Open Essential IPR Disclosure Database (OEIDD), the majority of patents currently claimed as essential are found precisely in the field of telecommunications.[50] In this regard, it is interesting to note that there was no differentiation at all between essential and non-essential IPR in the course of the promotion of

---

45 Justin P. Johnson, 'Open Source Software', in Martin Peitz and Joel Waldfogel (eds), *The Oxford Handbook of the Digital Economy* (Oxford University Press, 2012), p. 461.

46 See, e.g., W3C IPR policy, options of royalty-free licensing in IETF and OASIS IPR Policies.

47 E.g. Florian Müller, *IBM Breaks the Taboo and Betrays its Promise to the FOSS Community, FOSS Patents Blog,* available at http://www.fosspatents.com/2010/04/ibm-breaks-taboo-and-betrays-its.html; IBM *Statement of Non-Assertion of Named Patents Against OSS*, available at http://www.ibm.com/ibm/licensing/patents/pledgedpatents.pdf (last visited January 13, 2015).

48 The project was started by the Open Source Development Labs (OSDL): http://www.patent-commons.org.

49 See, e.g. Executive Office of the President, *Patent Assertion and U.S. Innovation* (2013), available at http://www.whitehouse.gov/sites/default/files/docs/patent_report.pdf (last visited January 13, 2015).

50 International Telecommunication Union, *Understanding Patents, Competition and Standardization in an Interconnected World* (2014), p. 52, available at http://www.itu.int/en/ITU-T/Documents/Manual_Patents_Final_E.pdf (last visited January 13, 2015).

the first Nordic Mobile telephone standard in the early 1970s.[51] Moreover, in spite of some subsequent instances of tensions between patents and standards in telecommunications, the issue of SEPs was not considered a major problem in the course of standardization in the sector.[52] This status quo has been challenged by the introduction of mobile telephony and the subsequent arrival of new players. Seen in this light, ongoing litigation and the practice of patent portfolio acquisitions in telecommunications can be interpreted as an industry 'entrance fee'.[53] The strategic purpose of IPRs in this context is to ensure freedom to operate. It implies that for the majority of companies active in telecommunications, IPRs are generally not seen as a primary source of revenue. Therefore, there is a strong incentive for producing entities to get into licensing agreements. On the other hand, a significant patent portfolio might become a more direct source of revenue in cases where companies' performance is less successful.[54]

The cited ICT sector example shows that technological convergence has brought together a variety of market players previously active in different industries. It is common that they represent different business models and have divergent opinions as to the role and ways of commercializing their IPRs.[55] Consequently, it has a considerable impact on SSOs. First of all, the number of patents claimed essential to standardization projects has increased significantly.[56] This is partly explained by the technological complexity of present-day standards and partly by the

---

[51] DongBak Seo, note 9 above, p. 60.

[52] Rudi Bekkers and Isabelle Liotard, 'European Standards for Mobile Communications: The Tense Relationship Between Standards and Intellectual Property Rights' (1999) *E.I.P.R.* 110, available at http://home.tm.tue.nl/rbekkers/EIPR Bekkers and Liotard.pdf (last visited January 13, 2015).

[53] Anne Layne-Farrar, 'The Brothers Grimm Book of Business Models: A Survey of Literature and Developments in Patent Acquisition and Litigation' (2012) 9(1) *Journal of Economics and Policy* 29, p. 54. More generally, the litigation in this case can be interpreted as a method of rebalancing the size and content of the patent portfolio of the ICT players.

[54] E.g. Nokia's deal with Microsoft closed on April 25, 2014.

[55] For a comprehensive discussion see Layne-Farrar, note 53 above.

[56] Timothy Simcoe, 'Explaining the Increase in Intellectual Property Disclosure' (December 1, 2005), available at http://ssrn.com/abstract=1396332 (last visited January 13, 2015).

strategic role patent portfolios play for firms in the ICT sector.[57] Second, the holders of those patents tend to value them more highly than other patents.[58] Third, the participation of companies operating with different business models has a potentially disruptive effect on subsequent SEP licensing practices.[59] It is reasonable to conclude that these factors have increased the incentive for the SSOs' participants to engage in rent-seeking, opportunistic behaviour. Such conduct might potentially lead to a less cooperative environment for the creation of standards.

How great, then, is this risk for SSOs? Should they intensify efforts to address it? We will address these questions by looking at SSOs and their IPR policies through the lenses of commons governance.

3.2 IPR Policy of SSOs as a Matter of Commons Governance

We have already noted that standards can be classified as non-pure private goods shared and governed by the companies that are often competitors in upstream and/or downstream markets. In principle, the input of such cooperation is information in the form of knowledge and expertise. Having said this, we should mention that a certain part of that information might relate to some patent applications and/or granted patents. In this framework, the collaboration in the course of standardization can be considered as a case of the open innovation model that emphasizes the benefits of sharing and exchanging technology across firm boundaries.[60] It follows, then, that as an example of R&D activity SSOs are particularly susceptible to commons management: IP boundaries are costly to define and defend, the cost of innovating is relatively

---

[57] Justus Baron et al., 'Joint Innovation in ICT Standards: How Consortia Drive the Volume of Patent Filings' (2012) CERNA Working Paper Series, 12-ME-03, available at http://www.law.northwestern.edu/research-faculty/searlecenter/innovationeconomics/documents/Standards_consortia_and_innovation_WP_2012.pdf (last visited January 13, 2015).

[58] Marc Rysman and Timothy Simcoe, 'Patents and the Performance of Voluntary Standard Setting Organizations' (2008) 54(11) *Management Science* 1920.

[59] See Anne Layne-Farrar, 'Moving Past the SEP RAND Obsession: Some Thoughts on the Economic Implications of Unilateral Commitments and the Complexities of Patent Licensing' (2014) 21 *Geo. Mason L. Rev.* 1093.

[60] This discussion is especially relevant in the case of anticipatory standardization.

high, but that of copying is low.[61] How should this mode of governance be transposed into the IPR policy of an SSO? Given the great number of technologies, markets and jurisdictions involved in a discussion on standardization, we will not attempt to provide concrete examples for every particular case. Rather, we would like to sketch out a general conceptual approach to IPR policy as seen from the SSO standpoint.

Recall, also, that commons management in our analysis refers to the situation in which a resource is shared among members of a community on non-discriminatory terms. Translated into the IPR policy of an SSO, such a governance model could be considered a form of cooperation where companies are not barred from access to the process based on their preferences with regard to the use of IP. In other words, it seems to be in an SSO's best interests to provide access to standards creation regardless of the business models of its potential participants. That said, it is important to take into account the previously outlined risk of a patent holder's opportunistic behaviour. As we shall see through some examples in section 4, this concern is commonly described in terms of patent holdup.

In general, the concept of patent holdup refers to a situation where a patent owner has the ability to extract a royalty which reflects not just the value of the patented technology but also a portion of the cost the infringer would incur by deciding to switch to a non-infringing alternative technology.[62] This risk can materialize either through a patent holder's deceptive conduct in the course of standard setting (the case of patent ambush)[63] or without fraud (examples of opportunistic behaviour linked to the breach of FRAND commitments).

In our discussion, we look at such cases from the perspective of the SSO and its members. It is evident that the patent holder's behaviour in cases of patent ambush has a negative impact on the process of the

---

[61] Christina Bohannan and Herbert Hovenkamp, *Creation without Restraint: Promoting Liberty and Rivalry in Innovation* (Oxford University Press, 2011), p. 333.

[62] For instance, this is the general approach to the patent holdup outlined in Norman Siebrasse and Thomas F. Cotter, 'A New Framework for Determining Reasonable Royalties in Patent Litigation' (2014) Minnesota Legal Studies Research Paper No. 14-45, p. 3, also available at http://papers.ssrn.com/sol3/papers.cfm?abstract_id=2528616 (last visited January 13, 2015).

[63] The notion of holdup with an element of surprise was first articulated by Nobel Laureate Oliver E. Williamson. See Oliver Williamson, *The Economic Institutions of Capitalism: Firms, Markets, Relational Contracting* (Free Press, 1985), pp. 61–3.

standards selection. It has real potential to undermine the SSO's efficiencies by preventing access to the information necessary to make informed decisions. In addition, it might have a disruptive effect on the SSO's members by compromising their trust in cooperation in good faith.

At the same time, the risk of patent holdup without deception seems to produce a less disturbing effect for the SSO. The abusive behaviour in this case is not so much associated with the process of the standards creation. More precisely, the prospects of such opportunistic behaviour (to a certain degree) are conditioned upon the adoption of standards by the market.[64] The extent to which one can exploit this position greatly depends on the scope of standards diffusion.[65] It follows that a patent holder generally has considerable incentives to cooperate, to share information and contribute to the quality of the standard in the phase of standards creation. In principle, the patent holder's interests coincide with those of the SSO at this stage: both parties work towards the standards promotion and its wide acceptance by the market. Furthermore, reputational costs in 'repeated game' setting[66] could be seen as an additional constraint for the patent holder with respect to participating in SSOs.

Thus, we may reasonably conclude that the principal concerns needing to be reflected in an SSO's IPR policy are centred upon two main issues: non-discriminatory access to the SSO and prevention of the patent ambush scenario. Assessed from the perspective of an SSO, the threat of a patent holdup without deceptive opportunistic behaviour issuing from a patent holder is rather insignificant.

It is commonplace that SSOs have IPR policies intended for mitigation of the outlined risks. The requirements of patent disclosure and licensing commitments are prevailing measures employed by SSOs in this regard. Generally speaking, the former refers to the obligation imposed on participants to disclose *ex ante* and *in good faith* any patents that might be essential for the implementation of the standard under consideration.

---

[64] For a discussion on the timeline of standards adoption and relevant factors see Kai Jakobs, *Standardization Research in Information Technology: New Perspectives* (IGI Global, 2008), p. 123.

[65] For an analysis of switching costs and corresponding value of the SEP, see, e.g. U.S. Department of Justice and the Federal Trade Commission, *Antitrust Enforcement and Intellectual Property Rights: Promoting Innovation and Competition* (2007), pp. 33–57, available at https://www.ftc.gov/sites/default/files/documents/reports/antitrust-enforcement-and-intellectual-property-rights-promoting-innovation-and-competition-report.s.department-justice-and-federal-trade-commission/p040101promotinginnovationandcompetitionrpt0704.pdf (last visited January 13, 2015).

[66] Wright, note 12 above.

Setting aside some thorny issues of the legal nature and content of SEP licensing commitments, it can therefore be generally stated that under a widespread model of FRAND commitments participants undertake that their IPRs (if incorporated into the standard) will be accessible on fair, reasonable and non-discriminatory terms.

In the next section we will look at the requirements of patent disclosure and licensing commitments more closely.

3.3 Patent Disclosure Policy and Licensing Commitments

In order to consider the extent to which SSOs take into consideration the identified concerns, we will employ the results of the empirical research on SSOs' IPR policies conducted by Rudi Bekkers and Andrew S. Updegrove. The following observations are important with respect to the patent disclosure policy:[67]

- All examined SSOs explicitly state that patent searches are not required, and that nothing in the policy would give rise to an obligation to perform such a search.
- In the case of W3C: when IPR owners are willing to license on royalty-free terms (which is sought by this SSO) they are relieved from a disclosure obligation.
- There are two types of disclosure and they are not intended to be alternatives. The first is often referred to as a patent call. It has a more informational (rather than formal and binding) nature. It usually serves at least two purposes: as a warning signal for the working group and as a factor that makes it harder for a member acting in bad faith to claim lack of awareness of the duty to disclose. The second type of disclosure refers to a later stage of standards development. It is usually linked to the requirement that the participant in standardization expresses preferences with regard to the licensing mode of disclosed essential claims.

These findings lead to the conclusion that, in principle, the disclosure requirement does not hamper access to the SSO. The absence of a duty to

---

[67] Rudi Bekkers and Andrew S. Updegrove, 'A Study of IPR Policies and Practices of a Representative Group of Standards Setting Organizations Worldwide' (September 17, 2012), available at http://ssrn.com/abstract=2333445 (last visited January 13, 2015) where IPR policies of the following SSOs are considered: ITU/ISO/IEC; IEEE; ETSI; ANSI; IETF; OASIS; VITA; W3C; HDMI Forum; NFC Forum.

conduct a thorough patent search implies that the adopted IPR policy model tends to err on the side of over-disclosure rather than under-disclosure.[68] However, there is no penalty if the result of such disclosure turns out to be inaccurate. These factors support the view that the adopted mechanism of patent disclosure does not represent a disproportionate burden for companies of different business models and thus provides non-discriminatory access to the SSO.[69]

As for the risk of patent ambush, it appears that the examined requirement of patent disclosure is a strong source of encouragement for SSO members to comply with it. Indeed, the incentive to observe the disclosure requirement lies in the very interest an SSO participant has in licensing those patents later. Moreover, the cases of non-compliance can potentially be scrutinized under the 'breach of good faith' notion. However, in order to provide for the realization of such investigation, it is important that the SSO articulates the requirement in a comprehensive manner.

Now we turn to the issue of licensing commitments. It is evident that the minimum goal of virtually all SSOs is to ensure that all known essential IPRs are available under FRAND licence terms,[70] without providing their exact meaning. Even though this SSO approach has been severely criticized, we believe that such critique does not take into consideration the position of SSOs and the interests of their members.

From an SSO perspective, the decision not to get involved in more specific elaborations of the exact provisions of FRAND commitments serves the purpose of providing access to an SSO on non-discriminatory terms. Considering the diverse business models of the companies involved in standardization, SSO adjustments of such a policy would bear risks of (1) discouraging companies from joining/subsequently participating in the SSO concerned; and (2) disincentivising the participation in

---

68 Ibid., p. 55.

69 The example of W3C policy is not an exception to this conclusion as was demonstrated through the story of Apple's participation in the Consortium. See Florian Müller, *Apple's Latest Patent Foe: The World Wide Web Consortium BM Breaks the Taboo and Betrays its Promise to the FOSS Community, FOSS Patents Blog*, available at http://www.fosspatents.com/2011/07/apples-latest-patent-foe-world-wide-web.html (last visited January 13, 2015). The fact that a patent holder incurs no obligation in cases of the default RF licensing is compensated by the option to withhold one's IPR from the offered licensing regime conditioned upon the disclosure of such IPRs.

70 Bekkers and Updegrove, note 67 above, p. 71.

SSOs altogether.[71] Seen in this light, the current widespread form of FRAND commitments allows for a certain flexibility and does not differentiate, for example, between manufacturing companies and companies engaged in the licensing of their IPRs only.

Relatedly, the concerns with regard to potential discrimination of FOSS followers in the FRAND framework should be noted.[72] However, empirical research[73] demonstrates that no inherent conflict exists between FOSS and FRAND.[74] Therefore, it appears that the FRAND framework presents a neat and elegant solution for market players in both the Telecommunications and IT sectors.

In principle, this matter is based on the assumption that no one has a right to exclude the implementers from SSO participation. In addition, the current form of the licensing requirement offers a certain degree of flexibility for subsequent licensing negotiations, including the potential for broad portfolio cross-licensing. It also provides an incentive for compliance: by committing to licensing its SEP on specified terms, the patent holder reduces the risk that the SSO will turn to alternative technologies. Finally, as we pointed out earlier, the patent holder's interests in the promotion of standards are in line with the nature and purpose of SSO cooperation.

Since the risk of a patent ambush is mostly linked to the disclosure requirement, analysing its permutations in terms of FRAND licensing commitments is less relevant. Overall, the disclosure and licensing

---

[71] See e.g. concerns voiced by Qualcomm in its letter to the IEEE with regard to the proposed changes, available at http://www.advancingengineering.org/sites/default/files/IEEE_IrwinLetter.pdf (last visited January 13, 2015).

[72] For a discussion see, e.g. Report by the European Commission and European Patent Office, *Implementing FRAND Standards in Open Source: Business as Usual or Mission Impossible?* (2012), available at http://ec.europa.eu/enterprise/sectors/ict/files/ict-policies/report-from-frand-os-conference-22nov12_en.pdf (last visited January 13, 2015).

[73] Jay P. Kesan, 'The Fallacy of OSS Discrimination by FRAND Licensing: An Empirical Analysis' (2011) Illinois Public Law Research Paper, No. 10-14, available at http://ssrn.com/abstract=1767083 (last visited January 13, 2015).

[74] See also Stephen Mutkoski, *Government Procurement Policy, Patent Royalties and the Myth of 'Discrimination' Against Free and Open Source Software Developers* (October 26, 2011), available at http://papers.ssrn.com/sol3/papers.cfm?abstract_id=1949832 (last visited January 13, 2015); Florian Müller, *Europe's Friend FRAND, FOSS Patents Blog*, available at http://www.fosspatents.com/2010/10/europes-friend-frand.html (last visited January 13, 2015).

requirements considered seem to confirm that SSOs do take the outlined concerns of open access and patent ambush into consideration in a fairly adequate way.

In the next section we will turn to competition law's treatment of SSOs and provide examples of antitrust investigations related to the identified risk of patent holdup.

4. OVERVIEW OF COMPETITION LAW PRACTICE

This section will provide a brief overview of competition law's treatment of SSOs as entities engaged in horizontal cooperation (section 4.1). It will also outline some cases concerning patent holdup behaviour through breaches of FRAND commitments (section 4.2). The section will serve as a basis for our concluding remarks.

4.1 Competition Law's Treatment of SSO Activity as Horizontal Cooperation

The model of SSO collaboration can raise antitrust concerns both with regard to associated collusive and exclusive risks.[75] There are a great number of cases relevant to the assessment of an SSO as a horizontal cooperation.[76] In addition, due to complexity and a great variety of facts involved in such an evaluation, it is possible for the same case to be considered under different categories.[77]

As established in previous sections, an SSO provides a platform for potential and/or actual competitors to decide on a solution to existent technical problems. Such cooperation may (1) facilitate collusion, (2) impose restriction on products or services that results in higher prices and

---

[75] As demonstrated by Peter Grindley et al., 'Standards Wars: The Uses of Standard Setting as a Means of Facilitating Cartels: Third Generation Wireless Telecommunications Standard Setting' (Summer 1999) 3 *International Journal of Commercial Law and Policy* 2.

[76] For a detailed overview of the relevant cases in the US one might refer to ABA, *Handbook on the Antitrust Aspects of Standards Setting* (American Bar Association, 2004), pp. 35–75.

[77] E.g. Qualcomm case litigated both in the US and the EU: *Broadcom Corp. v. Qualcomm Inc.*, 501 F. 3d 297, 314 (3d Cir. 2007); Press Release, European Commission, Antitrust: Commission Initiates Formal Proceedings against Qualcomm (October 1, 2007), available at http://europa.eu/rapid/press-release_MEMO-07-389_en.htm (last visited January 13, 2015).

(3) restrict product diversity and therefore consumer choice.[78] Notwithstanding these concerns, both courts and regulators seem to favour a flexible approach to assessing SSOs. In the US, for example, this is evidenced by a shift from the strict per se analysis to the rule of reason evaluation of an SSO in case development.[79] In the European Union, the pro-competitive benefits of SSO cooperation are outlined in the EU Commission Guidelines on horizontal cooperation agreements.[80]

Evidence suggests, then, that these antitrust risks could be well described using the notion of access. In general, by ensuring non-discriminatory access to a variety of market players, SSOs can thereby avoid being scrutinized under competition law with regard to the potentially anticompetitive effects of such horizontal collaboration. The US Supreme Court decision in the *Allied Tube*[81] case provides a good example confirming the link between access and legal compliance. The judgment concerns the SSO (National Fire Protection Association – NFPA) which sets and publishes product standards and codes related to fire protection. The Court established that NFPA's decision to not include a particular product in the standard was anticompetitive. In fact, it was deemed that this decision to exclude unreasonably restrained trade was in violation of the antitrust laws.

There were a number of factors that led the Court to reach this conclusion. First, the SSO decision under consideration had a significant effect on the market. The standard essentially demanded mandatory compliance due to its incorporation into the National Electrical Code and its wide acceptance in the building industry.[82] Second, despite the possibility of accommodating more than one technology in the standard,

---

[78] For the US practice see Herbert Hovenkamp and Mark A. Lemley, *IP and Antitrust: An Analysis of Antitrust Principles Applied to Intellectual Property Law* (Aspen Publishers Online, 2009), pp. 35–8. Similar concerns are outlined in the EU Commission Guidelines on the applicability of Article 101 of the Treaty on the Functioning of the European Union to horizontal cooperation agreements (hereinafter 'Guidelines') in paras 265, 266, 268.

[79] Hovenkamp and Lemley, note 78 above, pp. 32–7.

[80] Guidelines, paras 263, 308. For further information see Bjorn Lundqvist, *Standardization under EU Competition Rules and US Antitrust Laws: The Rise and Limits of Self-Regulation* (Edward Elgar, 2014), pp. 184–223.

[81] *Allied Tube & Conduit Corp. v. Indian Head, Inc.*, 486 U.S. 492 (1988), also available at http://caselaw.lp.findlaw.com/scripts/getcase.pl?court=US&vol=486&invol=492 (last visited January 13, 2015).

[82] Ibid. p. 496: the Code is the most influential electrical code in the nation: e.g. it gets adopted into law by a substantial number of state and local governments.

the decision to not include the plaintiff's solution precluded innovation[83] and potentially reduced the number of companies competing in the industry. In addition, the SSO's decision to exclude was reached through a manipulation of the standard setting process by the companies representing the production of technology competing with the plaintiff's company.[84]

Here, it is very important to differentiate this case of manipulation for anticompetitive reasons from the efforts a company may make in seeking to be part of standardization to achieve a particular, favourable outcome (such as the inclusion of a technology covered by this company's patent/patent application). When such a result is achieved on merit there should be no antitrust authority involvement.[85] By contrast, the cases of a wilful misrepresentation of the status of incorporated IPRs, (identified above as patent ambush cases) have been recently questioned in the course of antitrust investigations.

One of the most discussed and publicized FTC cases addressing this issue is *In re Rambus Inc.*,[86] where the FTC found Rambus liable for intentionally concealing a patent and relevant applications from the SSO concerned.[87] The EU Commission followed with its own action against Rambus, pronouncing a statement of objections against *Rambus* on July 30, 2007, and announcing its decision on December 9, 2009.[88] Although

---

[83] Ibid. p. 497: the plaintiff's polyvinyl conduit was claimed to offer significant advantages over steel conduit, including pliability, lower installed cost and lower susceptibility to short circuiting.

[84] Ibid. p. 497: they collectively agreed to exclude respondent's product from the 1981 Code by packing the upcoming annual meeting with new Association members whose only function would be to vote against the polyvinyl chloride proposal.

[85] See, e.g., Weiss and Toyokuku, note 40 above, discussing costs and benefits of participation in standard setting and pointing out the incentives provided by the inclusion of IP in such cases.

[86] *In re Rambus Inc.* 140 F.T.C. 1138 (F.T.C. 2005). A good overview of further cases addressing this issue, such as *In re Dell, Computer Corporation* 121 F.T.C. 616 (F.T.C. 1996) or *In re Union Oil Company of California* 138 F.T.C.1 (F.T.C. 2004) is given by Michael A. Carrier, *Innovation for the 21st Century: Harnessing the Power of Intellectual Property and Antitrust Law* (Oxford University Press, 2009), pp. 324–44.

[87] The SSO at issue was the Joint Electron Device Engineering Council (JEDEC), which sets and administers standards for the memory chip market, such as the case-relevant DRAM.

[88] European Commission Decision, Case COMP/38.636, *Rambus Inc.* (December 9, 2009), available at http://ec.europa.eu/competition/antitrust/cases/dec_docs/38636/38636_1203_1.pdf (last visited January 13, 2015).

the DC Circuit ultimately overturned the FTC's decision,[89] the FTC's analysis in *Rambus* paved the way for intensive academic debates.[90] The case also greatly influenced the US and EU competition authorities in their subsequent investigations. It also had a strong impact on the internal IPR policies of SSOs, which is a matter discussed in the next section.

Another challenge that IPR might present for SSOs involves instances where these entities may use formal and informal mechanisms to lessen the control an IP owner has over a standard that the SSO adopts.[91] This is a critical issue for understanding the limits of antitrust law on the practice of SSOs. As a point of departure, one should start from the assumption that IPR and competition law share a common goal in terms of promoting incentives to innovate and maximizing total societal welfare. The critical questions then become: how do SSO rules imposing a limitation on the IPRs of its participants affect innovation? Can these rules be deemed anticompetitive? Such questions are difficult to answer and we contend that there cannot be a 'one-size-fits-all' solution. Issues such as enforceability and membership structure[92] should be assessed on a case-by-case basis. It is impossible as yet to deduce any sort of conclusive guidelines from the practice of the competent authorities deciding on this matter. It seems that the rules restricting the exercise of intellectual property by the patent holders are generally permissible.[93] However, one should not underestimate the impact of some issues remaining unresolved as a result of the previously initiated antitrust investigations.[94]

---

[89] See *Rambus, Inc. v. F.T.C.*, 522 F.3d 456, 469 (D.C. Cir. 2008), cert. denied, 129 S. Ct. 1318 (2009).

[90] See e.g. Anne Layne-Farrar, *Viewpoint: What the Rambus Ruling Means for Intellectual Property in Standard Setting* (eSapience Center for Competition Policy, 2007).

[91] Hovenkamp and Lemley, note 78 above, pp. 35–7.

[92] It appears that the key matter in this case is to identify the risk of a buyers' cartel.

[93] E.g. DOJ business review letters to VITA and IEEE.

[94] E.g. Roger G. Brooks and Damien Geradin, 'Taking Contracts Seriously: The Meaning of the Voluntary Commitment to License Essential Patents on "Fair and Reasonable" Terms' (March 12, 2010), available at http://ssrn.com/abstract=1569498 (last visited January 13), discussing the complaint filed with the EU Commission by the Computer and Business Equipment Manufacturers' Association regarding the revision of ESTI IPR policy in 1993; Eric J. Iversen, 'Standardization and Intellectual Property Rights: ETSI's Controversial Search for New IPR-Procedures' (2000) *Informatik* IV.

4.2 Competition Law's Treatment of Patent Holdups through a Breach of FRAND Commitments

The second line of patent holdup cases does not involve a patent holder's deceptive behaviour. Rather, these cases concern 'pure' *ex post* contractual opportunism.[95] This includes attempts by patent holders to extract higher royalty fees by renegotiating or deviating from the original FRAND commitment made in good faith and without deception.[96]

A good example of the way competition authorities treat such conduct is provided by the FTC's enforcement action in *In re Negotiated Data Solutions LLC*.[97] The case concerned patents that were originally held by National Semiconductor which had disclosed its patents for the NWay Ethernet standard to IEEE and had also agreed to license the patents for a small fee under FRAND terms. It subsequently sold these patents to Vertical Networks, which, after getting into financial trouble, sold them to Negotiated Data Solutions (N-Data). After the purchase, N-Data claimed that it had not participated in IEEE and had not made any FRAND promise itself, so it was not bound by the FRAND commitment. As it turned out, the FTC did not accept such argumentation. On January 24, 2008, the FTC announced both a complaint and a settlement against N-Data deciding that a FRAND commitment was a pledge linked to the patent at issue, and that such a commitment did not depend on the party that had previously made the commitment.[98]

In this group of holdup cases much attention has also been given to the issue of injunctive relief in SEP cases. The controversy centres upon the litigation restrictions associated with a FRAND commitment, namely: does promising to license an SEP on FRAND terms to any licensee preclude the SEP holder from seeking an injunction against a third party or a licensee?[99] The issue has received an antitrust assessment in some recent cases by the EU Commission and the FTC.

---

95 Bruce H. Kobayashi and Joshua D. Wright, *Federalism, Substantive Preemption, and Limits to Antitrust* (Cambridge University Press, 2011), p. 501.

96 Ibid.

97 *In re Negotiated Data Solutions LLC (N-Data)*, No. 051-0094 (FTC, January 23, 2008).

98 See FTC's Analysis of Proposed Consent Order to Aid Public Comment: In the Matter of Negotiated Data Solutions LLC (2008), available at http://www.ftc.gov/os/caselist/0510094/080122analysis.pdf (last visited January 13, 2015).

99 Anne Layne-Farrar, 'Proactive or Reactive? An Empirical Assessment of IPR Policy Revisions in the Wake of Antitrust Actions' (2014) 59(2) *The Antitrust Bulletin* 373, p. 380.

In 2012, for example, the EU Commission initiated an investigation of Samsung, examining whether it had breached its commitment given to the European Telecommunications Standards Institute (ETSI) to license its patents related to the third generation (3G) mobile and wireless telecommunications systems on FRAND terms. More precisely, the Commission examined whether Samsung's attempts to seek injunctions against Apple before the courts of various Member States constituted an abuse of a dominant position prohibited by Article 102 of the TFEU.[100] It established that in the exceptional circumstances of the case under consideration, and in the absence of any objective justification, Samsung did indeed infringe Article 102 TFEU. Through its decision from April 29, 2014,[101] the Commission made binding the Final Commitments offered by Samsung for a period of five years. According to the commitments, Samsung will not seek injunctions in Europe on the basis of its SEPs for smartphones and tablets against licensees who sign up to a specified licensing framework. Under this framework, any dispute over what are FRAND terms for the SEPs in question will be determined by a court, or, if both parties agree, by an arbitrator.

On the same day, the Commission delivered a prohibition decision in a separate investigation concerning Motorola's enforcement of its two SEPs essential to the ETSI's GSM/GPRS standard[102] against Apple. In its decision, the Commission examined the issue of competition law defence in a case concerning a patent infringement under German and EU law. As a result of the investigation, the decision finding an infringement was adopted but no fine was imposed. According to the EU Commission, bringing an action for a prohibitory injunction was unlawful in the light of Article 102 TFEU, due to the following factors: (1) the case concerned an SEP, (2) the patent holder had indicated to ETSI its readiness to grant licences on FRAND terms, and (3) the infringer was itself willing to negotiate such a licence. However, the notion of 'willingness to negotiate' in the Commission's position was left without any substantial clarification.

---

[100] Consolidated Version of the Treaty on the Functioning of the European Union Art. 15, May 9, 2008, 2008 O.J. (C 115) 47 (hereinafter 'TFEU').

[101] The Commission Decision in the Case AT.39939 is available at http://ec.europa.eu/competition/antitrust/cases/dec_docs/39939/39939_1501_5.pdf (last visited January 13, 2015).

[102] The Commission Decision in the Case AT. 39985 is available at http://ec.europa.eu/competition/antitrust/cases/dec_docs/39985/39985_928_16.pdf (last visited January 13, 2015).

In this context, the request for a preliminary ruling from the Landgericht Düsseldorf (Germany) referred to CJEU in the case *Huawei Technologies Co. Ltd v ZTE Corp., ZTE Deutschland GmbH* (Case C-170/13) was foreseen. The opinion of the Advocate General delivered on November 29, 2014[103] appeared to be an attempt to find a middle path between the approach of the German courts, laid down in the Supreme Court Orange Book decision,[104] and the result of the EU Commission investigations in the Samsung and Motorola cases. The approach recommended by the Advocate General did not significantly differ from the solution offered by the Commission. The Advocate General, however, suggested a more elaborate legal test as to the assessment of a licensee's willingness. According to his opinion, an SEP holder can avoid the risk of abusing a dominant position by following some precursory steps before seeking injunctions. The highly anticipated judgment of the CJEU delivered on July 16, 2015[105] followed the overall approach proposed by the Advocate General. The Court established that the SEP holder's irrevocable offer to grant licences on FRAND terms implied a duty to comply with specific requirements when seeking a patent enforcement. The SEP owner has an obligation to properly inform the alleged infringer about the infringement prior to bringing an action for a prohibitory injunction. The SEP holder also has a burden of presenting an initial offer for a licence on FRAND terms. At the same time, the alleged infringer may not rely on an abusive nature of the SEP holder's behaviour without satisfying conditions of recognized commercial practices in the field and the requirement of good faith when responding to the offer proposed by the SEP owner.

Generally speaking, the judgment seeks to balance interests of both parties of the licensing arrangement. However, the proposed framework is rather general and does not offer much guidance on the issue of market dominance or matters of the scope and content of FRAND commitments.

---

[103] The Opinion of Advocate General Wathelet is available at http://curia.europa.eu/juris/document/document.jsf?text=&docid=159827&pageIndex=0&doclang=en&mode=lst&dir=&occ=first&part=1&cid=7191 (last visited January 13, 2015).

[104] English translation of the case is available at http://www.ipeg.eu/blog/wp-content/uploads/EN-Translation-BGH-Orange-Book-Standard-eng.pdf (last visited January 13, 2015).

[105] Judgment of the Court of Justice of the European Union in the case *Huawei Technologies Co. Ltd v ZTE Corp., ZTE Deutschland GmbH* (Case C-170/13) is available at http://curia.europa.eu/juris/document/document.jsf?text=&docid=165911&pageIndex=0&doclang=EN&mode=lst&dir=&occ=first&part=1&cid=190669 (last visited July 19, 2015).

Finally, it should be mentioned that similar issues have been examined in the course of FTC investigations in the cases of Bosch[106] and Google.[107] However, in spite of the seemingly active involvement of the FTC in the issue of SEP and injunctive relief, the prospects of the FTC taking a similarly aggressive policy regarding FRAND commitments in the near future is unclear.[108]

This brief summary of relevant cases and ongoing proceedings has demonstrated that the competition authorities and courts are very active in the area of standardization. The effect of such antitrust practices on SSOs and their IPR policies will be examined in our final section.

5. DISCUSSION

An overview of the cases in the preceding section identifies three main groups of antitrust concern in the context of standardization: (1) SSO activity as a form of horizontal cooperation, (2) cases of patent ambush and (3) potential risk of patent holdups through breaches of FRAND commitments.

To what extent should an SSO address these concerns in its IPR policy? Addressing this question involves multiple considerations. First of all, it is important to establish whether the SSO has a formal requirement to adjust its IPR policy to meet the highlighted antitrust concerns in every given case (the issue of autonomy spaces). Second, it is essential to find out whether these risks identified by the competition authorities correspond to the challenges that the SSO has as a form of self-governance. Third, it is necessary to determine if and how these threats have been accommodated through the SSO's IPR policy (issues concerning the efficiency of the SSO's private regulation). Once these

---

[106] Decision and Order, In the Matter of Robert Bosch GmbH, Docket No. C-437 (FTC April 24, 2013), available at http://www.ftc.gov/enforcement/cases-proceedings/1210081/bosch-robert-bosch-gmbh (last visited January 13, 2015).

[107] Decision and Order, In the Matter of Motorola Mobility LC and Google Inc. (FTC July 24, 2013), available at http://www.ftc.gov/enforcement/cases-proceedings/1210120/motorola-mobility-llc-google-inc-matter (last visited January 13, 2015).

[108] For a comparative analysis see Thomas F. Cotter, 'The Comparative Law and Economics of Standard-Essential Patents and FRAND Royalties' (2013) Minnesota Legal Studies Research Paper No. 13-40, p. 19, available at http://ssrn.com/abstract=2318050 (last visited January 13, 2015).

factors have been examined, we can draw some conclusions with regard to the appropriateness and desirability of changes to the IPR policies of SSOs.

Looking at SSOs in terms of horizontal cooperation, it is in an SSO's best interests to ensure compliance with the relevant competition law requirements. A failure to do so inevitably results in antitrust liability. Due to the mandatory nature of such compliance, we can conclude that an SSO has a formal obligation to accommodate the highlighted antitrust concerns. Translated into the terminology of user-generated law, it could be claimed that there is no real autonomy space for any private regulation model in this case. The State-enacted law in the form of antitrust provisions is based on public policy considerations concerning the protection of competition in a market. The benefits of the market competitive environment are generally acknowledged. The demand for law in this case is homogeneous. Therefore, the risks associated with the cooperation of actual or potential competitors are addressed through rather stringent State-enacted law with the potential for rigorous enforcement in cases of non-compliance.

However, it is important to consider the following factors. Despite the risks associated with collusive and exclusive behaviour of competitors affiliated with an SSO, the pro-competitive benefits of such cooperation are well-recognized. The shift from a strict per se analysis to an assessment under the rule of reason in practice of competition authorities might well be interpreted as adjustments of autonomy spaces for private regulation. The confines of the State-enacted law can be traced through the requirements that the SSO in question should operate:

> based on the merits of objective expert judgments and through procedures that prevent the standard-setting process from being biased by members with economic interests in stifling product competition.[109]

The exact methods of ensuring that this requirement is met appear to be left to an SSO's discretion. Generally speaking, the antitrust concerns associated with the horizontal collaboration correspond to the risk of over-exclusion inherent in the SSO as a form of self-governance. In this context, it could be concluded that in the majority of cases SSOs have addressed this risk and incorporated IPR policies that aim at providing for an open and non-discriminatory access to the SSO.

---

109 *Allied Tube*, note 81 above, p. 501. A similar approach can be found in the EU Commission Guidelines on horizontal cooperation, e.g. in para. 280.

As for the highlighted concern stemming from two identified patent holdup categories, there is no formal provision found in antitrust regulations that would require an SSO to introduce some special measures to combat these risks. In the light of user-generated law, one can interpret this as evidence of the existence of wide autonomy spaces for private regulation through the reactive process: the legislator has not defined the scope of the State-enacted law before the need for law materialized. Rather, the legislator left a legal vacuum later filled with different models of private regulation generated by the users. It appears that an SSO is generally better positioned in addressing the diverse needs and requirements of its users. Thus, seen from an SSO's perspective, cases of patent ambush have a potentially adverse effect on the process of standard setting. Generally, an SSO's requirement of patent disclosure takes the risk of such deceptive behaviour into account. However, the lack of a rigid and effective enforcement mechanism against potential abusers might be seen as an acknowledgement of the need for the State-enacted supplementary regulation.[110]

Finally, we turn to an examination of the patent holdup risk in cases where there has been a breach of FRAND commitments. Having considered this concern from the standpoint of an SSO, we established that these cases do not represent a significant threat to the SSO in terms of self-governance. In this regard, it is important to emphasize the lack of strong evidence supporting the prevalence of holdup behaviour in SSOs, or indeed for its negative impact on standard setting at large.[111] Moreover, the current framework of FRAND, where the exact meaning of such FRAND terms is not spelled out, provides an open access to SSOs on a non-discriminatory basis. This finding is well supported by the current climate in which the majority of SSOs have not introduced any additional measures to mitigate this risk of patent holdup despite a variety of proposed solutions.[112] We believe that one of the main reasons for this is

---

[110] However it should not be categorically interpreted as a confirmation of the inefficiency of the private regulation provided by the SSO. The scarce number of cases of patent ambush can be seen as indirect evidence that the existent mechanisms of regulation are enough.

[111] E.g. Wright, note 12 above; Alexander Galetovic et al., 'Patent Holdup: Do Patent Holders Holdup Innovation?', IP^2 Working Paper No. 14011, available at http://hooverip2.org/working-paper/14011/ (last visited January 13, 2015).

[112] For a comprehensive discussion on the measures and their potential impact see Damien Geradin, 'Standardization and Technological Innovation: Some Reflections on Ex-Ante Licensing, FRAND, and the Proper Means to Reward Innovators' (2006) TILEC Discussion Paper No. 2006-017; on *ex ante*

that the positive impact of the adoption of these solutions is not yet conclusively established.[113] It is not clear what effect such measures will have on the system of incentives for companies of different business models. Therefore, the general reluctance of SSOs to change their IPR policies to accommodate the potential risk of patent holdups could be explained by the unwillingness of SSOs to risk disrupting the balance of interests and incentives affecting their relevant stakeholders. Mandating onerous licensing requirements might make access to the given SSO less attractive and more burdensome. As a result, less innovation will be generated[114] and the SSO as a platform of innovation commons will become less effective. In addition, any negative IPR policy changes might confer a great competitive advantage on the holders of the patents not bound by strict FRAND commitments. Contrary to the expectations of the competition authorities seeking clarity on the meaning of FRAND commitments, this outcome would increase the odds of patent holdup and thus present unintended consequences.[115]

In view of the factors above, it appears that antitrust law has a rather limited role to play in shaping the IPR policy of SSOs concerning patent holdup in cases involving a breach of FRAND commitments.[116] The existing model of private regulation provides for a flexible and effective mechanism aimed at addressing the diverse needs and interests of the users involved. An SSO (as a form of self-governance) has no obligation to tackle the complexity of licensing after the standards adoption. In this

licensing negotiations in particular see Anne Layne-Farrar et al., 'Preventing Patent Hold Up: An Economic Assessment of Ex Ante Licensing Negotiations in Standard Setting' (May 5, 2008), available at http://ssrn.com/abstract=1129551 or http://dx.doi.org/10.2139/ssrn.1129551 (last visited January 13, 2015).

[113] See, e.g., the introduction of the *ex ante* disclosure of the licensing terms in ETSI. Despite an overall positive attitude towards the measure from the competition authority, to date no company has made a use of the offered measure: http://www.etsi.org/about/how-we-work/intellectual-property-rights-iprs/ex-ante-disclosures (last visited January 13, 2015).

[114] Anne Layne-Farrar et al, 'Payments and Participation: The Incentives to Join Cooperative Standard Setting Efforts' (2014) 23(1) *Journal of Economics & Management Strategy* 25, available at http://onlinelibrary.wiley.com/doi/10.1111/jems.12046/abstract (last visited January 13, 2015).

[115] Layne-Farrar, note 59 above, p. 11.

[116] The position on the limited role of antitrust law in informing SSOs' activities has been previously proposed by, e.g. David J. Teece and Edward Sherry, 'Standards Setting and Antitrust' (2003) 87 *Minn. L. Rev.* 1911 and Michael A. Carrier, 'Why Antitrust Should Defer to the Intellectual Property Rules of Standard-Setting Organizations: A Commentary on Teece & Sherry' (2003) 87 *Minn. L. Rev.* 2019.

regard, we believe that patent pools or other user-generated means might combine with such measures as improved pre-grant requirement mechanisms in patent law to produce better results.

6. CONCLUSIONS

In balancing the pros and cons of prospectively altering SSO IPR policies to accommodate antitrust concerns, we conclude that such development is not always beneficial to the SSO model of private regulation. In cases where the practices of the antitrust authorities provide solutions to the internal matters of SSO governance, the outcomes of such antitrust investigations should be carefully considered by the SSO concerned. However, an SSO should generally abstain from introducing any rigorous changes to its IPR policy in those situations where meeting antitrust concern has the potential to undermine the SSO's efficiency and innovation potential.

8. 'The rise of standardisation and the limits of self-governance': unilateral conduct under international standards from an EU competition law perspective

Björn Lundqvist

1. INTRODUCTION

Huawei is the latest EU case in the ongoing 'patent war' in the ITC (internet and telecom) industry. A patent war played out in courtrooms all over the world, yet fundamentally dealing with the same or similar issues. The cases gravitate around whether patents covering a technical detail, which is essential to a technology standard of infrastructure type, may be used to exclude competitors from an industry as a whole. For example, the current wireless technology used for mobile phone communication is a technical standard, the 4G technology/standard, which is covered by several patents, held by many firms. Can each of those firms refuse entering into licence agreements covering often narrow, yet necessary technology pieces of the over-arching infrastructure technology making up our telecom network standard? Can they thereby, by refusing to enter licences, exclude firms from, for example, the smart phone market as a whole, without infringing competition law?

The *Huawei* case deals with these hotly debated questions of access to international standards and standard essential patents on fair, reasonable and non-discriminatory (FRAND) terms. Thus, the main issues in the case were: when a technical standard that has been adopted by a standard setting organisation (SSO) is covering technology which mirrors certain patents (so-called standard essential patents (SEPs)), can the proprietor of said patents refuse entering into a licence agreement with a firm that would like to conduct business (sell products) under the standard? Especially, if the proprietor when the standard was agreed upon, to the

SSO committed that it would license its SEPs on FRAND terms? Or, should such refusal to license and thereby the proprietors' action for injunctive relief vis-à-vis the hopeful licensee be considered an abuse of dominant position under Article 102 TFEU?

The questions can generally be condensed into two. First, when may a SEP holder refuse access and obtain an injunction against an infringer, who is still a willing licensee? Second, what constitutes FRAND and who should bear the risk of defining FRAND for the licence to be entered – the proprietor or the potential licensee? These questions will be discussed in this chapter.

An additional focal point for this chapter is self-regulation and the limits of self-regulation (concerning the contractual procedural models to establish governance rules for standards which the stakeholders themselves create, rather than what the User Generated Law model calls 'State-enacted law'). The limits for the exercise of SEP and FRAND procedures are basically set by self-regulatory arrangements in SSOs. Hence, this chapter aims to analyse how FRAND should be interpreted in light of recent case law developments concerning what constitutes an abuse in regard to the terms for accessing SEPs. Having conducted this analysis, the chapter will return to and utilise the User Generated Law model in order to explain self-regulation in this context and also clarify why the courts reached these findings regarding the SEP and FRAND issues.

The chapter is divided in three main sub-chapters. First, we will discuss the background to the patent war and the European competition law starting point in trying to regulate the same in the seminal *Orange-Book-Standard* case from the German Federal Court. This case adjudicated upon the issue of when an SEP holder may obtain an injunction vis-à-vis an infringer; or, more accurately, the terms on which an SEP holder might withhold access to the patent. Second, the two investigations from the EU Commission, *Samsung* and *Motorola*, are analysed. Third, and perhaps most interesting, the recent Opinion of the Advocate General and the ECJ's judgment in *Huawei* are discussed. According to the ECJ, under what procedure should access to SEPs be negotiated and granted under EU competition law?

2. THE *ORANGE-BOOK-STANDARD* CASE AND BEYOND

An early but interesting European case showing the fundamental difficulties of gaining access to essential patents under a *de facto* standard is the German Federal Supreme Court *Orange-Book-Standard* case from 2009.[1]

In the *Orange-Book-Standard* case, which concerned the CD-R and CD-RW technologies, the question was whether a patentee could get injunctive relief following a patent infringement suit when the infringer had tried to obtain a licence on commercial grounds but the patentee had refused. Interestingly, the German Federal Supreme Court started by maintaining that licensing an essential patent under a standard is a market in itself and the proprietor is that market's sole supplier, and is thus a monopolist. The Court concluded that a defendant may successfully plead that the patentee is abusing its dominant position in the market if the patentee refuses to conclude a patent licence agreement with the defendant on non-discriminatory and non-restrictive terms and conditions. However, the alleged infringer has, under the rules of injunctive relief, the burden of offering evidence that the patentee was given an opportunity to grant a licence on fair terms. It is not the obligation of the patentee to offer such a licence, but if it refuses, the patentee may be abusing a dominant position, and the infringer may not face an injunction if it acts in the manner of a licensee (e.g. pays royalties to the patentee or into an escrow account and adheres to a general licence covenant, including a non-challenge obligation).[2]

This might be viewed as a narrow defence for the potential licensee. First, it is the licensee that must define (and bear the burden of stipulating) the boundaries of what constitutes the abuse. It is also the burden of the potential licensee to present a licence proposal containing the necessary terms to implicate the patentee in an abuse of its dominant

---

[1] Federal Supreme Court (Bundesgerichtshof) May 6, 2009 – Case No. KZR 39/06. For a lengthy discussion regarding the *Orange-Book-Standard* case and other German standard cases (such as the Federal Supreme Court (Bundesgerichtshof) 13 July 2004 – Case No. KZR 40/02 (*'Tight-Head Drum'*) (*Standard-Spundfass*)) cf. Björn Lundqvist, *Standardization under EU Competition Rules and US Antitrust Laws – The Rise and the Limits of Self-Regulation* (Edward Elgar, 2014), pp. 319 et seq. See also Björn Lundqvist, 'The Interface between EU Competition Law and Standard Essential Patents – From Orange-Book-Standard to the Huawei case' (2015) 11 *European Competition Journal* 367. Parts of this chapter are based on these works.

[2] Ibid.

position should it refuse these terms. This may constitute a heavy burden for the potential licensee. It may not know what FRAND or market terms ought to be for the patent at issue, and in practice this may force the potential licensee to present terms that do not equal FRAND, but rather FRAND + terms in an effort to abide with the *Orange-Book-Standard* test. It is possible that the patentee is in a better position to present a licence agreement which reflects the current market terms. However, the patentee might also exaggerate. Second, what terms, obligations and covenants can the potential licensee present and still adhere to the *Orange-Book-Standard* test? Can the potential licensee propose any conditions precedent? (For instance, can it propose that the firm will take out a licence under the condition that a court *ex post* establishes the validity of the patents and/or the fair royalty rate?) The answer to these queries is no. According to the Federal Supreme Court, the potential licensee only has two options: (i) it may offer the patentee a royalty rate that equals the royalty rate customarily applied in the industry; or (ii) it may propose a royalty rate to be determined by the patentee, applying the patentee's 'reasonable exercised discretion'.[3] Moreover, the potential licensee may not challenge the validity or essentiality of the patent, and should pay damages for any pre-licence, unauthorised use of the SEP. On the face of it, it seems that the *Orange-Book-Standard* case does not give much leeway for potential licensees to question validity, essentiality or rate. More recent German cases seem to verify this.

Several German cases which have followed in the wake of the *Orange-Book-Standard* case are pertinent regarding the stringencies and difficulties facing prospective licensees. Only in a few cases has the potential licensee actually fulfilled the requirements. In *Philips v. Sony Ericsson*[4] the District Court of Mannheim dismissed the injunction claim, finding that the defendant had fulfilled the requirements of *Orange-Book-Standard* by offering to license at a fixed rate and depositing the calculated royalties in an escrow account. More cases exist where the alleged infringers have not been able to meet the stringent requirements in *Orange-Book-Standard*. Motorola/Google, for example, obtained an injunction against Apple (based on cellular SEP under the General Packet Radio Service (GPRS) standard, connected to Global System for Mobile

3 Ibid. Lawrence R. Gabuzda et al., *Standard-Essential Patents and Injunctive Relief* (2013), April, Jones Day Law Firm Publications, available at http://www.jonesday.com/standards-essential_patents (last visited 24 February 2014).

4 District Court of Mannheim, *Philips v. Sony Ericsson*, 27 May 2011, Doc. No. 7 O65/10.

communication (GSM) in December 2011 in the Karlsruhe High Regional Court in Mannheim. The injunction was enforced for a while, until it was suspended for the case to be heard on appeal in February 2012.[5] The parties then agreed that Apple would take out a licence for a rate to be decided by a court. The court found that Apple had to withdraw its motion for nullification of Motorola's patent when Motorola accepted Apple's offer to license. In fact, Apple's licence offer was obligated to include a non-challenge termination provision to fulfil the *Orange-Book-Standard* requirements. The courts have also required that a licensee must accept liability for past damages in its licence offer.[6]

These cases have served to resolve some outstanding issues with *Orange-Book-Standard.* For example, the lower courts ruled additionally that a FRAND commitment is a declaration of intent by the patent owner to conclude a binding licence agreement in the future. It fulfils the patentee's obligation under antitrust law, but does not grant a right to use the patent to potential licensees. The potential licensee must still show that it is a 'willing licensee'.[7]

Regarding *Orange-Book-Standard*, there were many indications arising from both the *Google/Motorola* merger case[8] and the *Motorola* Statement of Objections (SO) that the EU Commission (while not inclined to dismiss the *Orange-Book-Standard* rule) did at least display some dissatisfaction with the case. Due to Apple's complaint, the EU Commission came to analyse the German case law development under the *Orange-Book-Standard* doctrine. The EU Commission seems to indicate that the requirements are too difficult to satisfy for the alleged infringer, especially in *de jure* standard-setting situations.

Under EU law, the infringer may have a case for accessing the standard-setting procedure and the result (*inter alia* the SEPs), or the patent pool, relying on the EU's 'exceptional circumstances' doctrine under the abuse of dominance rule (cf. *Magill*, *IMS Health* and to some extent *Microsoft*).[9] These cases lay down a three-part test: (i) the product

---

[5] Court of Appeal in Karlsruhe, *Motorola v. Apple*, 27 February 2012, Doc. No. 6 U136/11.

[6] Gabuzda et al., note 3 above.

[7] Ibid.

[8] Commission Decision Case No. COMP/M.6381 *Google/Motorola Mobility*, 13 February 2012.

[9] Joined Cases C-241 to 242/91 *RTE and ITP v. Commission* [1995] ECR I-743; Case T-418/01 *IMS Health Inc. & Co. v. NDC Health GmbH & Co.* [2001] ECR II-3193; Case T-201/04 *Microsoft v. Commission* [2007] ECR II-3601.

the infringer wants to market must relate to an indispensable input required for the marketing of the (new) product which the holder of the intellectual property right does not offer, and for which there is a demand; (ii) there is no justification for such a refusal; and (iii) the dominant firm has hence reserved for itself a secondary market. These requirements seem rather different to the *Orange-Book-Standard* conditions and possibly more easily fulfilled.[10] Moreover, the Commission may perhaps be purporting that refusing access in standard-setting scenarios not only implies refusal to access but also constitutes a misuse of the standard-setting procedure, and is thus deserving of escalated antitrust treatment. It is a stand-alone exceptional circumstance, disconnected from the *Magill* and *IMS Health* case law doctrine. In fact, the *Huawei* case would later verify that these cases and situations reflect a new 'exception circumstance'.

Compared to the EU case law which lays down the 'exceptional circumstances', the *Orange-Book-Standard* case, and even more so the earlier *Tight-Head Drum* case,[11] do not stipulate a new product requirement, but instead focus on whether competition by substitution is available.[12] If there is no substitute technology or standard available, a court may identify refusal to access the patent (at least discriminatory refusal) as an abuse. This test actually differs fundamentally from the exceptional circumstance test based on the new product requirement drawn up by the EU Courts.[13]

Yet in a legal context where any final EU judgment is still to be reached, the ruling in *Orange-Book-Standard* should not be underestimated. In essence, it implies that holders of SEPs cannot get permanent injunctions against infringers if the latter are satisfying the rules of *Orange-Book-Standard* (e.g. paying licence fees and acting as licensees). The impact of this is that a compulsory licence scheme has been created. Furthermore, more theoretically, it is an exemption from or

---

[10] James Venit, 'Article 82 EC: Exceptional Circumstances – The IP/Antitrust Interface after IMS Health', in Claus-Dieter Ehlermann and Isabela Atanasiu (eds), *European Competition Law Annual 2005: The Interaction between Competition Law and Intellectual Property Law* (Hart Publishing, 2007), pp. 7 et seq.

[11] Federal Supreme Court (Bundesgerichtshof) July 13, 2004 – Case No. KZR 40/02 ('*Tight-Head Drum*') (Standard-Spundfass). Cf. Hanns Ullrich, 'Patents and Standards – a Comment on the German Federal Supreme Court Decision Orange Book Standard' (2011) 41 *IIC* 337, pp. 339 et seq.

[12] Ibid.

[13] Josef Drexl, 'Abuse of Dominance in Licensing and Refusal to License: A More Economic Approach to Competition by Imitation and to Competition by Substitution', in Ehlermann and Atanasiu, note 10 above, p. 650 et seq.

a restriction on intellectual property. In these situations, intellectual property does not mirror property; instead, competition law transforms intellectual property laws to liability rules.[14]

There have been cases, for example the new *Motorola* and *Samsung* cases from 2014, where the EU Commission has had the opportunity to apply the *Orange-Book-Standard* doctrine, and where it has distanced itself from the German case law development.[15]

3. THE EU COMMISSION'S INVESTIGATIONS

As noted above, the EU Commission handed down a decision regarding Google and its use of Motorola's SEPs in April of 2014.[16] The 'talking point' prior to the EU Commission handing down its decisions revolved around whether the Commission would adopt the *Orange-Book-Standard* doctrine and/or whether it instead would follow the FTC *Google* consent order procedure.[17]

The Commission's investigation started in April 2012 when the EU Commission issued a statement that it was opening proceedings against Motorola (and in another case with similar circumstances against Samsung). The Commission was responding to complaints by Apple and Microsoft and it specifically undertook an investigation of whether Motorola had failed to honour its irrevocable FRAND commitments to

---

[14] Annette Kur and Jens Schovsbo, 'Expropriation or Fair Game for All? The Gradual Dismantling of the IP Exclusivity Paradigm', in Max Planck Institute for Intellectual Property, Competition & Tax Law Research Paper No. 09-14 (2009), available at http://ssrn.com/abstract=1508330 or http://dx.doi.org/10.2139/ssrn.1508330 (last visited 4 November 2013).

[15] Commission Decision of 29 April 2014, Case AT.39939 Samsung – Enforcement of UMTS Standard Essential Patents, available at http://ec.europa.eu/competition/elojade/isef/case_details.cfm?proc_code=1_39939 (last visited 28 September 2014). Commission Decision of 29 April 2014, Case AT.39985 Motorola Enforcement of GPRS Standard Essential Patent, available at http://ec.europa.eu/competition/elojade/isef/case_details.cfm?proc_code=1_39985 (last visited 28 September 2014).

[16] See the press release regarding Samsung of 31 January 2012, available at http://europa.eu/rapid/press-release_IP-12-89_en.htm?locale=en (last visited 10 July 2013).

[17] FTC, Statement In the Matter of Google Inc., FTC File No. 121-0120, 3 January 2013, available at http://www.ftc.gov/os/caselist/1210120/130103googlemotorolastmtofcomm.pdf (last visited 11 July 2013). For lengthy discussion regarding several FTC cases concerning standards and competition law, see Lundqvist, note 1 above, pp. 334 et seq.

SSOs by seeking and enforcing injunctions against Apple's and Microsoft's respective flagship products, such as iPhone, iPad, Windows and Xbox, on the basis of patents it had declared essential for producing standard-compliant products. The Commission examined whether Motorola's behaviour amounted to an abuse of a dominant market position as prohibited by Article 102 TFEU, and while addressing the *Orange-Book-Standard* case, it also addressed some specific licensing terms.[18]

In May 2013, the EU Commission issued a Statement of Objection against Motorola in reference to its Apple litigation.[19] The Commission's view was that a potential licensee's acceptance of a future binding third party determination (such as that of a court) stipulating the terms of a FRAND licence, in the event that bilateral negotiations do not come to a fruitful conclusion, still constitutes a clear indication that a potential licensee is 'willing' to enter into a FRAND licence. This could be interpreted as the EU Commission not accepting the *Orange-Book-Standard* test since in that case Germany's Federal Supreme Court indicated that the alleged infringer must actually state a royalty rate and stick to that (or accept whatever the patentee says is FRAND and thereafter litigate). Under such terms there does not seem to be any room for real negotiations. Yet contrary to this, the Commission states that FRAND is the *process* by which an adequate remuneration of the SEP holder is decided. If the potential licensee commits to the procedure,

---

[18] Ibid. See press release by the EU Commission regarding Motorola of 3 April 2012, available at http://europa.eu/rapid/press-release_IP-12-345_en.htm?locale=en (last visited 11 July 2013). The injunction relief in this case was based on SEPs for the H.264 video code. Microsoft here agreed to pay a royalty rate ten times the MPEG LA pool rate to Motorola and offered in addition a US$300 million bond, with room for discussion to increase the amount, as long as an injunction was not enforced during the appeal process. It seems Google refused and pushed for enforcement against Windows Operating System and the Xbox gaming consoles anyway. This was not successful, since a US District Court and Appeal Court barred the enforcement of the German injunctions. In turn, this allegedly attracted the interest of the EU Commission. It was actually the District Court in the Western District of Washington, with Judge Robart presiding, that entered into a preliminary relief to extend an earlier temporary restraining order for Google/Motorola. It was now extended also to include the injunction by the Mannheim Regional Court.

[19] 'Antitrust: Commission Sends Statement of Objections to Motorola Mobility on Potential Misuse of Mobile Phone Standard-Essential Patents – Questions and Answers', Reference: MEMO/13/403, 6 May 2013, available at http://europa.eu/rapid/press-release_MEMO-13-403_en.htm (last visited 11 July 2013). For discussion, see Lundqvist, note 1 above, pp. 341 et seq.

while not necessarily accepting every term presented, it is still adhering to FRAND. Indeed, the EU Commission seems to accept that FRAND implies a flexible procedure to determine terms on a case-by-case basis. During this period an SEP holder may not enforce injunctions.

Additionally, in the Commission's view the fact that the potential licensee challenges the validity, essentiality or infringement of the SEP does not make it 'unwilling' to license if it otherwise agrees to be bound by the determination of FRAND terms by a third party (e.g. an arbitrating panel).[20] In the case before the Commission, Motorola required non-challenge covenants that prohibited challenges by Apple, even after Apple had agreed to be bound by a third party determination of the FRAND terms. According to the Commission, it is in the public interest that licensees should be able to challenge the validity, essentiality or infringement of SEPs. Indeed, the Commission seems to be more lenient than the German *Orange-Book-Standard* court. Hence, the hypothetical licence agreement may not include a non-challenge clause and the hypothetical licensee may still try to get a low royalty rate as long as the undertaking commits to a licence and to a process for establishing FRAND.

The Commission also mentioned *Orange-Book-Standard* and stated: 'The [German] Supreme Court's ruling did not specifically relate to SEPs'.[21] It should be clear that because the German cases following the *Orange-Book-Standard* did not distinguish between SEPs and other essential patents, the Commission seeks to use this fact to distance its investigation from the *Orange-Book-Standard* case. This accords with the Commission's interpretation of the ruling 'whereby a willing licensee is essentially not entitled to challenge the validity and essentiality of the SEPs in question is potentially anti-competitive'.[22]

It seems that the EU Commission is taking inspiration from the FTC *Google* Consent order. The Commission is trying to assert that FRAND represents a procedure in a similar vein to the FTC. If the patentee has agreed to FRAND then this implies that it has agreed to enter into a procedure to establish FRAND in which it will abide by the outcome of the court or arbitration panel proceedings, while still not making use of the injunctions. Yet under what rule or doctrine is the EU Commission stating this?

---

[20] Ibid.

[21] Ibid.

[22] Ibid.

The EU Commission delivered its decision in 2014. It is evident that it is using the doctrine of 'refusal to license' or exceptional circumstances (i.e. *IMS Health* and *Microsoft*) and is focusing on the fair terms for accessing the standard essential or interoperability essential patents. Moreover, the EU Commission seems to believe that a non-challenge clause is an unfair term to the degree that inclusion of such a clause in the licence may amount to abuse of dominance. Thus, it is an unfair trading condition under Article 102(a) TFEU.

The EU Commission addressed the issue of dominance in the *Samsung* case[23] and in the *Motorola* case[24] which were delivered on the same day. The Commission begins in both cases by stating that standards ensure 'compatibility and interoperability' and it proceeds to describe the role of the European Telecommunications Standards Institute (ETSI) and standard-essential patents. The Commission reached the finding that Samsung and Motorola respectively were dominant in their similar but separate relevant markets. The Commission stated that an implementer of a standard has to use the technology protected by an SEP when manufacturing a standard-compliant product and is therefore locked-in to the technology. According to the Commission, the relevant product markets encompass the licensing of the technologies as specified in the Universal Mobile Telecommunications System (UMTS) or GPRS standard technical specifications on which Samsung's UMTS SEPs read and Motorola's Cudak GPRS SEPs read.[25] There was no demand-side substitutability in either case. Both companies held a 100% share of respective markets (licensing of the technologies specified in the standard). Dominance was reinforced by the widespread adoption of these standards through market penetration and by a legal requirement to use the standards.

In both cases, the Commission identified that seeking preliminary and permanent injunctions against a 'willing' licensee was an abuse since the exceptional circumstance doctrine was available. The Commission stated in the Samsung case 'the exceptional circumstances in this case are: (i) the UMTS standard-setting process; and (ii) Samsung's commitment to ETSI to license its UMTS SEPs on FRAND terms and conditions'. The EU Commission also noted in its *Motorola* decision that a willing

---

23 Commission Decision of 29 April 2014, Case AT.39939 Samsung – Enforcement of UMTS Standard Essential Patents, available at http://ec.europa.eu/competition/elojade/isef/case_details.cfm?proc_code=1_39939 (last visited 28 September 2014).

24 Ibid.

25 Geographic markets were at least EEA-wide. See e.g. ibid., paras 214–20.

licensee can still (i) disagree regarding the validity of the SEP, and the patentee (Motorola) should not be allowed to terminate the agreement; a potential willing licensee does not (ii) need to acknowledge past infringements and can disagree (iii) on the right FRAND level. Thus, a patentee demanding disadvantageous terms can be considered abusing its dominant position even if is an abuse prior to the more openly combative step of seeking of a court injunction.

In addition, the Commission's ruling in the *Samsung* case establishes a safe harbour (namely, a procedure for how potential licensees may obtain licence agreements based on FRAND terms without the risk of facing injunctions, while concurrently the SEP holder may avoid violating Article 102 TFEU). The procedure is complicated and based on the settlement proposed by Samsung, and is clearly inspired by the FTC *Google* decision. The main features are as follows.

The SEP holder (Samsung) is committed to a negotiation period of up to 12 months. If no licensing agreement or alternative process for determining FRAND terms and conditions has been agreed upon at the end of the negotiation period, the determination of FRAND terms and conditions should be submitted to arbitration or to court adjudication in order to determine the FRAND terms and conditions of either a unilateral licensing or cross-licensing agreement.

Samsung could seek an injunction against a potential licensee on the basis of Samsung's Mobile SEPs in instances where two cumulative conditions were met: (i) a potential licensee has sought an injunction against Samsung on the basis of some of its Mobile SEPs; and (ii) Samsung has agreed to be bound by the Licensing Framework for its own Mobile SEPs and some of the Mobile SEPs of the potential licensee as covered by the reciprocity rules of SSOs.

The *Motorola* decision and the *Samsung* settlement have been accused of being potentially too licensee friendly, and the most recent development is that the ECJ received a request for a preliminary ruling from a court in Düsseldorf regarding the interface between competition law and intellectual property law with reference to an injunction based on an SEP. This offered the ECJ some scope and opportunity to develop the EU FRAND rules.[26] The Advocate General has given its Opinion in that case discussing both the *Orange-Book-Standard* case and the *Samsung* and *Motorola* investigations; and the ECJ recently delivered its judgment.

---

[26] See AG Opinion in Case C-170/13 *Huawei Technologies v. ZTD*, not yet published.

4. THE OPINION OF THE ADVOCATE GENERAL IN *HUAWEI*[27]

In the spring of 2013, the Düsseldorf regional court sent the ECJ specific questions regarding injunctive relief and SEPs. They were specific in the sense that the national court wanted to get an answer regarding whether it should use the *Orange-Book-Standard* test or the EU Commission's procedure described in the *Samsung* safe harbour. The *Huawei* case pitted Huawei Technologies, a multinational company active in the telecommunications sector, and the proprietor of, *inter alia*, the European patent registered under reference EP 2 090 050 B 1, bearing the title 'Method and apparatus of establishing a synchronisation signal in a communication system', granted by the Federal Republic of Germany, a Contracting State of the EPC (hereinafter 'the patent').

The patent is essential for one of the fundamental telecom standards, the 4G or 'Long Term Evolution' (LTE) standard. Huawei notified it to the ETSI on 4 March 2009 as a patent essential to the LTE standard. At the same time, Huawei undertook to grant licences to third parties on FRAND terms.

More than 4,700 patents have been registered as essential for the 4G or LTE standard and if the patent held by Huawei is essential to that standard, it implies that anyone using the LTE standard inevitably uses the teaching of that patent.

Between November 2010 and the end of March 2011, Huawei and ZTE Corp., a company belonging to a multinational group active in the telecommunications sector and which markets, in Germany, base stations equipped with software using technology covered by the LTE standard, engaged in discussions concerning, *inter alia*, the infringement of said patent and the possibility of concluding a licence on FRAND terms in relation to those products.

Huawei indicated the amount, which it considered to be a reasonable royalty. For its part, ZTE Corp. sought a cross-licensing agreement. In the end, the negotiations failed and no licensing agreement was finalised. Nonetheless, ZTE still marketed its base stations in Germany, thus using the technology covered by the patent, without paying a royalty.

On 28 April 2011, on the basis of German patent law and the European Patent Convention, Huawei brought an action for infringement against

---

[27] Björn Lundqvist, 'The Interface between EU Competition Law and Standard Essential Patents – From Orange-Book-Standard to the Huawei Case' (2015) 11 *European Competition Journal* 367. Parts of this section are based on this work.

ZTE before a German court, seeking an injunction prohibiting the infringement, the presentation of accounts, the recall of products and an award of damages. The national court considered that the decision on the substance in the main proceedings turned on whether the action brought by Huawei constituted an abuse of that company's dominant position. It thus observed that it might be possible to rely on the mandatory nature of the grant of the licence in order to dismiss the action for a prohibitory injunction – in particular, on the basis of Article 102 TFEU – if, by its action, Huawei were to be regarded as abusing its dominant position.

Advocate General Wathelet has delivered his Opinion, which notes, first, that the *Orange-Book-Standard* case and the case before the Düsseldorf Court (and thereby, indirectly, the investigations conducted by the EU Commission) dealt with different factual situations. He states:

> [a]s regards *Orange-Book-Standard*, the significant factual differences between that case and the dispute before the referring court should be noted. The patent at issue here is essential to the LTE standard which was developed as a result of an agreement concluded between the undertakings (including Huawei and ZTE) involved in the standardisation process within ETSI, whereas the standard at issue in the *Orange-Book-Standard* case before the Bundesgerichtshof was a *de facto* standard. It follows that, in *Orange-Book-Standard*, the owner of the patent at issue had not given any commitment to grant licences on FRAND terms.[28]

The Advocate General proceeds to state:

> [i]t is only natural that, in those circumstances, the patent owner will have greater negotiating power than in the case of an SEP the owner of which is, like the licence applicant, a member of a European standardisation body, and that an action for a prohibitory injunction on its part will ultimately be regarded as abusive only if the royalty it demands is clearly excessive.[29]

Whether the specific CD technology described in the Orange Book was *de jure* or *de facto* standard depends on interpretation. The Orange Book is in itself a written description for a specified technology standard agreed upon by the founders Philips and Sony. Moreover, the Orange Book (which is the combination of CD-R and CD-RW technologies) had been *de jure* standardised in fragments before SDOs. It is derived from the two forms of CD standards: Red and Yellow, both *de jure* standardised by SDOs. It has been recognised by ISO/IEC, through the work of

---

28 Ibid., para. 48.
29 Ibid.

regional SDOs, where *inter alia* representatives of its developers Philips and Sony had been taking an active part.[30] Moreover, there have been patent pools established that used the Orange Book to define the pool technology where the royalty rate reflected an agreement to license on fair terms vis-à-vis any comer to the pool. In regard to these earlier CD-ROM technology pools, the parties later had to dissolve the relevant technology pool, and the Commission in its 2003 investigations did analyse the levels of the royalty rates, and the parties seem to have then stated that they would only license on fair terms.[31] Hence, there are clear indications that the Orange Book should be regarded as encompassed by *de jure* standards and that there was a requirement (based on competition law) to only license to fair return. Notwithstanding this, the technology was standardised so long ago that it seems clear that neither the parties nor the SSOs at that time implemented IP policies including FRAND commitments. Thus, no FRAND commitment has been made to an SSO, and that makes a huge difference according to the Advocate General and the ECJ in the *Huawei* case.

The Advocate General clearly wanted to distance the *Huawei* case from the *Orange-Book-Standard* case, the probable reason being that utilising the *Orange-Book-Standard* doctrine would lead to over-protection of SEP holders.

On the other hand, as noted by the Advocate General, using the *Samsung* safe harbour would lead to under-protection of SEP holders. The *Samsung* case concerns an SEP dispute in which the SEP owner has

---

30 It was recognised by ISO/IEC, ECMA, and the TC31-optical disks and cartridges committee chaired by a representative of Philips. Cf. Hanns Ullrich, 'Patents and Standards – a Comment on the German Federal Supreme Court Decision Orange Book Standard' (2011) 41 *IIC* 337, fn. 18. See also http://en.wikipedia.org/wiki/Red_Book_(CD_standard)#cite_note-3 (last visited 20 November 2014).

31 See EC Commission Press Release IP/03/1152, 7 August 2003, 'Commission Clears Philips/Sony CD Licensing Programme' and EC Commission Press Release IP/06/139, 9 February 2006, 'Commission Closes Investigation Following Changes to Philips CD-Recordable Disc Patent Licensing'. See the ITC case, 'Notice of Commission on Determination of No Violation of Section 337, In the Matter of Certain Recordable Compact Discs and Rewritable Compact Discs', Investigation No. 337-TA-474. See also US Court of Appeals for the Federal Circuit *U.S. Philips Corp. v. International Trade Commission*, 424 F.3d 1179 (Fed. Cir. 2005). The US FTC also undertook an early analysis of the licensing agreements for the CD-ROM pool in the 1980s. See Carl Shapiro, 'Navigating the Patent Thicket: Cross Licenses, Patent Pools and Standard Setting', in Adam Jaffe et al. (eds), *Innovation Policy and the Economy* (MIT Press, 2001), p. 20.

given a commitment to a standardisation body to grant licences on FRAND terms. Nonetheless, the mere willingness on the part of the infringer to negotiate in a highly vague and non-binding fashion cannot, according to the Advocate General, in any circumstances be sufficient to limit the SEP holder's right to bring an action for a prohibitory injunction.[32] The Advocate General is therefore right to stake out a middle ground between *Orange-Book-Standard* and *Samsung* safe harbour.

The Advocate General also addresses the issue that an SEP holder, according to some findings, *ipso facto* holds a dominant position. He states that in his view a dominant position must be based on factual finding of dominance and that it must be feasible to rebut the presumption of dominance in these cases.[33]

Thereafter, the Advocate General turns to the issue of abuse. The identification of such abuse by the Advocate General is, however, not based on exclusionary effects but rather on a pure legal analysis: namely, 'the right to intellectual property and the SEP holder's (Huawei's) right of access to the courts, on the one hand, and the freedom to conduct business which economic operators such as the undertakings implementing the LTE standard (ZTE) enjoy under Article 16 of the Charter, on the other hand'.[34] This is of greatest importance.[35]

The Advocate General's view supports the right to conduct business and the doctrine of exceptional circumstances may be used to access SEPs. Under exceptional circumstance the right to conduct business trumps the right to property. He uses this as a platform to draw up an abuse test.

According to Advocate General Wathelet, when an infringer is technologically dependent following the incorporation into a standard of the patent, and is subjected to unfair or unreasonable conduct by the SEP holder inconsistent with its commitment to grant licences on FRAND terms towards the infringer concerned (which has shown itself to be

---

32 AG Opinion in Case C-170/13 *Huawei Technologies v. ZTD*, para. 50.

33 Ibid., paras 53 et seq.

34 Ibid., para. 59.

35 The AG then argues in a way which exhibits similarities to the EU doctrine of existence/effect, and to the US inherency doctrine. The AG seems to convey that the right to exclude is the very essence of intellectual property rights, which thus interpreted should rarely be restricted. The AG then proceeds to hint that an analogy might be possible comparing commitments reached under IP guides to SSOs with commitments made to Patent Offices under 'license of rights' rules: ibid., paras 59 et seq., para. 65.

objectively ready, willing and able to conclude such a licensing agreement) then the bringing of an action for a prohibitory injunction constitutes recourse to a method different from those governing normal competition. It has an adverse effect on competition to the detriment, in particular, of consumers and the undertakings which have invested in the preparation, adoption and application of the standard; and it must therefore be regarded as an abuse of a dominant position for the purposes of Article 102 TFEU.

After defining abuse in such terms, Advocate General Wathelet draws up the method for establishing FRAND, namely the procedural (good governance) rules designed to avoid a finding of abuse. The procedure is similar to both the FTC *Google* Opinion and the EU Commission's decision in *Samsung* and *Motorola*, but remains different in some aspects: first, unless it is established that the alleged infringer is fully aware of the infringement, the SEP holder must alert it to this fact in writing, giving reasons, and specifying the SEP concerned and the way in which it has been infringed. Second, the SEP holder must, in any event, present to the alleged infringer a written offer for a licence on FRAND terms that contains all the terms normally included in a licence in the sector in question, in particular the precise amount of the royalty and the way in which that amount is calculated.[36] Third, the alleged infringer must respond in a diligent and serious manner to the offer made by the SEP holder. The Advocate General takes a step beyond the EU Commission in this respect, also stating that the potential licensee does indeed need to show a willingness to enter into an agreement. In this part of the Opinion the Advocate General is closer in his argumentation to the FTC *Google* consent order than to the *Samsung* safe harbour. If an alleged infringer does not accept a particular offer, it must promptly submit to the SEP holder, in writing, a reasonable counter-offer relating to the clauses with which it disagrees. However, the Advocate General still puts the initial burden of defining FRAND royalty rates on the SEP holder. What will happen if neither the proprietor nor the willing licensee makes an offer that corresponds to FRAND? The parties then should go to arbitration. The proprietor should not take action for obtaining an injunction with the risk of conducting an abuse.

The Advocate General does not stipulate a clear time-frame for how long the parties should negotiate the FRAND terms (compare, here, the FTC and the EU Commission requirements about six or 12 months

---

[36] Ibid., paras 84 et seq.

respectively). The time-frame for the exchange of offers and counter-offers and the duration of the negotiations must instead be assessed in the light of the 'commercial window of opportunity' available to the SEP holder for securing a return on its patent in the sector in question.[37]

An additional set of concerns emerging from the Advocate General's Opinion is that the court must determine whether there was a real possibility of negotiating FRAND terms based on the terms and rate offered. In this regard, the Advocate General takes the view that the referring court must assess whether proposals are genuine and not merely tactical efforts by the potential licensee to stall the litigation. Furthermore, if negotiations are not commenced or are unsuccessful, the conduct of the alleged infringer cannot be regarded as dilatory or lacking serious intent if it asks for those terms to be fixed either by a court or an arbitration tribunal. In that event, it would be legitimate for the SEP holder to ask the infringer either to provide a bank guarantee for the payment of royalties or to deposit a provisional sum at the court or arbitration tribunal relating to its past and future use of the SEP. The same would apply if, during the negotiations, the infringer reserved the right, following the conclusion of a licensing agreement, to challenge before a court or arbitration tribunal either the validity of that patent or alternatively the illegality (or the very existence) of the use it had made or would make of the teaching protected by the patent.[38]

Concerning the validity of the SEP, the wrongful issue of a patent may constitute an obstacle to the legitimate pursuit of an economic activity. Moreover, if undertakings supplying standard-compliant products and services cannot call into question the validity of a patent declared to be essential to that standard, then according to the Advocate General it may prove effectively impossible to verify the validity of that patent because other undertakings would have no interest in bringing proceedings in that regard. As regards the use of the teaching of a patent, it is clear that undertakings which implement a standard do not have to pay for intellectual property which they are not using. It follows that the alleged infringer can call into question *ex post* its supposed use of the teaching of a patent and the nature of that patent as being essential to the standard in question.

---

37 Ibid.

38 Ibid., paras 93 et seq.

The Advocate General's Opinion is interesting in multiple respects:

(1) It is clearly arguing for a per se use of Article 102 TFEU. If the requirements for the test of abuse are fulfilled, then *ipso facto* it is to the detriment of consumers and competitors. For example, an SEP holder must provide the opportunity to enter into a FRAND licence irrespective of the number of licensees already appointed or the market share held by the SEP holder or potential licensee.
(2) The requirement to negotiate FRAND also implies that there are naked restrictions that may not be used (e.g. it would constitute an abuse if the SEP holder required a non-challenge clause to be incorporated in the licence agreement).
(3) Generally, and more importantly, the whole FRAND procedure drawn up by the Advocate General is very indebted to legal, procedural/governance frameworks. It is somewhat different from what we are accustomed to in antitrust law: a clear test which identifies anticompetitive conduct and/or effect. In fact what Advocate General Watherel does and also the ECJ did in the final decision (see below) is to create a mini block exemption under Article 102 TFEU, stipulating a safe harbour based on some few procedural rules that the parties need to follow. The procedural rules create somewhat of a black list of conduct that would render a finding of abuse, should the SEP holder violate the procedure described.

The Advocate General's Opinion mirrors the idea behind the *Samsung* commitment decision, but this is clearly juxtaposed with the FTC *Google* decision where the FTC ruled according to a violation of unfair competition law but not US antitrust regulations. The fact that the FTC did not use antitrust law creates notable complications when the decision is invoked in this connection.

5. THE ECJ'S JUDGMENT IN *HUAWEI*[39]

On 16 July 2015, the ECJ delivered its judgment in *Huawei*, and commentators who expected a long discussion mirroring that of the

[39] Björn Lundqvist, 'The Interface between EU Competition Law and Standard Essential Patents – From Orange-Book-Standard to the Huawei Case' (2015) 11 *European Competition Journal* 367. Parts of this section are based on this work.

Advocate General's Opinion were greatly disappointed.[40] In fact, the ECJ judgment transposed the feeling of a Court that does not want to state too much, nor interfere more than necessary in an ongoing multinational business development. The ECJ only focused on the essential points: answering the referring court's questions, while leaving room for further speculations.

The Advocate General had an interesting discussion regarding identifying dominance, and emphasised that dominance, based on the identification of the relevant market, also needs to be established in these SEP cases.[41] The ECJ left this issue untouched. In contrast to the Advocate General, the ECJ did not mention how to establish dominance in reference to SEPs, and the Court only focused on the existence of abuse in its judgment.[42]

When focusing on the abuse, the ECJ seemed to accept that there might be a dichotomy between *de facto* standards and *de jure* standards. It stated that the dispute before the court dealt only with a *de jure* standard where the proprietor had agreed to an SSO (in this case ETSI) to irrevocably license on FRAND terms. The ECJ did not mention the German precedent regarding SEPs, the *Orange-Book-Standard* case,[43] and thus avoided the discussion of how to deal with *de facto* standards under competition law. It is also apparent that the ECJ did not take into consideration the development of national (German) case law.

The ECJ thus took great effort not to go beyond what the referring court had requested. In one way, the ECJ took the easy way out and left the field open to the arguments put forward not only by the Advocate General, but also by the Commission in *Samsung* and *Motorola*, yet the ECJ did not distance itself from *Orange-Book-Standard* by stating that it is only applicable to *de facto* standards. How to square *Huawei* and *Orange-Book-Standard* will be an issue for the German Court to iron out.

Furthermore, the ECJ agreed with the Advocate General that there is a need to weigh rights and freedoms to obtain the right answer; and there

---

40 Case C-170/13 *Huawei Technologies v. ZTD*, 16 July 2015, ECLI: EU:C:2015:477.

41 AG Opinion in Case C-170/13 *Huawei Technologies v. ZTD*.

42 Ibid., para. 43.

43 Federal Supreme Court (Bundesgerichtshof) May 6, 2009 – Case No. KZR 39/06 (*Orange Book Standard*). For a lengthy discussion regarding the *Orange-Book-Standard* case and other German standard cases (such as the Federal Supreme Court (Bundesgerichtshof) July 13, 2004 – Case No. KZR 40/02 (*Tight-Head Drum*) (Standard-Spundfass)) cf. Lundqvist note 1 above, pp. 319 et seq.

was no mention of economics. There was no discussion of whether a finding of abuse requires a finding of exclusionary effects or anti-competitive effects. Instead, freedom to compete must be weighed against the constitutional character of intellectual property rights. However, there is a difference between the Advocate General and the ECJ regarding what should be weighed. According to the Advocate General, the freedom to conduct business which economic operators such as the undertakings implementing the LTE standard (ZTE) enjoy under Article 16 of the Charter of Fundamental Rights of the European Union, should be included in the weighing.[44] According the ECJ, it:

> must strike a balance between maintaining free competition – in respect of which primary law and, in particular, Article 102 TFEU prohibit abuses of a dominant position – and the requirement to safeguard that proprietor's intellectual-property rights and its right to effective judicial protection, guaranteed by Article 17(2) and Article 47 of the Charter, respectively.[45]

Does the ECJ imply that the freedom of conducting business is not under threat in the case, or, even that freedom to conduct business is not a right to take into consideration under antitrust law? We do not know.

Referring to its established case law, the ECJ continued that the exercise of an exclusive right to bring an action for infringement which is directly linked to the owner's intellectual property rights can only amount to abuse under exceptional circumstances.[46] This focus on the exclusive rights conferred on intellectual property owners, and not on the right of access to courts, together with the omission of any reference to *ITT Promedia/Protégé International* seems to confirm the implications of the judgment in *Micro Business Leader*.[47] The ECJ did not consider the use of injunctions by SEP owners to amount to abusive litigation, but focused on the exclusionary effects the use of injunctions produce on the product market when the proprietor has agreed to license on FRAND terms, but refuses such licence.[48]

---

[44] See AG Opinion in Case C-170/13 *Huawei Technologies v. ZTD*, para. 59.

[45] Case C-170/13 *Huawei Technologies v. ZTD*, 16 July 2015, ECLI: EU:C:2015:477, para. 42.

[46] Ibid., paras 46–7.

[47] Case T-111/96 ITT *Promedia v. Commission of the European Communities*, 17 July 1998, ECLI:EU:T:1998:183 (*'ITT Promedia'*) and Case T-198/98 *Micro Leader Business v. Commission of the European Communities*, 16 December 1999, ECLI:EU:T:1999:341 (*'Micro Leader Business'*).

[48] Iva Svobodová, 'Seeking injunctions in SEPs' infringement proceedings as an abuse of dominant position under Article 102 TFEU', Master's thesis.

Only in exceptional circumstances may the constitutional character of intellectual property rights be restricted, and the ECJ agreed that in the dispute before the Court, a new exceptional circumstance scenario was at hand. First, by the fact that the patent at issue was essential to a standard established by a standardisation body, and the use of the patent was rendering its use indispensable to all competitors which envisaged manufacturing products that complied with the standard to which it was linked.[49] Second, the case should be distinguished by the fact that the patent at issue obtained SEP status only in return for the proprietor's irrevocable undertaking, given to the standardisation body in question, that it was prepared to grant licences on FRAND terms.[50] These two circumstances caused the triggering of the exceptional circumstance doctrine.[51]

Thereafter, the ECJ stipulated the good governance procedural rules, to which the parties in these situations must adhere, so as not, on the one hand, abuse a dominant position, or, on the other, cause the national court to agree to order an injunction or removal of goods.[52] In this part of the judgment the ECJ followed the few procedural rules stipulated by the Advocate General, which in turn, to a large extent, mirrors the outline in the *Samsung* decision by the Commission and the FTC *Google* settlement. The proprietor should offer a licence on FRAND terms. The willing licensee should diligently reply and accept or otherwise produce a counter-offer. However, the ECJ was also somewhat more conservative.

According to the ECJ, in the event that an agreement on FRAND terms is not reached after the infringer has presented his counter-offer, a third party determination of an appropriate royalty may be requested by the parties.[53] The wording of the judgment suggests that unlike in the Commission's and Advocate General's approach, third party determination of FRAND royalty should rather be a voluntary step to take for the parties: a step not relevant for the competition law evaluation of whether or not there is an abuse. The competition law evaluation will be based solely on the offer and the counter-offer, and whether or not any of those should have been accepted. Has the ECJ thereby removed the SEP implementers' safe harbour created by the Commission and the Advocate

---

49 Ibid., para. 49.

50 Ibid., para. 51.

51 This seems to imply that for *de facto* standards, the old exceptional circumstances cases, e.g. *Magill*, *IMS Health*, still apply.

52 Case C-170/13 *Huawei Technologies v. ZTD*, 16 July 2015, ECLI: EU:C:2015:477, paras 61 et seq.

53 Ibid., para. 68.

General that an injunction cannot be issued against them as long as they agreed to third party determination of FRAND terms?[54] That seems to be the case. If the national procedural and intellectual property rules allow for it, the proprietor may risk taking action for injunctive relief and still wrestle the issue of FRAND in arbitration with the potential licensee.

Nonetheless, the alleged infringer may, according to the ECJ, still challenge the validity of the SEPs. Whether such action would trigger the safe harbour and cause the proprietor to abuse its dominant position were it to seek an injunction is moreover not entirely clear. The ECJ seems to have removed this from the competition law analysis. The ECJ concluded by stating:

> Article 102 TFEU must be interpreted as meaning that the proprietor of a patent essential to a standard established by a standardisation body, which has given an irrevocable undertaking to that body to grant a licence to third parties on fair, reasonable and non-discriminatory ('FRAND') terms, does not abuse its dominant position, within the meaning of that article, by bringing an action for infringement seeking an injunction prohibiting the infringement of its patent or seeking the recall of products for the manufacture of which that patent has been used, as long as:
>
> - prior to bringing that action, the proprietor has, first, alerted the alleged infringer of the infringement complained about by designating that patent and specifying the way in which it has been infringed, and, secondly, after the alleged infringer has expressed its willingness to conclude a licensing agreement on FRAND terms, presented to that infringer a specific, written offer for a licence on such terms, specifying, in particular, the royalty and the way in which it is to be calculated, and
> - where the alleged infringer continues to use the patent in question, the alleged infringer has not diligently responded to that offer, in accordance with recognised commercial practices in the field and in good faith, this being a matter which must be established on the basis of objective factors and which implies, in particular, that there are no delaying tactics.

The second bullet point makes no reference regarding counter-offers. Instead, it is referring to recognised business practise and good faith. The ECJ then, given the discussion in the body of the judgment, presumes that commercial practices often include counter-offers. However, it makes

---

[54] Cleary & Gottlieb, Alert Memorandum, 'Enforcing Standard-Essential Patents – The European Court of Justice's Judgment in Huawei v ZTE', 3 August 2015, available at http://www.cgsh.com/files/News/d23034e9-186e-4b11-a120-b3acfb065e45/Presentation/NewsAttachment/cbc6c8d2-4f4a-418c-a0ad-b549088 30217/Alert%20Memo%20(PDF%20Version)%202015-62.pdf (last visited 16 August 2015).

no reference to third party arbitration or suit validity. So, what happens if such actions are recognised commercial practice in an industry? Are they also encompassed by the safe harbour? Probably not, but this is not entirely clear from the judgment.

6. ANALYSIS[55]

Generally, the ECJ's judgment is balanced, clear, yet conservative enough that the Court will not likely be forced to abandon or divert from the decision going forward. The ECJ, together with the Advocate General and the Commission in the *Samsung* and *Motorola* decisions, has begun to carve out a 'mini block exemption' or safe harbour for these circumstances under Article 102 TFEU. What good governance or procedural rules should the parties abide to so as not to violate Article 102 TFEU or be slapped by an injunction order, respectively? The ECJ in *Huawei* is clearly more restrictive in this regard, and the 'mini block exemption' is narrow. It only creates a minimum of safe harbour for the infringer as well as for the proprietor. The ECJ, by drafting the procedure so narrowly, is strongly encouraging the parties to settle disputes quickly.

The most contentious issues before *Huawei* were: first, when may an SEP holder refuse access and obtain an injunction against an infringer, who is still a willing licensee? Second, what constitutes FRAND and who should bear the risk of defining FRAND, the proprietor or the potential licensee? According to the ECJ in *Huawei* these questions should be rephrased as: 'Under what procedure should access to SEPs be granted under EU competition law?' By rephrasing these issues as issues regarding procedure, the ECJ has circumvented several difficult topics.

Nonetheless, some answers may be identified. First, only actions for injunctions (injunctive relief) and recall of products may amount to an abuse if the proprietor has made a FRAND commitment to an SSO or similar. Actions for damages and presentations of accounts may not amount to an abuse. Second, the burden of defining the FRAND royalty rate seems to have been placed on the proprietor. However, it should be noted that in paragraph 66 of the ECJ judgment, the willing licensee only can successfully claim to be an victim of an abuse if its counter-offer has identified the FRAND royalty rate. What if neither the offer nor the counter-offer corresponds to FRAND? Is an action for injunctive relief

---

[55] Björn Lundqvist, 'The Interface between EU Competition Law and Standard Essential Patents – From Orange-Book-Standard to the Huawei Case' (2015) 11 *European Competition Journal* 367. Parts of this section are based on this work.

under these circumstances still an abuse? This is still unclear. However, it seems that the ECJ actually put some weight behind the notion that the willing licensee should produce a FRAND counter-offer. Perhaps, the licensee is not a willing licensee if it does not produce a FRAND counter-offer to the proprietors possibly FRAND + offer? Notwithstanding this, the ruling ultimately still seems to put the burden on the SEP holder to produce a FRAND offer.

If the EU agencies and now the ECJ have defined the procedure for gaining access on FRAND terms, the national courts may thus still, in the end, be forced to define significant details: chiefly the FRAND royalty rate, but also other FRAND terms. Or, at least, depending on how the parties make their arguments, the national court must choose between what the proprietor believes is FRAND and what the potential licensees think is FRAND. This issue will now mirror the issue whether or not there is an abuse, and whether or not the court should order an injunction. However, to do this the court needs to define FRAND, or, logically, it must know what FRAND is so as to be able to say that either the offer or the counter-offer represents FRAND, or that neither offer represents FRAND.

Moreover, according to *Huawei*, the national court or an arbitration panel may also be faced with two parties wanting it to define FRAND. How should the court or panel proceed when establishing these terms and the right FRAND royalty rate? What is a FRAND royalty on a case-by-case basis? It is difficult to see that the ECJ in *Huawei* helped these courts. Rather, the idea seemed to be in *Huawei* that the parties will, by following the procedure, agree on FRAND and not go to court. But, we cannot take that for granted. There will be parties that do not agree and a national court will ultimately have to define FRAND.

7. USER GENERATED LAW MODEL

It is clear that the protagonists in the IT/telecom sector have self-regulated the sector to the extent that standard essential patents have lost some of their property character and instead are liability rights. The FRAND procedure can be understood as a kind of user generated and agreed-upon compulsory licensing scheme, where a larger part of the regulatory model is left to the parties concerned rather than to a court to determine. This in turn poses two questions concerning why this type of regulation occurs under EU competition law and why parties do not use common compulsory licence schemes. In a broader context, there is a similar user generated procedure being developed in the United States.

However, in this setting it is emerging according to flexible doctrines under intellectual property and contract law. Why is that? If the User Generated Law model can provide the answer to such questions, it would probably include the following considerations: (1) there is a great need for flexibility and speed in the relevant legal regulation (heterogeneous demands); (2) the parties, patentees and licensees each stand to gain from this solution (expectation of benefits) since they benefit from easy adoption of technology and access to the same; (3) the parties have better information and knowledge than the legislature and the courts (asymmetric information); and (4) the US private standard-setting model and the way in which ETSI works have proven that private standard setting works, and ETSI was a pioneer for establishing how to develop private technical standards in a European setting.

'Adoption' in the User Generated Law model corresponds well to the courts' limited intervention and correction in determining remuneration (restricting autonomy). Drawing upon the model's terminology further, the regulatory process is thus deemed 'reactive' rather than 'proactive'. As such, in many ways the User Generated Law model fits well in explaining the development of the regulation of SEPs under FRAND commitments made to SSOs.

8. CONCLUSION

In my humble opinion it is unfortunate that the development of the standardisation/intellectual property/competition law interface has developed in ways which mean that national courts and arbitration panels will now indirectly become pricing authorities. It does indicate that the standardisation system we have built is beset with problems and has involved misconceptions from the outset. The legal system fails because of the way standardisation is becoming the arena for global self-regulation, while patents are still too easily obtainable, and competition law under Article 101 TFEU and its equivalents is not utilised in a manner promoting innovation and competition. We do not have the space to develop this line of reasoning further here;[56] but given the level of systemic failure, the FRAND procedure requiring access to patents through a process in which national courts will ultimately set the royalties remains the 'best' outcome in the sense that existing alternatives are worse.

---

[56] Discussed further in Lundqvist, note 1 above.

Moreover, a question could be raised as to what incentives the new exceptional circumstance doctrine creates for proprietors of future potential dominant technologies. According to the EU case law as it stands now, a proprietor may, thus, have more and extended rights connected to its patents if it keeps them out of the SDOs and outside any irrevocable undertaking to license on FRAND terms. The optimal source of wealth would be to obtain a *de facto* SEP instead of a *de jure* SEP. To create such an incentive, for example for patent trolls, is not benevolent if the goal is to promote the work of SDOs and SSOs and to protect the integrity of the standard-setting procedure. The ECJ states that the patents in the dispute obtained SEP status because they made the irrevocable undertaking to license on FRAND terms. However, that does not necessarily always have to be the case. Moreover, large proprietors may even get an incentive to go for the optimal goal of obtaining the whole market by getting a market to 'tip' in the favour of its technology, i.e. to get the whole market to adopt the proprietor's technology. That creates monopolies both in the technology market and in downstream product markets, while the SDO and standard-setting route often creates, and aims to create, oligopolies in technology markets and downstream competition.

9. The private legal governance of domain names

Jens Schovsbo

1. INTRODUCTION

Domain names serve as "human friendly"[1] "mnemonic labels that assist in identifying the locations of resources on the internet".[2] Although their importance as a means for navigating the Internet has diminished with the development of effective search engines,[3] an effective system for the management of domain names remains crucial for the functioning of the Internet.[4]

In spite of their continuing importance, and in spite of burgeoning potential for conflicts concerning trademark rights, the intervention of traditional State-enacted law has been very limited in terms of regulating domain names. National legislators have been almost totally absent from the process and relatively few conflicts have reached national courts considering that a staggering 270+ million domain names are registered. While the traditional means for creating legislation and resolving conflicts have remained peripheral, we have seen the emergence of what has been described as "a cosmopolitan and uniform system of rules that

---

[1] World Intellectual Property Organization (WIPO), *The Recognition of Rights and the Use of Names in the Internet Domain Name System* (Report of the Second WIPO Internet Domain Name Process, 2001), para. 54.

[2] Dan L. Burk, 'Cybermarks' (2010) 91 *Minnesota Law Review* 1375, pp. 1376 et seq.

[3] Ibid., and Frederick M. Abbott, 'On the Duality of Internet Domain Names: Propertization and Its Discontents' (2013) 3 *N.Y.U. Journal of Intellectual Property and Entertainment Law* 1.

[4] For an account of the technical aspects and for the distinction between "domain names" and "IP addresses" see David Lindsay, *International Domain Name Law – ICANN and the UDRP* (Hart Publishing, 2007), pp. 1 et seq.

transcends local rules and nation states".[5] Hence, conflicts involving domain names are being decided by special private tribunals or panels such as the Uniform Domain Name Dispute Resolution Policy (UDRP). These are bodies which have been developed by communities of users within complicated systems of self- and co-regulation such as ICANN (the Internet Cooperation for Assigned Names and Numbers). Such bodies have authorized a number of private institutions ("Providers") to decide disputes over domain names. Normally, these dispute resolution bodies do not derive their competences from legislation. Instead, they are instituted by the contracts which registrants entered into when they registered their domain names and which do not allow for the individuals who register a domain name to opt out of the dispute resolution mechanism provided for under that Top Level Domain (TLD) or to tailor their own system.[6]

In practice, the tribunals have come to serve as alternatives to courts which has meant that a whole class of legal disputes has in effect been kept out of the regular court system. In principle the tribunals' decisions may be brought before national courts, but this rarely happens. Therefore, the decisions of the tribunals normally remain the final word in these cases. This development raises some concern since the character of the UDRP does not incorporate the legal guarantees of *inter alia* fairness and impartiality which are intrinsic to "real" courts that are anchored in national constitutions. Since the dispute system is mandatory and parties cannot opt out (except by creating a whole new name-space), it is also impossible for users of domain names to vote with their feet and to design alternative models. Finally, because of their central importance as decision-makers the tribunals have come to take on a function of "rule makers" in the void left by the lack of traditional legislative activities and ministerial (executive) powers. These elements have fuelled a critique which has been voiced consistently throughout the (short) history of the

---

[5] Leon E. Trakman, 'From the Medieval Law Merchant to E-Merchant Law' (2003) 53 *University of Toronto Law Journal* 265, pp. 287 et seq. (comparing also the result with *lex mercantoria*). See also Chapter 1 of this book.

[6] Laurence R. Helfer and Graeme B. Dinwoodie, 'Designing Non-National Systems: The Case of the Uniform Domain Name Dispute Resolution Policy' (2001) 43 *Wm. & Mary L. Rev.* 141, pp. 199 et seq. (on UDRP). In a similar vein, the Danish system does not provide for opting out.

UDRP, *viz.* the lack of legitimacy not only of ICANN[7] but also of the UDRP.[8]

The purpose of this chapter is to evaluate how these institutions perform. More concretely, it will describe and scrutinize how and to what extent the domain name system balances interests between trademark owners and other users of domain names and secures the rule of law (legal certainty and predictability). I will compare and contrast two different dispute resolution models, *viz.* the UDRP (WIPO) and the Danish Complaints Board for Internet Domain Names ('the Board'). This comparative process will be used to evaluate the effects of the institutional design featuring a contractual starting point and varying international panels (UDRP) vs. a legislative starting point and a permanent board (DK); it will also investigate the normative design characterized by assessment based on "bad faith" (UDRP) vs. evaluation based on a norm defined by the legislator ("good domain name practices") (DK). For the discussion of substantive law, I will focus on cases where trademarks are used as (parts of) domain names to express criticism of the trademark holder or the trademark itself (e.g. "TMsucks.com"/"lorteTM.dk"). These cases involve free speech issues and have been described as being both hard to deal with and important. Finally, I will use the accumulated insights to reflect on how these institutions have had an impact on the ways the relevant systems perform. I will then assess the extent to which the general methodology of user generated law (UGL) is applicable and suitable for explaining the "emergence", "diffusion" and "adoption" of these norms.

---

[7] ICANN itself, along with the process that led to its establishment, has been described as a "revolutionary departure from traditional approaches to global governance. It significantly reduced the power of national governments and existing intergovernmental organizations over communication and information policy": Milton L. Mueller, *Networks and States – The Global Politics of Internet Governance* (The MIT Press, 2010), pp. 60–61. Presently, initiatives are underway to "enhance ICANN accountability", see https://www.icann.org/public-comments/enhancing-accountability-2014-05-06-en (last visited November 17, 2014). The focus of this chapter's discussion will not be ICANN as such but rather the UDRP.

[8] Laurence R. Helfer, 'International Dispute Settlement at the Trademark-Domain Name Interface' (2001) 29 *Pepperdine Law Review* 87, p. 89; and Alpana Roy, 'Reflections on the Uniform Domain Name Dispute Resolution Policy as It Enters its Second Decade' (2012) 1(1) *Int. J. Technology Policy and Law* 20.

2. THE INSTITUTIONAL FRAMEWORK FOR DISPUTE RESOLUTION OF DOMAIN NAMES

ICANN was established in 1998 and is a not-for-profit entity which still coordinates and oversees the Internet's underlying address book, namely the Domain Name System (DNS). This includes administering the DNS root zone management such as generic (gTLD) and country code TLDs (ccTLD). In October 1999, ICANN approved the *UDRP Policy* ("The Uniform Domain Name Dispute Resolution Policy") which sets out the legal framework for the resolution of disputes between domain name registrants and third parties over any abusive registration and use of a domain name in the gTLD and those ccTLD or other top level domains which have adopted the UDRP Policy on a voluntary basis. The *UDRP Rules* lay down the procedures for the dispute resolution administrative procedure.

Administrators of ccTLDs can establish their own policies and rules and dispute resolutions systems. Some countries (such as Germany[9]) do not provide for specific resolutions mechanisms but leave it to normal courts to decide conflicts over domain names. Other countries (such as Denmark) have instituted specified dispute resolution mechanisms. The Danish ccTLD (".dk") is administered by the not-for-profit organization DIFO (Dansk Internet Forum). DIFO was established in 1999, and in 2009 it was awarded the administrative task after a public invitation to tender for the role which followed the adoption of the Act on Internet Domains Specifically Allocated to Denmark in 2005. DIFO consists of members who represent a wide range of the Danish Internet community (i.e. suppliers and professional and private users of the Internet). Furthermore, DIFO owns the subsidiary "DK Hostmaster A/S" which manages the operation of all domain names in the ccTLD ".dk".

2.1 The UDRP System

The UDRP is designed to provide solutions in clear cases involving cybersquatting. The central substantive rules of the UDRP are found in section 4(a) of the UDRP Policy. This stipulates that the UDRP Administrative Procedure is only available for a dispute in which the alleged abusive registration of a domain name meets the following criteria:

[9] See https//www.denic.de (accessed January 26, 2016).

(i) the domain name registered by the domain name registrant is identical or confusingly similar to a trademark or service mark in which the complainant (the person or entity bringing the complaint) has rights; and
(ii) the domain name registrant has no rights or legitimate interests in respect of the domain name in question; and
(iii) the domain name has been registered and is being used in bad faith.

Prior to the establishment of the UDRP system, conflicts were dealt with either informally ("netiquette") or through national courts.[10] Both of these methods have obvious flaws. Netiquette depends on the goodwill of the parties and their willingness to cooperate and work towards a perceived common goal, yet for cases involving obvious conflict this is not an efficient approach. For national courts the main problem is that the costs of bringing action are often prohibitive even in clear-cut cases of bad faith registration and use. The UDRP system was put together in order to prepare for an anticipated floodgate of cases involving conflicts with trademark holders which could not be effectively dealt with in the existing system. Rapidly, a wholly new system which placed a private organization (ICANN) in charge of the development process was assembled by national governments, national institutions (the US Department of Trade), and an intergovernmental organization (WIPO). Only two years after the US Department of Commerce launched the process with its "White Paper",[11] the first proceeding commenced.[12]

Under the UDRP, cases are decided by administrative panels which are composed of either one or three persons ("panellists"). Administrators for one-person panels are appointed by the dispute resolution service provider that has been selected by the complainant. In the case of three-person panels, one panellist is appointed by the provider and the two others by the complainant and the respondent respectively. The WIPO Center's list of Domain Name Panellists consists of some 400 panellists from over 50 countries. A panel must evaluate complaints on the basis of "the statements and documents submitted and in accordance with the

---

[10] Dan L. Burk, 'Trademarks Along the Infobahn: A First Look at the Emerging Law of Cybermarks' (1995) 1 *Rich J. L. & Tech.* 1.

[11] 'Statement of Policy on the Management of Internet Names and Addresses', June 5, 1998, available at http://www.ntia.doc.gov/federal-register-notice/1998/statement-policy-management-internet-names-and-addresses (accessed January 26, 2016).

[12] December 9, 1999 ("worldwrestlingfederation.com"); see Timeline for the Formulation and Implementation of the Uniform Domain-Name Dispute-Resolution Policy, available at http://www.icann.org/en/help/dndr/udrp/schedule (accessed January 26, 2016).

UDRP, the UDRP Rules, and any rules and principles of law that it deems applicable".[13] In this way the UDRP does not depend on norms derived from traditional State-enacted norms but is *sui generis*. It is also unique in terms of its institutional design and has been described as a "hybrid" containing elements from three decision-making models: judicial, arbitral, and ministerial.[14]

It is evident that panels are not instructed to seek guidance from sources such as national law but nor are they barred from doing this. The same discretion applies regarding whether to consult previous decisions by other UDRP panels. Since there is no general principle of "precedents" or a doctrine of *stare decisis* which obliges individual panels to follow previous decisions,[15] the UDRP system contains risks regarding legal uncertainties and inconsistencies[16] which are increased by the lack of an appeal system within the UDRP.[17] It was also pointed out very early on that the composition of the panels and the number of panellists deciding the cases profoundly affect the outcome of complaints.[18] Additional variations may stem from the different resolution providers[19] selected by the complainant who would normally choose "friendly" providers.[20] Results may also vary because of individual panellists[21] while the nationality of panellists and parties may affect both the reasoning of the panels and the concrete decisions (see below). For these reasons legal certainty and predictability of complaints are inherently difficult to achieve in the UDRP system. Since a "legislator" in the traditional sense is absent from the governance structure and parties cannot opt out, achieving consistency and coherence is left to the governance system itself.

---

13 UDRP, para. 15(a).

14 Helfer and Dinwoodie, note 6 above, p. 149.

15 Lindsay, note 4 above, pp. 128, 130.

16 E.g. Anette Kur, *UDRP: A Study by the Max Planck Institute for Foreign and International Patent, Copyright and Competition Law* (Max Planck Institute, 2002); Michael Geist, 'Fair.com?: An Examination of the Allegations of Systemic Unfairness in the ICANN UDRP' (2001) 27 *Brook. J. Int'l L.* 903.

17 Roy, note 8 above.

18 Geist, note 16 above, p. 922.

19 Kur, note 16 above, para. 2.2.

20 Jay P. Kesan and Andres A. Gallo, 'The Market for Private Dispute Resolution Services – An Empirical Re-Assessment of ICANN-UDRP Performance' (2005) Law and Economics Working Papers, Paper 22, p. 15.

21 Ibid., p. 31.

Interestingly, it has also been reported that "panels have taken it upon themselves to follow previous UDRP decisions"[22] and that in practice an "informal doctrine of precedent"[23] has developed. Such a process of inspiration may result in a tendency either to follow previous cases or to distance oneself from those. Both effects may result in patterns. Such patterns are clearly visible and can be substantiated by statistical analysis of sources such as WIPO's list covering the "25 Most Cited Decisions in Complaint". Here, the top case is D2000-0003 telstra.org (on the issue of passive holding) which has been cited more than 4,000 times.[24]

A very important factor in the drive towards a "system of precedents" has been the "WIPO Overview of WIPO Panel Views on Selected UDRP Questions, Second Edition" ("Overview").[25] The Overview is said to be based on a "careful and conservative evaluation of some 20000 UDRP cases". The Overview's purpose is to build awareness of panellists' views on certain questions that commonly arise in proceedings under the UDRP in order to maximize the consistency of the UDRP system and create predictability.[26] This is deemed to be particularly pertinent in situations where panellists and parties come from a multitude of jurisdictions.[27] It is expressly stated that the Overview does not create "rules" which are binding on panellists, but Lindsay reports that in practice panellists "will not generally depart from a Consensus View, even if they disagree with it".[28]

As far as references to national law are concerned, it is explained in the Overview that:

> where panels have chosen to apply national law in UDRP decisions, they have done so on grounds including the location or nationality of the parties, or where a specific concept of national law is judged germane to an issue in dispute, or bearing in mind, in certain circumstances, the mutual jurisdiction

---

22 Zinatul A. Zainol, Wan M. H. W. Hussain and Noor InayahYaakub, 'WIPO Panels' Interpretation of the Uniform Dispute Resolution Policy (UDRP) Three-Prong Test' (2011) 33 *World Patent Information* 275, p. 280.

23 Lindsay, note 4 above, p. 131.

24 See http://www.wipo.int/amc/en/domains/statistics/cases_cited.jsp?party=C (on the day of writing (November 17, 2014) the case had been cited 4,410 times) (URL accessed January 26, 2016).

25 The latest version is from 2011 and can be found at http://www.wipo.int/amc/en/domains/search/overview2.0 (accessed January 26, 2016).

26 Ibid.

27 Ibid.

28 Lindsay, note 4 above, p. 128.

election in the UDRP proceeding that would likely govern the location (and therefore the law) of any subsequent court case.

2.2 Denmark (.dk)

In the short history of Danish domain name regulation there are two basic watershed dates.

The first occurred on January 15, 1997. Prior to this date, the right to register domain names had been limited to "legal entities" which in addition could only register one domain name each (i.e. their "name" or trademark).[29] After this date, no restrictions applied regarding the registrants (private or legal parties), the number of names to be registered, or the character of domain names (except for openly offensive words or expressions involving matters such as racism). As a consequence of this liberalization, a need quickly arose to rein in the area to prevent misuses. In order to serve this need, the private organization DIFO ("Dansk Internet Forum") was entrusted by the political system (through a Memorandum of Understanding) with building a system of "self-regulation". As part of this, a complaints board for domain names was instituted and implemented through the contracts between users and registrars.[30]

The second watershed occurred in 2005 when the Act on Internet Domains Specifically Allocated to Denmark (Domain Names Act) was adopted.[31] The Domain Names Act established the sovereign ownership over the ".dk-" domain by the Danish State and provided both the administrator (DIFO) and the Complaints Board with a solid legislative underpinning (not contract). The Act maintained the principle of "self-regulation" as the basis for the administration and in this way sought to vest legitimacy directly in the "Danish Internet community" and not just

[29] Geographical names and "concepts" could not be registered.

[30] The competence of the Complaints Board to act on the basis of contracts which did not originally foresee the existence of such a board was disputed. However, in 2006 the Supreme Court found that DIFO – because of the nature of the contractual relationship it had with registrants – was competent to change the terms for the use of a domain name in cases of "special need": *Ugeskrift for Retsvæsen* 2006, p. 1189. That competence is normally assumed to also include the instituting of the Complaints Board.

[31] Lov nr. 598 af 24. juni 2005 om internetdomæner, der særligt tildeles Danmark. The 2005 Act was based on *Betænkning nr. 1450 om administration af domænenavne i Danmark* (2004). The 2005 Act was amended by Lov nr. 164 af 26. februar 2014 om internetdomæner (making only slight modifications in the rules and principles discussed here).

(indirectly) in the traditional legislative process. It also included a new provision on "good domain name practices" (see below). The Danish regulation only addresses domain names which have been allocated especially to Denmark or are in other ways associated with Denmark.[32]

The Danish Complaints Board is independent of the administrator and the Minister for Science, Technology and Innovation and it consists of three members who are appointed by the Minister. Overall, the Board should exhibit theoretical and practical legal expertise, including expertise regarding names and trademark rights. The Minister also appoints two members with business- and consumer-related expertise, who must assist in dealing with cases bearing on non-commercial users or registrants and in dealing with cases of general importance. The chairman of the Board must be a judge. Unlike the UDRP, the Board's competence is not restricted to cases of "cybersquatting". Instead, the Board is competent to decide (1) disputes between registrants and third parties, (2) disputes between registrants and the registry (i.e. "DK-Hostmaster"), and (3) complaints about the administrator's decisions. In cases between registrants and third parties the Complaints Board may decide to suspend, withdraw or transfer a domain name registered and used contrary to regulations such as the rule on good domain names practices or "other legislation" (notably the Trade Marks Act and the Marketing Practices Act). The decisions of the Complaints Board are binding and cannot be brought before any administrative authority. The decision may, however, be brought before the courts within eight weeks of the date on which the decision was communicated to the party concerned. Complainants pay a fee of 200 DKR (around 25 Euro) in consumer cases and 500 DKR (approximately 60 Euro) in commercial cases. A complaint may be lodged by any person who has an individual and significant interest in the outcome of the case, and may also be lodged by the registry. Since 2000,

---

32 Domain Names Act, para. 2. This includes the ccTLD ".dk" and any future domain names such as "dk.eu" or those containing Danish geographical locations (e.g. ".jylland"). For domain names registered under a TLD governed by the UDRP, Danish courts rely on the UDRP. See the decision of the Supreme Court reported in *Ugeskrift for Retsvæsen* 2005, p. 3262. The Supreme Court refused to base its argumentation on a decision by a WIPO panel, and instead expressed its own understanding of the UDRP.

the Board has decided around 2,500 cases.[33] Around 1 percent of the decisions made by the Board have been brought before a court.[34]

The Domain Act provided the already existing system with bullet-proof legislative backing. At the same time, a rule on good domain name practices was adopted. According to this (section 25):

> (1) Registrants must not register and use Internet domain names contrary to good domain name practice.
> (2) Registrants must not register and maintain registrations of Internet domain names solely for the purpose of selling or renting to other parties.

The purpose of this rule was to provide the Board with a more solid legal grounding for deciding cases involving non-commercial parties (where neither the Trade Marks Act nor the Marketing Practices Act applies) and to provide the panel with a "legal platform" for the further development of the law by "balancing the interests of the involved parties" in what the legislator acknowledged to be a special area.[35] This balancing should involve all interests including those of private and commercial parties. The Act does not prioritize any of these interests, which should all be given equal weight.[36] As far as "valuable" domain names are concerned (e.g. generic terms) these should be used in the way which will most benefit the Internet society.[37]

The rule on good domain name practice constitutes the centrepiece of the Domain Names Act since it is precisely through this mechanism that the Board is supposed to "develop" the law in accordance with the values of the Internet community. One avenue for achieving this is the way that

---

[33] Including cases decided in 2014 at the time of writing (primo December 2014), see information at http://www.domaeneklager.dk (accessed January 26, 2016).

[34] Based on a count from DIFO's yearly reports, available at http://www.difo.dk/om_difo/bestyrelse_og_ledelse/aarsrapporter/ (accessed January 26, 2016) for the period 2008–2013 (17 out of 1,576 decisions are reported to have been brought before a court).

[35] Betænkning nr. 1450, note 31 above, pp. 288 et seq.

[36] Ibid., p. 291. This principle has been repeated in the 2014 revision. See the comments to the 2014 Act, 2013/1 LSF 66 from 13 November 2011 ad § 25, available at https://www.retsinformation.dk/Forms/R0710.aspx?id=158868 (accessed January 26, 2016).

[37] See for an English language study of the Danish system Knud Wallberg in Torsten Bettinger (ed.), *Domain Name Law and Practice* (Oxford University Press, 2005). For a recent and comprehensive analysis in Danish see Peter Møgelvang-Hansen, Thomas Riis and Jan Trzaskowski, *Markedsføringsretten* (Ex Tuto Publishing, 2nd edn, 2011), pp. 603 et seq.

the Board's two members with business- and consumer-related expertise assist in dealing with cases bearing on non-commercial users or registrants and in dealing with cases of general importance; a second avenue for development is the invitation by the legislator for the Board to balance the involved interests against the overall interests.

2.3 Perspectives and Implications

Legal certainty and predictability are inherently difficult to achieve in the UDRP due to the lack of a principle of precedents and the multinational composition of the panels. Because of the international and hybrid nature of the system, the traditional "checking functions"[38] such as legislating or opting out are not in place. National courts could perform an *ex post* control function as to the decisions by panels within their jurisdictions. In practice, however, this rarely seems to happen. The costs of traditional court actions mean that such initiatives would normally be reserved for cases involving substantial economic interests and for this reason national courts cannot be conceived of as a comprehensive way of monitoring panel decisions. Hence, little external control regarding the policy direction of panel decisions is in place. At the same time, both informal and formal pressures have developed from within the system itself which encourage panels to decide cases on a de-nationalized basis and to follow precedents. As a result, the body of case law developed by the panels is more coherent than one might have expected. The Overview seems to have been central in this regard and to have taken on a statute-like character. Unlike traditional law making ("from the top") the Overview is – at least in principle – in constant flux as it develops through case law ("from the bottom"). In this way, the Overview functions like a feed-back loop between the different layers of the communities which consist of "legislator" (ICANN) and "judiciary" (panels), and it creates consistency between the decisions of the various panels. Concurrently, the Overview may also in this subtle way amend the UDRP informally.

In Denmark, the Board came about in 1999 as a private dispute resolution model without direct government involvement as a direct consequence of the liberalization of the registration system. Since 2005, the Board has been part of a legislative package. The purpose of the legislation was partly to solidify the existing system (both in terms of institutions and substantive law) and partly to provide the basis for a further development of the law. The presence of the legislature in the

[38] Helfer and Dinwoodie, note 6 above, pp. 189 et seq.

Danish development has led to a rather sophisticated model that combines traditional legislative techniques with dynamic elements from the UDRP. The self-governance envisaged by the Act relies on a combination of governance mechanisms (self-regulation) and a substantive law provision. The general clause helps drive future development to create feed-back loops between the different layers of the communities: the "subjects" (the Internet community), the "legislator" (acting through DIFO/ICANN), and the "judiciary" (the Board).[39] By expanding the mandate of the Board beyond cases of cybersquatting, the legislator sought to institute the Board as the central arbitrator for all conflicts involving domain names.[40]

3. SUBSTANTIVE LAW CONFLICTS: USE OF TRADEMARK IN A DOMAIN NAME TO EXPRESS CRITICISM

3.1 Introduction

Apart from functioning as locators/addresses, domain names may also serve as signs to identify goods or services that are being offered on the Internet (e.g. via a webpage operated from the IP address identified by the domain name). Unless authorized, such commercial uses normally

[39] In Norway an ADR-system is provided for (domeneklagenemda). Compared to Denmark, the Norwegian Board has heard relatively few cases (since 2003 just 456), see http://www.norid.no (accessed January 26, 2016). An important reason for this would seem to be that the requirements for applicants are relatively strict in Norway where only organizations that are registered in Norway's Central Coordination Register for Legal Entities, run genuine operations and/or have activities of substance, are able to provide evidence that they "genuinely exist [sic!]" and have a Norwegian postal address may register up to 100 domain names: "Domain name policy for .no", points 5.1. and 5.2. Private individuals who are 18 years or older and possess a Norwegian identity number and a Norwegian postal address may register up to five domain names directly under ccTLD ".no": ibid., points 5.3 and 5.4. These stringencies probably account for the fact that the number of domain names registered under the ".no" is approximately half the number which have been registered under the ccTLD ".dk". For ".no" the number was 646,749: ibid. (under "statistik"). For ".dk" 1,274,695 names had been registered by October 2014, https://stats.dk-hostmaster.dk/domains/total_domains/yearly (accessed November 14, 2014).

[40] However, the Board cannot decide on issues such as compensation for unlawful use of a domain name.

constitute trademark infringements. In addition, since registrants often chose trademarks as domain names, and the use of a domain name as an identifier may by itself trigger trademark protection, the overlap between trademark law and domain names is very high.[41]

The overlaps are also reflected in situations where third parties register the trademarks of others as domain names or as parts thereof. These cases cover a broad spectrum of situations. At one end of this spectrum situations arise where different owners of similar trademarks in different jurisdictions (or in the same jurisdiction for different goods or services) accidently seek to register their trademarks and thus compete for the same domain name. It follows from the first-come-first-served principle that the first registrant past the pole wins the domain name. At the other end of the spectrum one finds "cybersquatting" ("domain name grabbing") cases where trademarks are being registered as domain names only to be sold at an inflated price to their rightful owners.[42] In the grey area between these points on the spectrum lie the difficult cases where both parties claim legitimate but competing interests and where panels must decide whether the interests of the complainant are substantial enough to trump those of the first-past-the-registration-pole respondent. The conflicts between groups of users are particularly hard to resolve in cases involving genuinely political or critical uses of trademarks as part of domain names[43] where claimants have registered a domain name with the intention of creating a link in the mind of the public to a specific trademark. For this reason, I will focus on such cases in the ensuing discussion.

Some commentators have alleged that a bias towards commercial interests and, in this way, trademark holders (claimants) is systemic to the UDRP.[44] Also notable in this vein are the risks arising from the specialized nature of the domain dispute system which may contribute to a "tunnel-vision" favouring right holders' interests.[45] Such claims are

---

41 E.g. Burk, notes 10 and 2 above; Helfer, note 8 above; Abbott, note 3 above; and Chih-Hong (Henry) Tsai, 'The Trademark/Domain Name Protection War: A Comparative Study of the U.S., UDRP and Taiwanese Law' (2013) 12 *J. Marshall Rev. Intell. Prop L.* 350. The mere registration of a domain name does not normally amount to a trademark violation. For this to happen, the name has to be used as an indicator of source.

42 This is explicitly prohibited by section 25 of the Danish Domain Names Act, 2.2.

43 Kur, note 16 above, para. 3.2.3.1.1.

44 Helfer and Dinwoodie, note 6 above, pp. 210 et seq.

45 Kesan and Gallo, note 20 above.

hard to substantiate since the success rate of claimants does not in itself signify very much as claimants would arguably only pursue cases which they have a good chance of winning.[46] By contrast, others have claimed that the system does not go far enough in protecting trademark holders.[47] I will not address these issues directly. Nor will I provide a detailed analysis of the substantive issues. Rather, I will focus on illustrating how the two different dispute resolution models function in practice with a view to assessing how and to what extent the domain name system balances interests between trademark owners and other users of domain names and secures the rule of law (legal certainty and predictability) in cases involving the use of trademarks in domain names to express criticism.

3.2 UDRP

The archetypical examples of domain names which express criticism of the trademark holder involve "TMsucks[.com]" or "fuckTM[.com]" registrations. The first question under the policy is to establish whether such names imply a risk of confusion with the trademark in question.[48] The "risk of confusion" standard is well known in trademark law where it constitutes the basic norm for trademarks which are not well known. For trademarks which are famous, trademark law normally provides for extended protection. Under the UDRP, the risk-of-confusion standard is the only one utilized. Even though it is debatable whether one would find a trademark to be "confusingly similar" with a domain name that combines the trademark with a derogative but also generic term, it follows from the WIPO Overview that normally panels do find that a risk of confusion exists.

Since such panels normally find that a risk of confusion exists, most cases involving critical uses are subsequently decided under the "legitimate interest" principle (i.e. "the domain name registrant has no rights or legitimate interests in respect of the domain name in question"). Article 4(c) of the policy contains examples of considerations which would normally demonstrate the domain name holder's rights or legitimate

[46] Both Kur, note 16 above and Lisa M. Sharrock, 'The Future of Domain Name Dispute Resolution: Crafting Practical International Legal Solutions from Within the UDRP Framework' (2001) 51 *Duke Law Journal* 817 came away unconvinced that substantial problems existed.

[47] Geist, note 16 above, p. 904, with references.

[48] See UDRP Policy, 2.1, para. 4(a).

interests concerning the domain name. These include "making a legitimate non-commercial or fair use of the domain name, without intent for commercial gain to misleadingly divert consumers or to tarnish the trademark or service mark at issue". This is obviously a complicated legal starting point. Given that a risk of confusion has been established in the process of a panel not granting the complainant's request, the use should therefore not simply be "non-commercial or fair"; it should also be "legitimate" in this connection. Also, it is not clear whether the last stipulation ("without ...") constitutes an extra requirement (so as to ban "fair commercial speech"). Seen from the perspective of a panel, the most vexing problem, however, is probably the inherent vagueness of the legal concepts which are being used ("fair" and "legitimate"). This problem is further exacerbated – and this is a central point to make for the present purposes – because of the *de-nationalized* nature of the rules and the *international* character of the dispute in which the claimant and the defendant may come from different jurisdictions and cultures. For panels consisting of one panellist, no clear national sources are available. For panels with three members, no firm basis for consensus in traditional legal sources exists.

For these reasons it is perhaps not surprising that according to the WIPO Overview no clear view has developed:

> In the event that a domain name identical or confusingly similar to a trademark is being used for a genuine noncommercial free speech website, there are two main views. In cases involving only US parties or the selection of a US mutual jurisdiction, panelists tend to adopt the reasoning in View 2 (though not universally).
>
> View 1: The right to criticize does not necessarily extend to registering and using a domain name that is identical or confusingly similar to the complainant's trademark. That is especially the case if the respondent is using the trademark alone as the domain name (i.e, <trademark.tld>) as that may be understood by Internet users as impersonating the trademark owner. Where the domain name comprises the protected trademark plus an additional, typically derogatory term (*e.g.*, <trademarksucks.tld>), some panels have applied View 2 below.
>
> View 2: Irrespective of whether the domain name as such connotes criticism, the respondent has a legitimate interest in using the trademark as part of the domain name of a criticism site if such use is fair and noncommercial.[49]

---

[49] References to cases omitted. To this the Overview adds the following: "Additional Considerations": "Some panels have opted to assess questions of

According to Lindsay, the different views reflect "a fundamental tension in the interpretation and application of the UDRP",[50] *viz.* tension between a viewpoint which maintains that the registration of a domain name reflecting a trademark by someone other than the trademark owner is inherently suspect ("View 1") and a viewpoint asserting that people should be free to register and use trademarks as part of domain names unless it is abusive and in bad faith ("View 2").[51] The difference between the two views matters in practice since according to the second view the use of a trademark as part of a domain name for the purposes of criticism is recognized as a defence if the use is fair and non-commercial *even if* the use involves an element of consumer confusion or is detrimental to the trademark. According to this view, free speech interests effectively serve as a "defence" that trump the interests of the trademark holder.

The position in the Overview contains several interesting points. First, it is clear that sometimes the nationality of the parties does matter and "cases involving only US parties or the selection of a US mutual jurisdiction" are singled out as constituting a special (though not exclusive) group. For such cases, national norms rather than de-nationalized ones apply. Next, the fact that two fundamentally different "views" exist parallel to each other is challenging on the level of predictability and legitimacy since it is openly acknowledged that the outcome of a concrete case depends on the nationality of the parties and that two panels will not necessarily decide the same under identical circumstances. The existence of different norms developed through variant

---

whether a respondent may have a legitimate interest in using a trademark as part of the domain name of a criticism site by reference to additional considerations, including whether: (i) the domain name has been registered and is used genuinely for the purpose of criticizing the mark owner; (ii) the registrant believes the criticism to be well-founded and lacks intent for commercial gain; (iii) it is immediately apparent to Internet users visiting the website at the domain name that it is not operated by the owner of the mark; (iv) the respondent has refrained from registering all or most of the obvious domain names reasonably suitable for the owner of the mark; (v) where appropriate, a prominent and appropriate link is provided to the relevant trademark owner's website; and (vi) where there is a likelihood that email intended for the complainant will use the domain name in issue, senders are alerted in an appropriate way that their emails have been misaddressed." According to Lindsay, note 4 above, pp. 335 and 342 et seq., some panellists have adopted a "third view" which is a hybrid of the two views mentioned above (the "totality of circumstances" approach).

50 Lindsay, note 4 above, p. 345.

51 Ibid., pp. 345 and 123 et seq.

"centres" within what would seem to be "the same legal system" also challenges traditional legal thinking, since two opposing decisions may be "correct" at the same time.[52] The Overview in this way simultaneously enacts both its own strengths and its inherent weaknesses. By clarifying the differences, the Overview invites panellists to orient themselves towards either of the two views and thus channels decisions in two directions. Consistency, in other words, is not primarily linked to a specific outcome but rather to the choice by a panel which reflects one of the two indicated views. The UDRP does not provide for a way to resolve this conflict by providing for one authoritative answer through authoritative interpretation by an appellate body or via "legislation". Also, since any juridical review of the decision from the UDRP takes place on a national basis, no real correction aimed at the level of the Overview follows from that.

3.3 Denmark

The first Danish case regarding what are normally called "hate sites" arose in 2003 and concerned the domain name "lorte-seat.dk" (English: "shitty-seat.dk").[53] The name had been registered and was being used by a private person for a webpage where he expressed his dissatisfaction with the quality of his Seat vehicle and the service offered to him by his Seat car dealership. On the webpage users could share similar stories. The page also contained links to commercial websites of general interest to the car business (such as that of "FDM", the Danish "Automobile Owners Association"). The Board found that the use was legal. It first explained that as a matter of principle "a private use of someone else's trademark is normally not illegal, if the purpose of the use is to express an opinion about the trademark holder or its products and the normal

[52] This development could be explained under the theory of legal polycentricity, which recognizes the multi-faceted origins of regulation as opposed to monopolistic statutory law including a position according to which there is a sole provider of law for each jurisdiction, e.g. Henrik Zahle, 'Polycentri i retskildelæren', in Anders Bratholm et al. (eds), *Samfunn, Rett, Rettferdighet* (TANO, 1986) p. 752.

[53] Case 2000-208 (lorte-seat.dk) of March 24, 2003, available at https://www.domaeneklager.dk/ (accessed January 26, 2016). As a declaration of interest the author of this chapter has been a member of the Board since 2003 and took part in the lorte-seat.dk decision and in most of the decisions mentioned in the following (and many more).

limitations of freedom of speech are respected".[54] The limitations mentioned in the latter part include libel. Even though the registrant could no doubt have found a more elegant way of phrasing his criticism, the use of the term "lort(e)" (English: "shitty") did not, according to the Board, in itself amount to libel. Since the site, in spite of the links, was considered to be non-commercial and to have the character of a "consumer information site", and also since the use of the derogatory term clearly indicated the nature of the domain name as a reference to a "hate site", the registration and use were deemed not contrary to "general legal principles".

The Board relied on "general legal principles" since neither the Trade Marks Act nor the Marketing Practices Act applies in non-commercial cases and because no statutory norm existed for non-commercial uses. The Board's reference to "general legal principles" met with some criticism as it was thought to be vague and imprecise. In the preparatory work leading to the Domain Names Act in 2005, "hate site" cases were highlighted as being of great general importance and the position taken by the Board was implicitly accepted. At the same time, a need to have a clear legal basis for deciding cases involving only private parties was recognized and the general clause was formulated to "fill the hole" in the legislation regarding non-commercial uses. Yet interestingly, the scope of the general clause was not limited to non-commercial parties. It also applies in commercial cases where it replaced the general clause in the Marketing Practices Act. The purpose of the general clause is therefore to serve as the basic norm for *all* cases involving domain names that do not fall to be dealt with under special rules according to the normal principle of *lex specialis derogat legi generali.* Apart from providing the Board with a statutory norm, the legislator also gave rather detailed directions for the Board to use the "platform" provided by the rule on good domain name practices in future cases to develop the area in a way which corresponds with the changing needs. In order to do this, the Board must balance all of the involved interests, including commercial and private and general societal ones. In practice, when dealing with such "hate site" cases the Board normally refers directly to the wording of the preparatory work to the 2005 Act to support its finding (i.e. this is the Board's means of setting the scene for the balancing of interests evaluation). Finally, cases which involve private parties or are of "general importance" are

---

[54] Author's own translation of: "(e)n rent privat brug af en andens varemærke er imidlertid ikke i almindelighed retsstridig, hvis formålet med brugen er at ytre sig om den pågældende varemærkeindehaver eller dennes produkter og ytringsfrihedens almindelige grænser i øvrigt respekteres."

always decided by the "Grand Board", which includes two members with business- and consumer-related expertise. In this way users' involvement in the Board is guaranteed in almost all cases involving free speech concerns.

Later cases have confirmed the early patterns and it is now firmly established that the use of a trademark as part of a domain name to express criticisms is normally allowed provided that the use is non-commercial and does not go further than is deemed reasonable (using very derogatory language is not allowed).[55] Use which implies a risk of confusion is not, however, considered as being fair. For this reason, registration of a domain name that consists only of the trade mark ("TM.dk") for critical use is not permitted.[56] The critical purpose of the site should be apparent from the name itself. In addition, the content of the websites to which the names refer is normally not taken into account.

3.4 Perspectives and Implications

Both the UDRP and the relevant Danish legislation recognize that cases involving genuine non-commercial free speech websites which use trademarks as (parts of) relevant domains constitute special cases which involve a balancing of free speech interests and the interests of trademark holders.

The UDRP is aimed at cybersquatting cases and is formulated in a number of discreet steps. As a consequence of this, the free speech interests come into play only *after* it has been established that the interests of the trademark holder are being jeopardized by a risk of confusion. The risk implicit in this sequence is that the interests of the respondent may be viewed as constituting not only the literal second step but also as being of secondary value compared to those of the trademark holder. On the other hand, the Danish Domain Names Act provides for a more neutral starting point since it is clearly stated that the application of the rule involves a balancing of all the involved interests – i.e. "commercial", "private", and "societal" – and that none of these are to be given *a priori* priority. While this allows for an overall assessment of the case at hand, it arguably also blurs the different interests. Additionally, the free speech interests of the private holder of the domain name involved in expressing critique are not in themselves viewed as being decisive. They

---

55 E.g. Case 2013-0114 (eniro-nej.dk) of October 4, 2013. Commercial use would normally be considered as constituting a trademark infringement: see Case 536 and 537 (fuckseoghor.dk) of December 2, 2004.

56 E.g. Case 2014-0098 (frijsendal.dk) of October 9, 2014.

merely constitute one element in an overall balancing of interests. In spite of the neutral starting point, the position of the Danish Board is closer to the UDRP View 2 than to View 1 since the registration of domain names which include trademarks for the purposes of expressing critique is accepted *unless* it is considered to be abusive. In accordance with View 1, however, the Board does not accept the naked registration of a trademark to express criticism (which is deemed to be abusive).

It is obviously more difficult for the UDRP than it is for the Danish Board to provide for clarity and predictability. The main difference is the absence in the UDRP of an arbitrator to overcome the "fundamental tensions" between different views. This is not necessarily a critique but more a reflection of the international nature of the UDRP. The two different views (and the contextual points made regarding the US position) clearly highlight the limits as to harmonization in terms of substantive law. This is not unique to the area of domain names. Arguably, it would be impossible even through international law making (treaties) to arrive at consensus and generally acceptable substantive legal norms in the area of the protection of free speech (and other fundamental rights). For the Danish Board the situation is profoundly different. It is interesting that the Danish legislative initiative involved a combination of different means. The introduction of the rule on good domain name practices in 2005 was combined with the statutory backing of the already existing system for dispute settlement. In this way, the legislator sought to combine the clarity of a statutory norm with the dynamics of a constant development through the case law of the Board. The choice not to limit the competence of the Board to cybersquatting cases but to endeavour instead to concentrate all cases involving domain name conflicts within the Board's jurisdiction has meant that the Board has become the central institution in Denmark for the development of the law in these areas.

4. REFLECTION: DOMAIN NAMES AND USER GENERATED LAW

As explained in Chapter 1, UGL can be described as developing through three phases: emergence, diffusion, and adoption. The current chapter on the legal governance of domain names has provided examples of all three phases.

Since the late 1990s, a system for deciding cases involving domain names and trademarks has "emerged". ICANN was a "lead actor" on the international level and has served as a channel for the ensuing international development by allocating the rights to administer ccTLDs with accompanying legal obligations. Both internationally and in Denmark, developments in terms of domain name dispute resolution systems were prompted primarily by "users" (i.e. the actual and potential registrants affected by the law). Part of this dynamic was a realization that the traditional court system would not be able to deal with these cases in a sufficiently cheap and clear way. For Denmark, the decision to liberalize the policy for registration under the ccTLD ".dk" provided a special impetus since the sudden lack of *ex ante* control mechanisms highlighted the need for *ex post* control to prevent abusive registrations involving trademarks and cronyism. This realization would clearly seem to have originated amongst the users themselves, and the involvement of the legislator was prompted by users. In this way, some degree of "asymmetric information" was present and pertinent in the sense that the users (the Internet community) were more aware of the emerging problems and had better knowledge about the necessary legal solutions. The same drivers were also present at the international level which rapidly led to the creation of ICANN. Functioning concurrently to the process of similar solutions developing, ICANN's allocation of ccTLDs to national administrators has contributed to the carving up of the Internet into the distinct spheres or virtual spaces governed by different rule-sets described by Thomas Schulz.[57] National legislation such as the Danish Domain Names Act, which is based on rules and systems that are different from the UDRP, has added to this process. The price paid for increased legal clarity and certainty within the ccTLD ".dk" has therefore been increased legal uncertainty on the general level of domain name governance.

National legislators have taken very different stances on law making for the ccTLDs. In regard to the adoption of the Domain Names Act, the Danish legislator chose an active role. Given Denmark's history of rather intense public involvement and extensive regulation in this sphere, this may not seem surprising. Yet the interesting aspect is the extent to which the legislator has chosen to bolster the user element in the regulatory model and has relied on a user driven model not only to develop practices but also to secure legitimacy of the legal development in the "Danish Internet society". In this way, the 2005 Danish Domain Names Act is

57 Thomas Schultz, 'Carving up the Internet: Jurisdiction, Legal Orders, and the Private/Public International Law Interface' (2008) 19(4) *The European Journal of International Law* 799, p. 805, see also pp. 828 et seq. and Riis, Chapter 1, section 8 of this book.

also a clear example of "adoption" whereby the legislation incorporates a user generated institutional device. By combining the Board with the general clause on good domain name practices the legislator has sought to create a legal *perpetuum mobile* to constantly develop the law in this area without direct legislative involvement at the micro level. The general clause in this way has increased the "autonomy space" in a proactive way for the Board to develop the law within the very broad limits indicated in the Act (i.e. the balancing of the involved interests).

"Diffusion" has taken place in a number of different ways. On an overall level, the decision by the Danish legislator to opt for a special Board as an institutional device for deciding domain name conflicts is very likely inspired by the UDRP. ICANN does not require national administrators to copy the UDRP and the Danish legislator decided to take a different approach. Seen from a Danish perspective, the "diffusion" of the ICANN model was in this way limited to the institutional level and did not extend to the concrete norms. For those ccTLDs that have decided to choose the UDRP, clear-cut diffusion has taken place.

Unsurprisingly, the national system is more transparent and its decisions are more consistent than those reached by the UDRP. In addition, the presence of a legislator has provided the Danish Board with much more solid legal ground under its feet than the WIPO panels. The international character of the UDRP and the varying, international composition of the panels is challenging for the UDRP in terms of legal predictability. The WIPO Overview, however, has taken on a quasi-legislative character and principles of legal interpretation known to traditional national legal systems (precedents) have developed in the UDRP in a guided process of self-ordering where the Overview has served as a feed-back loop between the different layers of the communities. The role of WIPO as a moderator and the amount of cases on which the Overview is based would seem to have been central for this development. In a similar way, the general clause in the Domain Names Act through the decisions of the Board has braided together the different layers of the Danish communities.

10. Private enforcement of IP law by internet service providers: notice and action procedures

Clement Salung Petersen and Thomas Riis

1. INTRODUCTION

Internet service providers (ISPs) play a significant role in our current knowledge-based society by providing services for internet access, use, or participation. ISPs facilitate structured exchange of information for the benefit of internet users and are able to control information exchange within their services. As a response to the inefficiency of litigation and other traditional means of law enforcement, private forms of dispute resolution and law enforcement have emerged which have largely replaced traditional means of law enforcement when it comes to dealing with allegedly illegal content and activity in internet services.

This chapter concerns one significant example of private means devoted to law enforcement: the so-called *notice and action* (N&A) procedures. ISPs use N&A procedures to handle notifications from third parties about allegedly illegal content or activity on an internet platform, usually in order to avoid liability for making such content available for the public. When notified of illegal content, the ISP may, for example, remove the content (notice-and-takedown procedure), block access to the content, or request that it be voluntarily taken down by the person who posted it online.[1] Organizations using N&A procedures include providers of hosting services, social media (such as Facebook and YouTube), search engines (such as Google and Bing), P2P file-sharing services and cyberlockers.

[1] See e.g. European Commission, 'A coherent framework for building trust in the Digital Single Market for e-commerce and online services', COM(2011) 942 final, p. 13.

In this chapter, we will use the user generated law model presented in Chapter 1 to analyse the emergence and development of these N&A procedures. We will also analyse some of the significant problems related to these procedures and discuss the need for legislation in this respect (i.e. the question of "adoption" in the user generated law model). We will focus on the role that these procedures play as a private means of enforcing intellectual property (IP) law.

2. EMERGENCE OF N&A PROCEDURES

The emergence of N&A procedures is closely related to two factors: (1) the practical difficulties encountered in traditional law enforcement regarding internet users who infringe IP law; (2) the central role that ISPs play as intermediaries in connection with such infringements.[2]

2.1 The Autonomy Spaces: Standards of Liability for ISPs

State-enacted laws define a space within which ISPs may act autonomously (i.e. without fear of State intervention).[3] This *de jure* autonomy space is defined, in particular, by the standards of liability for ISPs. These standards differ across jurisdictions and they are often subject to legal uncertainty.[4] Since the late 1990s, legislators in many jurisdictions have acknowledged that this can seriously harm innovation in the field of internet services and that there is a need to define liability exemptions ("safe harbours") for specific types of internet services. In the United States, significant examples of such exemptions include the Communications Decency Act (which does not apply to IP law) and the Digital Millennium Copyright Act (DMCA); in Europe, the E-Commerce Directive has been enacted by the European Union.[5] Liability provisions similar to those found in the DMCA are included in several US free trade

---

[2] See references in section 2.1 below.

[3] This *de jure* autonomy space is described in Chapter 1, section 4.1 of this book.

[4] As an example, see the divergent US case law prior to the enactment of the DMCA mentioned by Jennifer M. Urban and Laura Quilter, 'Efficient Process or "Chilling Effects"? Takedown Notices under Section 512 of the Digital Millennium Copyright Act' (2005) 22 *Santa Clara High Tech. L.J.* 621, pp. 631–3.

[5] See, in particular, Directive 2000/31/EC of the European Parliament and of the Council of 8 June 2000 on certain legal aspects of information society

agreements.[6] Today, similar safe harbours have been adopted by nations which include China, India, Japan, South Korea, Taiwan and Australia.[7]

The DMCA not only defines four "safe harbours", but also includes a notice-and-takedown system that must be used by ISPs in order to benefit from three of the four "safe harbours".[8] The EU E-Commerce Directive defines liability exemptions without any specific notice-and-takedown system.[9] Instead, the Directive explicitly encourages voluntary self-regulatory N&A procedures for removing and disabling access to illegal information.[10]

As explained in Chapter 1 (section 4.1), the *de facto* autonomy space may differ from the *de jure* autonomy space. The economic incentives for complying with the level of care established by law depend on many factors: these include balancing the actual risk and costs of incurring such liability against the benefits for ISPs of not complying with the established level of care. It is unlikely that ISPs will be sued and incur liability for each and every infringement of IP law in their internet services, which suggests that the *de facto* autonomy space could be *wider* than the *de jure* autonomy space.

Several other factors combine to suggest that the *de facto* autonomy space is *narrower* than the *de jure* autonomy space. First, in many cases it is difficult to determine whether or not specific content is actually infringing, and it may require significant resources to actually resolve this question. Hence, in the face of this uncertainty and the risk of liability, it must be assumed that ISPs will generally avoid investing in

services, in particular electronic commerce, in the Internal Market ("E-Commerce Directive"), recital 40; and US Senate Report No. 105-190 (11 May 1998), p. 8.

[6] Daniel Seng, 'The State of the Discordant Union: An Empirical Analysis of DMCA Takedown Notices' (2014) 18 *Va. J. L. & Tech.* 369; Andrew Christie, Sophie Waller and Kimberlee Weatherall, 'Exporting the DMCA through Free Trade Agreements', in Christopher Heath and Anselm Kamperman Sanders (eds), *Intellectual Property and Free Trade Agreements* (Hart Publishing, 2007).

[7] The Department of Commerce, Internet Policy Task Force, *Copyright Policy, Creativity, and Innovation in the Digital Economy* (July 2013), p. 53; and OECD, *The Role of Internet Intermediaries in Advancing Public Policy Objectives* (OECD Publishing, 2011), Chapter 4.

[8] See 17 U.S.C. §§ 512(c), 512(f) and 512(g).

[9] See Arts 12–15 of the Directive.

[10] See E-Commerce Directive, recital 40 ("rapid and reliable procedures for removing and disabling access to illegal information"). See also Art. 17 of Directive 2004/48/EC on the enforcement of intellectual property rights ("Enforcement Directive").

significant evaluation efforts and will simply remove material or prevent access to it in order to be on the safe side.[11] Second, many ISPs operate on a global level and can thus potentially incur liability in all jurisdictions of the world. The various jurisdictions may have different rules on liability, so in order to minimize the risk of liability ISPs are likely to comply with the strictest liability system (the lowest/safest common denominator).

Narrowing down the *de facto* autonomy space can lead to *over-deterrence*, which means that the ISP removes or blocks content that is not officially infringing any rights but is merely alleged to do so. The effect of over-deterrence is that the *de facto* scope of protection is expanded beyond the scope of the substantive rights.[12] This effect is enhanced by the fact that there are minimal costs to the right holder in sending a takedown notice requesting removal of infringing content from the relevant ISP's platform, and therefore the number of such notifications is likely to be large.[13] Unlike public court proceedings, the administration of private N&A procedures is usually not transparent, and therefore it is difficult to determine the actual degree of over-deterrence. However, it has been reported that approximately one-third of takedowns are without merit.[14] We will return to these problems in section 4.2 below.

In summary, the *de jure* autonomy space of ISPs is defined by the applicable liability standards (levels of care); but since these standards differ across jurisdictions and are often subject to legal uncertainty, ISPs,

---

[11] Mark A. Lemley, 'Rationalizing Internet Safe Harbors' (2007) 6 *J. on Telecomm. & High Tech. L.* 115; Wendy Seltzer, 'Free Speech Unmoored in Copyright's Safe Harbor: Chilling Effects of the DMCA on the First Amendment' (2010) 24(1) *Harvard Journal of Law & Technology* 171, p. 178.

[12] Ira S. Nathenson, 'Civil Procedures for a World of Shared and User-generated Content' (2010) 48 *University of Louisville Law Review* 911, pp. 916, 919.

[13] Wendy Seltzer, 'Free Speech Unmoored in Copyright's Safe Harbor: Chilling Effects of the DMCA on the First Amendment' (2010) 24(1) *Harvard Journal of Law & Technology* 171, p. 176.

[14] Jennifer M. Urban and Laura Quilter, 'Efficient Process or "Chilling Effects"? Takedown Notices Under Section 512 of the Digital Millennium Copyright Act' (2006) 22 *Santa Clara Computer & High-Technology Law Journal* 621, pp. 666–7.

to the greatest extent possible, are likely to prefer operating within applicable liability exemptions ("safe harbours").[15]

2.2 Heterogeneous Demands

There are three groups of actors who are affected by N&A procedures and as such can be considered users of the regulatory model: ISPs, users of the internet services concerned, and third parties whose rights are enforced by way of N&A procedures. It is not a very felicitous notion that ISPs and users of the supplied internet services will exhibit a pronounced demand for legal regulatory models designed to enforce intellectual property rights in internet services. Enforcement by ISPs usually concerns rights owned by third parties and is for the benefit of such parties. In this sense, heterogeneous demands are not an essential driver for the emergence of N&A procedures. However, as already indicated, there is a close and distinct relationship between the liability standard of ISPs and the emergence of N&A procedures. An ISP will seek to minimize its legal risks by adhering to applicable liability standards. Hence, the demands for N&A procedures are products of the State-enacted liability standards and the possible heterogeneity in demands translates into variations in the applicable liability standards.

The liability exemptions mentioned above only apply to specific activities that are intermediary (meaning that the service provider transmits or hosts information from third parties). Some ISPs may limit their business to such activities, such as providers of traditional hosting services. Other ISPs will conduct various activities which are not (necessarily) covered in their entirety by the liability exemptions (such as the "AdWords" service offered by Google).[16] In such situations, the ISP needs to take other liability issues into consideration when drafting its N&A procedure.

The demand for N&A procedures also depends on the jurisdiction(s) in which the ISP operates. For ISPs operating in the United States, the DMCA regime is usually unavoidable. In the European Union, an ISP needs to take account of the framework established by the E-Commerce

---

15 In the European Commission's public consultation on e-commerce, stakeholders indicated that liability exemptions are "essential for the provision of intermediary activities", see SEC(2011) 1641 final, p. 24.

16 For an overview of different types of internet services and the liability exemptions of the E-Commerce Directive, see SEC(2011) 1641 final, pp. 26–32.

Directive. For some ISPs, other rules can also influence N&A procedures, such as the EU rules on data protection.[17]

The scopes of different liability exemptions may also create heterogeneous demands for N&A procedures. As an example, the US Communications Decency Act and the DMCA leave ISPs with different autonomy spaces which could lead to different demands for N&A procedures relating *inter alia* to notices regarding libel and copyright infringement.

As such, differences in the functioning, scope and level of ambition of ISPs as entities, along with differences in the legal climates these bodies inhabit, create variations when it comes to handling notifications about allegedly illegal content or activity in internet services.

2.3 Expectation of Benefits

Third party right owners are provided with an alternative and effective means of rights enforcement and clearly enjoy benefits. However, they are not directly involved in the establishment and workings of the N&A procedures. Users of internet services may suffer economic harm from removals of content (and this includes unmerited removals because ISPs will typically exclude liability for any such unmerited removals in the relevant terms of service). This will often leave users of the internet platform with no legal remedy in cases of unmerited removals by the ISP.[18] By signing up for the internet service, the users of the service accept the terms and conditions of the ISP including the N&A procedure. These terms and conditions are non-negotiable. The users of the service would be better off without the N&A procedure but the ISP exploits the attractiveness of its service to impose the N&A procedure on the users by means of a one-sided adhesion contract. That leaves the ISPs as the central actors when it comes to the establishment and workings of N&A procedures.

Most ISPs are profit-seeking companies and benefit from N&A procedures by bringing all or some of the relevant activities within a "safe harbour" which thus minimizes their legal risks, as discussed above. Rational ISPs will implement N&A procedures that bring the largest volume of their activities within a "safe harbour" at the lowest

---

[17] See, e.g., CJEU judgment in Case C-131/12 *Google Spain SL, Google Inc.*, on "the right to be forgotten".

[18] Wendy Seltzer, 'Free Speech Unmoored in Copyright's Safe Harbor: Chilling Effects of the DMCA on the First Amendment' (2010) 24(1) *Harvard Journal of Law & Technology* 171, p. 203.

cost. The administration costs of running the N&A procedure may be minimized by standardization of notifications and the implementation of a fast and crude process of handling and deciding on notifications.

2.4 Asymmetric Information

The liability exemptions ("safe harbours") for ISPs aim to encourage innovation in the field of internet services.[19] Since these exemptions were introduced, the market for internet services has developed rapidly.[20] In short, the internet, including its expanding array of internet services, has revolutionized the everyday lives of citizens globally in a way comparable to the industrial revolutions of the previous centuries.[21] Internet innovation has brought with it not only new internet services, but also new ways for ISPs to "take action" against illegal content and activity on their internet platforms. Examples include new technologies for automatic filtering of illegal content, technologies for Domain Name System (DNS) blocking of specific domains or websites, and the "Content ID" system established by YouTube.[22] These filtering technologies are not flawless.[23]

The speed of technological innovation within this field creates an information asymmetry between legislators and ISPs because legislators do not have an insider's knowledge of new services and technologies and thus cannot keep abreast of the most cost effective procedures for enforcement of rights.

The safe harbour provisions mitigate this information asymmetry by leaving it to each ISP to decide the exact form and content of its N&A procedure. When the ISPs develop these specific N&A procedures so as to minimize their own legal risks and associated costs, there is a risk that the general societal objectives of the law enforcement systems are ignored. This may create problems: particularly in relation to the users of the internet services.

---

[19] See section 2.1 above.

[20] See, e.g., SEC(2011) 1641 final, pp. 26–31, mentioning new search engine and hyperlinking services, video-sharing sites, online selling platforms, file-sharing services, and social media (blogs, discussion forums and social networks).

[21] Compare COM(2011) 942 final/2, p. 1.

[22] See https://support.google.com/youtube/answer/2797370?hl=en (last visited in 1 July 2015).

[23] See, e.g., SEC(2011) 1641 final, pp. 50–51, referring to the fact that "[a] wide variety of stakeholders mentioned several disadvantages of filtering techniques and confirmed that Article 15 [of the E-Commerce Directive] is still relevant today".

It has been noted above that safe harbour provisions differ across jurisdictions. The safe harbour provisions of the E-Commerce Directive grant a wider scope of discretion for ISPs than the safe harbour provisions of the DMCA.

2.5 Lead User

Due to the general lack of transparency in N&A procedures it is difficult to assess the role of lead users within this field. In the European Commission road map "Initiative on a clean and open Internet: procedures for notifying and acting on illegal content hosted by online intermediaries", the Commission reports on a public consultation concerning electronic commerce and the E-Commerce Directive that was held in the second half of 2010. The vast majority of the 420 respondents expressed concerns about the fragmentation of N&A procedures throughout the EU.[24] On the strength of this, the European Commission concluded that the E-Commerce Directive provides the basis for a multitude of procedures which are often very different in practice.[25]

Yet this does not exclude the possibility of lead users in regard to certain types of ISP activities with similar demands for an N&A procedure.[26] The DMCA notice-and-takedown (NTD) system forms the basis for the N&A procedures applied by YouTube, Facebook and Google.[27] It is likely that many other ISPs adhere to this basis when offering their services to customers both in the United States and

---

[24] According to Thomas Schulz, 'Carving up the Internet: Jurisdiction, Legal Orders, and the Private/Public International Law Interface' (2008)19(4) *The European Journal of International Law* 799, p. 830f: "certain marketplaces have developed highly detailed user policies used in the dispute resolution process as the applicable 'law', to the exclusion of many of the normally applicable national laws, including their mandatory non-derogable rights. Such constructions cause their normative environments to be largely divorced from public legal systems: a private dispute resolution mechanism applies privately developed norms and the outcome of the procedure is enforced through private means. Such constructions create marketplace-specific legal systems. From an external and global point of view, these systems form a patchwork of private legal orders each specific to an online marketplace or to an equivalent context of Internet activities. They form 'layers' as they can pile up so as to be several which apply to the same individual, governing different facets of her life."

[25] SEC(2011) 1641 final, pp. 25, 43.

[26] Compare section 2.2 above regarding the heterogeneous demands.

[27] P. Bernt Hugenholtz, 'Codes of Conduct and Copyright Enforcement in Cyberspace', in Irini Stamatoudi (ed.), *Copyright Enforcement and the Internet* (Wolters Kluwer, 2010), pp. 314–15.

internationally because it is necessary to use the DMCA NTD system to stay within the DMCA safe harbours.[28]

2.6 Conclusion

Our analysis shows that State-enacted laws have been the initiating factor for the emergence of N&A procedures but this process has left a significant autonomy space for user generated law. A number of the four determinants for user generated law have been present in a modified form during the emergence of N&A procedures. State-enacted laws (rather than the four determinants) have prompted the introduction of N&A procedures as a private means of enforcing IP law in internet services, but the determinants have influenced the procedures actually used by the ISPs and can therefore be said to contribute to an understanding of how such law has evolved.

3. DIFFUSION

The lack of transparency in the content and workings of N&A procedures makes it difficult to ascertain whether the existing procedures are directly copied and diffused from one ISP to another. Given the variations in the services supplied, it is likely that diffusion of any specific N&A procedure, if it exists, takes place between ISPs offering the same type of internet services.

In Europe, there are several national associations and at least one European association of ISPs (EuroISPA).[29] The policy objectives of EuroISPA include promoting self-regulation by the internet industry, contributing to the regulatory process on behalf of the internet industry, developing professional standards for the industry and contributing to the development of technical standards.[30] Nevertheless, we have not been able to identify that EuroISPA promotes any specific N&A procedures. The Swiss Internet Industry Association (simsa) has adopted a "Hosting

[28] See section 2.1 above.

[29] See, e.g., the UK Internet Service Providers Association (ISPA), at http://www.ispa.org.uk, the Swiss Internet Industry Association (simsa), and the Danish Association of IT-hosting companies in Denmark, at http://www.bfih.dk. See also the website of EuroISPA at http://www.euroispa.org.

[30] Cf. EuroISPA Articles of Association, para. 1.3, retrieved from http://www.euroispa.org (last visited 1 July 2015).

Code of Conduct".[31] In the Netherlands, the National Infrastructure against Cyber Crime (a public-private partnership which includes several branches of the Dutch government and internet providers) has developed a NTD code of conduct which includes a common general framework for procedures designed to allow intermediaries to deal with reports of unlawful content on the internet.[32] In 2011, several right holders and some ISPs signed a Memorandum of Understanding that established a code of practice in the fight against the sale of counterfeit goods over the internet. This code also included provisions on N&A procedures.[33]

Hence, there is evidence of some diffusion of N&A procedures – at least at the level of frameworks. Still, public consultations held by the European Commission in 2010 and 2012 showed that there is little cooperation within this field in Europe and that most N&A procedures result from the unilateral policy of individual ISPs.[34] These consultations also indicated diversity and "considerable differences" among the policies actually used by different ISPs.[35] The majority of stakeholders who responded to the public consultation said that "NTD procedures are heavily fragmented".[36]

In the United States, the NTD system set forth in the DMCA seems to constitute the basis for many of the N&A procedures applied by ISPs. Nevertheless, the DMCA leaves ISPs with a "margin of appreciation" (though a smaller one than in the EU) as regards the precise implementation of N&A procedures, and recent reports suggest that there is also diversity in the United States among the policies actually used by different ISPs.[37] A number of initiatives seeking to develop a common

---

31 As outlined at https://www.swisscom.ch/content/dam/swisscom/en/biz/sme/it-hosting/pdf/wh_verhaltenskodex-simsa_en.pdf (last visited 1 July 2015).

32 An English translation is available at http://www.ecp.nl/sites/default/files/NTD_Gedragscode_Engels.pdf (last visited 1 July 2015).

33 See http://ec.europa.eu/internal_market/iprenforcement/docs/memorandum_04052011_en.pdf (last visited 1 July 2015).

34 SEC(2011) 1641 final, p. 41.

35 See European Commission, *Summary of the results of the Public Consultation on the future of electronic commerce in the Internal Market and the implementation of the Directive on electronic commerce (2000/31/EC)*, p. 11, and SEC(2011) 1641 final, pp. 25, 42.

36 SEC(2011) 1641 final, p. 43.

37 See, e.g., the Green Paper from the US Department of Commerce, Internet Policy Task Force, *Copyright policy, creativity, and innovation in the digital economy* (July 2013), and the outcomes of the meetings in the "Multistakeholder Forum on Improving the Operation of Notice and Takedown System" set up by the Department of Commerce Internet Policy Task Force in 2014, available at

framework for N&A procedures have been launched. Multiple large content owners and ISPs have created the Copyright Alert System (CAS) based on a common Memorandum of Understanding.[38] CAS is a graduated response scheme which sends out a series of six alerts to potentially infringing subscribers. Depending on the ISP in question, this sequence may *inter alia* lead to a temporary reduction in internet speed, a temporary downgrade in internet service tier, or a redirection to a landing page for a set period of time. Within a narrower field, a similar instrument named "Principles of User Generated Content Services" has been produced by a number of copyright owners and ISPs offering user generated content services (including Microsoft, myspace.com and youku.com).[39] In 2013, US companies that offer "Ad Networks" in the United States adopted "Best Practice Guidelines for Ad Networks to address piracy".[40] Since 2014, a "Multistakeholder Forum", under the US Department of Commerce, has worked on defining best practices and/or developing voluntary agreements for improving the operation of the DMCA NTD system.[41]

As such, although we have been unable to find convincing evidence that a specific model of an N&A procedure has been diffused large-scale among ISPs, it seems plausible that ISPs exchange information about self-regulatory models for N&A procedures and that the various initiatives (codes of conduct, guidelines, memoranda of understanding, etc.) aim to establish a common framework and to mainstream the procedures implemented by the individual ISPs. Such initiatives are clearly still at a nascent stage because in 2010, at an OECD workshop on the role of internet intermediaries, participating stakeholders expressed the need for an international convergence of approaches to developing policies involving ISPs.[42]

---

http://www.uspto.gov/learning-and-resources/ip-policy/copyrights (last visited 1 July 2015).

[38] See more on CAS on the "Center for Copyright Information" website at http://www.copyrightinformation.org/ (last visited 27 January 2016).

[39] See http://www.ugcprinciples.com (last visited 27 January 2016).

[40] See http://www.2013ippractices.com/bestpracticesguidelinesforadnetworkstoaddresspiracyandcounterfeiting.html (last visited 3 February 2016).

[41] Ibid.

[42] OECD, *The Role of Internet Intermediaries in Advancing Public Policy Objectives* (OECD Publishing, 2011).

4. ADOPTION

So far, our analysis has focused on the emergence and possible diffusion of N&A procedures. Under the theory of user generated law, the remaining question is whether N&A procedures – when viewed as user generated legal innovations – are "adopted".[43]

Both in the United States and the EU, the liability exemptions ("safe harbours") have remained as they were when originally adopted. However, this does not mean that these legislators have decided that N&A procedures are currently functioning well and that there are no grounds for legislative corrections. Since the liability exemptions were adopted, there has been increasing criticism from right holders, ISPs and NGOs about the functioning of N&A procedures, and legislators in both the United States and the European Union are currently considering the need for legislative corrections (adjustments) of the present autonomy spaces (see section 4.3 below).

Below, we will analyse the significance of N&A procedures and examine some of the pertinent problems associated with them. We will also explore current discussions about legislative adjustments of the autonomy spaces in the European Union and the United States.

4.1 Significance of N&A Procedures

Infringements of IP rights in internet services, especially copyright infringements, constitute a substantial problem for right holders. Yet quantitative information about the extent of the problem remains limited.[44] Today, N&A procedures are usually the primary means of IP law enforcement on internet platforms and the use of N&A procedures is extensive. In 2013, Google received notifications for removal of approximately 230 million items.[45] The vast majority of notifications led to action by ISPs, typically in the form of removing specific content. In this way, N&A procedures play a significant role in modern knowledge societies with implications for all internet users. In practice, too, very few disputes about N&A procedures seem to be brought before the courts.

---

[43] See Chapter 1, section 7 of this book.

[44] See, e.g., OECD, *The Role of Internet Intermediaries in Advancing Public Policy Objectives* (OECD Publishing, 2011), pp. 144, 155.

[45] Hearing on 13 March 2014 before the Subcommittee on Courts, Intellectual Property, and the Internet of the Committee on the Judiciary, House of Representatives (Serial No. 113-86), p. 3.

Thus, N&A procedures have generally replaced traditional means of law enforcement on internet platforms.

Users of the relevant internet services are the parties directly affected by N&A procedures. In principle, users can avoid N&A by simply not using the services supplied by the ISPs. However, since more and more information is exchanged in services supplied by ISPs (search engines, social media, market places, etc.), such an internet user strategy will steadily isolate the user from the internet community and the rest of the world to an extent that makes this path unviable for many users.

Thus far, users of internet services have often accepted terms and conditions with clauses on jurisdiction and applicable law that can make it very onerous for a user to pursue any litigation strategy vis-à-vis the ISP in cases concerning (allegedly) unmerited removal of content.[46] Litigation against the third party right holder, who has notified the ISP and requested action against the content, is often unlikely to remedy the unmerited removal because such litigation will not in itself bring back the removed content, and also because the third party is not generally liable for the ISP's unmerited removals. Hence, in the vast majority of disputes about N&A procedures, litigation is not a real option. Consequently, these actions are governed only by the ISP's terms and conditions, including N&A procedures, not by the general law.

Third party right holders who find that an N&A procedure is not sufficiently effective to (permanently) remove infringing content can litigate against the ISP. However, since the safe harbours will often still apply, such litigation can generally only result in injunctions. In the European Union, such injunctions are available but will often not be more effective than typical "action" as a result of an N&A procedure because of the limitations imposed by the E-Commerce Directive (Article 15). This is supported by the case law of the CJEU according to which Member States may not impose general duties on providers to act.[47] Nevertheless, due to concern about the potential costs of such litigation, ISPs receiving notifications from right holders who are likely to start

[46] As an example, any dispute between Facebook and its users shall be governed by the laws of the State of California and must be exclusively resolved in the US District Court for the Northern District of California or a state court located in San Mateo County; see "Statement of Rights and Responsibilities" used by Facebook.

[47] See, in particular, CJEU judgment of 12 July 2011, Case C-324/09 (*L'Oréal*), judgment of 24 November 2011, Case C-70/10 (*Scarlet Extended*), judgment of 16 February 2012, Case C-360/10 (*Sabam*), and judgment of 27 March 2014, Case C-314/12 (*UPC Telekabel*).

such litigation, in particular from financially strong companies or organizations that own or manage IP rights, are likely to apply their N&A procedures in a way which imposes a more strict enforcement regime.

4.2 Problems Related to N&A Procedures

Concerning the role and legal responsibilities of ISPs for allegedly infringing content in internet services, N&A procedures seek to strike a balance between the interests of ISPs, right holders and internet users. In the past decade, there has been an increasing volume of criticism from right holders, ISPs and NGOs about the current functioning of N&A procedures. At a hearing before a committee of the US House of Representatives in 2014, witnesses presented divergent views on the functioning of the DMCA NTD system. One commentator argued that it was "not working for anyone", while another argued that this system "has proven to be remarkably resilient in the face of the Internet's evolving culture and technology".[48] In 2011, the OECD concluded that N&A procedures "appear workable and balanced, but are limited in their application and effect for many of the principal forms of online infringement".[49] Civil rights and consumer organizations on both sides of the Atlantic complain that N&A procedures are used to take action against content or activities which are in fact legal; that they take disproportionate action against illegal content or activity; and that they sidestep fundamental procedural guarantees such as the right to be heard and to defend the legality of specific content.[50] They also complain that there are examples of persons using N&A procedures to submit outright fraudulent notices with no risk of penalties.[51]

Based on recent research and administrative reports, we will now present an overview of the main problems related to N&A procedures, all of which can influence the "adoption" of these procedures. On this basis, we will subsequently explore topical discussions in the United States and the European Union about prospective legislative action within this field that will correct the current autonomy spaces.

---

[48] See the witness testimony of Professor Sean M. O'Connor, University of Washington (Seattle), at the 2014 US hearing, note 45 above, pp. 15, 19.

[49] OECD, *The Role of Internet Intermediaries in Advancing Public Policy Objectives* (OECD Publishing, 2011), p. 155.

[50] See, e.g., SEC(2011) 1641 final, pp. 41, 44; and 2014 US Hearing, note 45 above, p. 5.

[51] Ibid.

4.2.1 Lack of transparency

N&A procedures are private procedures: the use and impact of these procedures is usually subject to a significant lack of transparency (though some ISPs have started to publish certain limited information about their application of N&A procedures).[52] In the 2011 OECD study "The Role of Internet Intermediaries in Advancing Public Policy Objectives", it is stated that (1) "[t]here is little public information on the number of take-down notices filed; (2) [t]he number of take-downs in response to these notices is not known; (3) [t]he number or percentage of counter-notices requesting put-back of allegedly infringing material is not known; (4) neither the costs to copyright owners nor the costs to the service providers of complying with the notice and take-down requirements have been publicly estimated".[53]

The existing lack of transparency means that it is difficult to assess the actual implications of N&A procedures. This impedes evaluating just how effective and widespread the procedures are; assessing how they work in terms of accuracy; and monitoring their adherence to general standards of fair process. It is also difficult to assess how this system affects right holders, ISPs and internet users in general. In terms of users, concern has been voiced that N&A procedures negatively affect the freedom of expression (right to impart and receive information) of internet users. On these grounds, scholars have called for greater transparency in N&A procedures.[54]

---

52 See, e.g., the Google Transparency Reports. Some research projects are also endeavouring to shed light on the actual functioning of these procedures. See, in particular, the "Takedown Project", available at http://www.takedownproject.org (last visited 27 January 2016), which is a project that aims at mobilizing the global research community to explore how NTD procedures operate, and to examine how these procedures resolve conflicts between copyright and freedom of expression. The project looks to create greater transparency on these issues with respect to technology sector norms and law, and specifically seeks an improved knowledge of takedown notices and takedown procedures. See also the related US research project at http://www.chillingeffects.org (last visited 27 January 2016).

53 OECD, *The Role of Internet Intermediaries in Advancing Public Policy Objectives* (OECD Publishing, 2011), p. 146.

54 Daniel Seng, 'The State of the Discordant Union: An Empirical Analysis of DMCA Takedown Notices' (2014) 18 *Va. J. L. & Tech.* 369; Annemarie Bridy, 'Graduated Response American Style. "Six Strikes" Measured Against Five Norms' (2012) 23 *Fordham Intellectual Property, Media & Entertainment Law Journal* 1, pp. 62 et seq; Mary LaFrance, 'Graduated Response by Industry Compact: Piercing the Black Box' (2012) 30 *Cardozo Arts & Entertainment Law*

4.2.2 Fair process

Enforcing IP rights through N&A procedures is a way to resolve disputes between parties (i.e. the right holder, the ISP and the internet user(s) concerned). Without N&A procedures, such disputes would eventually have to be decided through civil litigation or arbitration. As noted above, N&A procedures have largely replaced other means of dispute resolution, and it is thus pertinent to scrutinize whether N&A procedures comply with core values of "due process". In this connection, at least some types of N&A procedures have attracted significant criticism.[55]

A concept of "due process" exists in most modern societies. Under the European Convention on Human Rights, everyone is entitled to "a fair and public hearing within a reasonable time by an independent and impartial tribunal established by law", and judgments must generally be pronounced publicly. Similar rights follow from the European Charter of Fundamental Rights. As regards arbitration, Article 18 of the UNCITRAL Model Law on International Commercial Arbitration sets out fundamental requirements of procedural justice: "The parties shall be treated with equality and each party shall be given a full opportunity of presenting his case." A somewhat similar concept of due process has been developed in US Constitutional law.[56]

Core aspects of these different notions of "due process" are included in Lawrence B. Solum's theory of procedural justice which is based on the two general principles of "accuracy" and "participation". Accuracy refers to the accurate application of substantive law and the correctness of outcomes of the legal processes. When N&A procedures are used to enforce IP law on internet platforms, "accuracy" means that infringing material is removed or blocked, whereas non-infringing material is not. (To the extent that infringing material is not removed or blocked and non-infringing material is removed or blocked, the procedures are less accurate.) However, in a model of procedural justice, accuracy is not an

---

Journal 165; and Special Rapporteur (Frank La Rue), *Report on the promotion and protection of the right to freedom of opinion and expression*, Human Rights Council, UN Doc. A/HRC/17/27 (16 May 2011), p. 12.

[55] See, e.g., Nicolas Suzor and Brian Fitzgerald, 'The Legitimacy of Graduated Response Schemes in Copyright Law' (2011) 34(1) *University of New South Wales Law Journal* 1: "In most common forms, graduated response schemes are highly problematic with regards to due process, the proper exercise of the judicial power of the Commonwealth, and respect for the rights of Australian internet users" (at p. 2).

[56] See also the EU Telecoms Package, Art. 3a of Directive 2002/21/EC as amended by Directive 2009/140/EC.

absolute value since it must be modified by the rule of diminished marginal return. Obtaining accuracy requires resources, and the rule of diminished marginal return indicates that an increase in the resources invested in the legal process results in a decreasing marginal improvement in accuracy. Hence, procedural costs in the broad meaning of the term must be taken into account, and a fair and reasonable balance between accuracy and the costs of procedure must be found.[57]

The summary nature of N&A procedures makes them comparable to provisional (sometimes protective) measures such as *ex parte* preliminary injunctions. However, there is no requirement for N&A procedures to offer procedural safeguards comparable to those usually related to the granting of a preliminary injunction.

Solum's "participation" requires that persons affected by the procedures are granted an active role (e.g. by receiving advance notice of matters of importance and having an opportunity to be heard). This participation principle can be interpreted in several ways, but essentially it is claimed that procedures that purport to be binding without affording any meaningful rights of participation are fundamentally illegitimate.[58]

Legal certainty can be subsumed under the principle of accuracy and is actually a part of accuracy if the degree of accuracy is high. With lower degrees of accuracy, legal certainty in the sense of predictability, equality and non-discrimination cannot be ensured. Since the outcomes of legal processes are never fully accurate due to the rule of diminished marginal return, an additional principle is required for a just procedural system. The highest degree of predictability regarding the outcomes of legal processes is obtained by adopting a rigid and fixed rule, but such a rule is not always in conformity with the policy objectives behind the law. In some cases, the overriding value of substantial justice is better promoted by a flexible legal standard. Hence, as an element of procedural justice, legal certainty shall not be supported by the adoption of fixed rules; instead, legal certainty shall be ensured by a principle of transparency in the legal processes and the legal system so the subjects can assess the possible outcomes of those processes.

As mentioned in section 4.2.1 above, the lack of transparency makes it difficult to ascertain whether N&A procedures accommodate these fundamental notions of due process. However, it is reasonable to assume that this is not the case because ISPs do not have real incentives to spend time

---

[57] Lawrence B. Solum, 'Procedural Justice' (2004) 78 *Southern California Law Review* 181, p. 273.

[58] Ibid., p. 274.

and other resources on making comprehensive investigations of possible IP infringements; nor do they possess an incentive to hold a fair hearing involving the alleged infringer.[59] Disregarding due process creates a risk of N&A procedures being abused.[60] This risk of abuse is increased by the fact that notices are often generated automatically in large numbers by a computer using automated web crawler technology and databases of digital fingerprints. As emphasized by William Patry, this technique is notoriously inaccurate.[61]

We recall here, too, that it is also a general notion of due process that parties should be treated with equality, and that disputes should be decided by a neutral third party. The opportunity to send a counter-notification under the US DMCA seeks to strike a fair balance between the interests of the parties. However, even if the right holder does not take (further) legal action, the ISP has no obligation to restore any removed content. Generally, there are thus no procedural safeguards to ensure that parties are treated with equality in N&A procedures. The fact that one group of actors (financially strong companies or organizations) is willing to litigate claims (and counterclaims) related to an ISPs' N&A procedure while other groups of actors (private persons and possibly also small and medium-sized companies) are not, implies that there are severe biases built into the system.[62] As a commercial profit-seeking entity, an ISP minimizes cost, and one way to do that is to avoid litigation. Hence, an ISP is more likely to react to claims (and counterclaims) from financially strong companies or organizations than similar claims from private persons and other financially weak parties. As such, the ISP can hardly be regarded as a neutral third party under fundamental notions of due process.

---

[59] E.g. Nicolas Suzor and Brian Fitzgerald, 'The Legitimacy of Graduated Response Schemes in Copyright Law' (2011) 34 *University of New South Wales Law Journal* 1, pp. 20, 26–7.

[60] Ibid., p. 25; and Special Rapporteur (Frank La Rue), *Report on the promotion and protection of the right to freedom of opinion and expression*, Human Rights Council, UN Doc. A/HRC/17/27 (16 May 2011), p. 12.

[61] William Patry, *Moral Panics and the Copyright Wars* (Oxford University Press, 2009), p. 13. See also Peter K. Yu, 'The Graduated Response' (2010) 62 *Florida Law Review* 1373, pp. 1395 et seq.

[62] See Rebecca Giblin, 'Evaluating Graduated Response' (2014) 37 *Columbia Journal of Law & the Arts* 147, pp. 203 et seq.

4.2.3 Freedom of expression

Action against content or activities on internet platforms may have a negative impact on internet users' rights to receive and impart information (freedom of expression). It is far from clear which (if any) obligations private ISPs are subject to in relation to ensuring the fundamental rights of their users. In recital 46 of the EU E-Commerce Directive, it is stated that ISPs should take action "in the observance of the principle of freedom of expression", and the CJEU has emphasized similar obligations in its recent case law.[63] Any such obligations are unlikely to have any substantial influence on private systems of enforcement of rights which for all practical purposes are not going to be subject to litigation.

4.2.4 Risks of over-deterrence of IP protection

From a utilitarian perspective, substantive IP law is construed as a balancing mechanism that provides economic incentives to engage in many forms of innovation while ensuring that others are granted access to this new knowledge, information, technology, and so forth. The actual functioning of this balancing mechanism significantly depends on the way substantive IP law is enforced (i.e. whether the enforcement procedures reflect the public policies behind substantive IP law).[64]

As noted at section 2.1 above, it must be expected that the use of N&A procedures results in *de facto* extension of substantive IP protection by way of over-deterrence; but the lack of transparency related to the use of such procedures makes it difficult to determine the actual extent of over-deterrence. As an indication, though, it has been reported that approximately one-third of takedowns are without merit.[65]

4.2.5 Democratic governance

From a broader societal perspective, the functioning of N&A procedures has implications for the democratic governance of internet platforms. Our analyses above illustrate the extent to which ISPs, through their N&A procedures, often function both as lawmaker and judiciary. We have also

---

[63] See CJEU judgment of 27 March 2014, Case C-314/12 (*UPC Telekabel*).

[64] E.g. Roger Blair and Thomas F. Cotter, *Intellectual Property. Economic and Legal Dimensions of Rights and Remedies* (Cambridge University Press, 2005), pp. 60, 258.

[65] Jennifer M. Urban and Laura Quilter, 'Efficient Process or "Chilling Effects"? Takedown Notices Under Section 512 of the Digital Millennium Copyright Act' (2006) 22 *Santa Clara Computer & High-Technology Law Journal* 621, pp. 666–7.

seen that N&A procedures are often used to enforce private norms which differ from those found in democratically enacted laws. Additionally, our analyses show that N&A procedures clearly do not fulfil the democratic role of civil litigation in courts.[66] Given the important role that internet services play in modern knowledge societies, it is no surprise that the functioning of these procedures remains controversial.

4.3 Adoption: Legislative Correction of Autonomy Spaces?

Today, N&A procedures are a natural part of ISPs' terms and conditions. They are, in general, accepted as a regulatory model by all parties involved, and they are supported by State-enacted law. In this sense, N&A procedures can be considered "adopted" according to the terminology established by the model of user generated law. However, the optimal form and contents of N&A procedures are disputed.

Given the widespread use of N&A procedures, and given the aforementioned problems associated with them, it is not surprising that the procedures have now attracted significant attention from legislators in major jurisdictions, including the United States and the Europe Union, as well as on the global agenda under the auspices of the OECD. Various interest groups present opposing views on the most expedient legal framework for N&A procedures, and such views feed the ongoing policy discussion concerning how to adjust the autonomy spaces for these procedures. In general, groups of right holders tend to push for a more rigid liability norm that will incentivize a more thorough ISP policing of their internet platforms and prevent further IPR infringements, while groups of ISPs and other intermediaries argue that their freedom to conduct businesses is a prerequisite for the further development of internet based services, and that such development relies on ISPs and other parties not being burdened with the practical means of rights enforcement for the benefit of third parties.

We will now proceed to a consideration of the current policy discussions in the European Union and the United States concerning the need for new State-enacted laws in this domain in order to estimate the prospective adjustment of the autonomy spaces for N&A procedures.

---

[66] See *inter alia* Judith Resnik, 'The Democracy of Courts: Jeremy Bentham, "Publicity", and the Privatization of Process in the Twenty-First Century' (2013) *NoFo (No Foundations)* 10, pp. 100 et seq.; Trevor C. W. Farrow, *Civil Justice, Privatization, and Democracy* (University of Toronto Press, 2014); and Dame Hazel Genn, *Why the Privatization of Civil Justice is a Rule of Law Issue*, 36th F. A. Mann Lecture, Lincoln's Inn, 2012.

4.3.1 Recent developments in the European Union

In the public consultation on the E-Commerce Directive in 2010, a majority of the respondents proposed a European NTD procedure, either on a voluntary or on an obligatory basis; but views about the desirable specifics of such a common procedure were divided.[67] On the basis of this consultation, the European Commission identified a number of "persisting issues" that create a significant fragmentation of N&A procedures and concluded that an analysis of the need for EU action in this field was justified.[68] The European Commission promised an impact assessment on N&A procedures in 2012 and emphasized the need to ensure "the transparency, effectiveness, proportionality and fundamental rights compliance of NTD procedures" as well as the need for "a balanced and workable approach towards NTD procedures, with a focus on the impact on innovation and growth, while ensuring respect of fundamental rights".[69] On the basis of this impact assessment, the Commission would try to adopt "a horizontal initiative on notice and action procedures".[70] After yet another public consultation in 2012 (on "a clean and open internet"), which generated a significant volume of responses, in April 2013 the Commission repeated its endeavours in terms of working on an impact assessment on N&A procedures and of adopting, on this basis, a horizontal initiative on N&A procedures.[71]

According to various rumours, the European Commission worked on a "Notice and Action Directive" which has been dropped – or at least put on hold – because of significant lobbyism and the divergent interests of stakeholders involved. In a speech in the European Parliament on 6 February 2014, Michel Barnier, European Commissioner for Internal Market Services, said that work on a Commission initiative within this field shall continue, but so far no other official information about the current plans of the European Commission have surfaced.

It remains to be seen whether any initiative will involve new legislation or focus on encouraging further self-regulation. It also remains to be seen

---

67 SEC(2011) 1641 final, p. 43. Some stakeholders ("a search engine and two video platforms") have suggested a number of specific principles defining a potential European NTD procedure: see "Summary of the results of the Public Consultation on the future of electronic commerce in the Internal Market and the implementation of the Directive on electronic commerce" (2000/31/EC), p. 12.

68 Ibid.

69 Ibid., p. 46.

70 COM(2011) 942 final/2, p. 15.

71 "E-Commerce Action Plan 2012–2015, State of play 2013", SWD(2013) 153 final, pp. 17–18.

whether any such initiative will result in legislative amendments to the liability exemptions of the E-Commerce Directive and/or a more specific regulation of N&A procedures which might include adopting current best practices.

4.3.2 Recent developments in the United States

In 2010, a US "Internet Policy Task Force" was created to conduct "a comprehensive review of the nexus between privacy policy, copyright, global free flow of information, cybersecurity, and innovation in the Internet economy".[72] After public consultation and symposiums regarding, *inter alia*, the role and responsibilities of internet intermediaries and experiences with DMCA NTD procedures, the task force presented a number of recommendations in three groups. One group of recommendations concerned "assessing and improving enforcement tools to combat online infringement and promote the growth of legitimate services while preserving the essential functioning of the Internet", and this included recommendations to establish a multi-stakeholder dialogue on how to improve the operation of the DMCA NTD system. The task force would also support and encourage "the development of appropriate voluntary private sector initiatives to improve online enforcement, and will monitor and evaluate the effectiveness of such initiatives to determine whether additional action should be considered".[73]

In 2013, the US Department of Commerce concluded that it was time "to assess whether the current balance of rights, exceptions and responsibilities is still working for creators, rights holders, service providers, and consumers". The task force concluded that the problems related to the DMCA NTD system "taken together may be undermining the benefits of the notice-and-takedown system".[74] As potential solutions, the report suggested, *inter alia*, creating best practices for NTD procedures to support a more efficient and reliable NTD system.[75] To this end, the task force intended to convene a multi-stakeholder dialogue involving right holders, ISPs, consumer representatives and companies in the business of identifying infringing content, in order to discuss improvements to the current NTD system.[76] A multi-stakeholder forum was subsequently

---

[72] See http://www.ntia.doc.gov/category/internet-policy-task-force (last visited 1 July 2015).

[73] Ibid., pp. 3–4.

[74] Ibid., p. 58.

[75] Ibid., p. 58.

[76] Ibid., p. 58.

established, and in a series of four roundtables the forum has duly discussed draft guidelines (best practice) for NTD procedures.[77]

4.3.3 Future perspectives

A possible correction of the autonomy spaces for N&A procedures must be expected to counterbalance the advantages of more effective enforcement of intellectual property rights by ISPs against the disadvantages represented by any increased disregard of procedural guarantees and the increased burden placed on ISPs by IPR enforcement. It is hard to imagine an extension of these autonomy spaces in the future based on present, ongoing political initiatives. It is more likely that legislators will limit the autonomy spaces by introducing additional demands on the ISPs – whether this involves increased ISP responsibility for liability avoidance or increased procedural guarantees in the implementation of N&A procedures. In each case, such amendments will raise the costs for ISPs in managing the procedures.

5. CONCLUDING REMARKS

The practical significance of N&A procedures has increased and it can be expected that this development will continue in the future. The procedures are prime examples of self-regulation which supplants State-enacted law. Yet they differ from many other forms of self-regulation in one important aspect: the groups primarily affected by N&A procedures, ISPs and the ISPs' customers, do not have a foundational, instigating demand for this regulatory model in the sense that the ISPs want as much freedom as possible in conducting their businesses, and their customers are the stakeholders who are "harmed by the actions" when the procedures are applied. It is a natural part of the business of ISPs to lay down terms and conditions for the use of their services, and N&A procedures are a sub-set of such terms and conditions. The risk of being held liable for infringements that take place in relation to the ISPs' services is the reason why they have incorporated N&A procedures into their terms and conditions, and the risk of being held liable is determined by the liability standard which is applicable to ISPs, in particular the safe harbour provisions of the DMCA.

This characteristic feature of N&A procedures as a mode of self-regulation has implications when it comes to applying the user generated

---

[77] See section 3 above. See also section 4.2 above concerning the recent hearing in the US House of Representatives.

law model. The primary driver for the emergence of N&A procedures is the State-enacted liability standard for ISPs rather than a demand for law among the persons affected by the law. Obviously, right holders derive benefits from a more effective enforcement of rights due to N&A procedures, but ISPs also expect benefits from implementing N&A procedures because the procedures shield them from liability. Accordingly, we can conclude that "expectation of benefits" is a driver for the emergence of N&A procedures, as well as "asymmetric information" which is reflected in the superior information that ISPs possess on the most cost effective procedures. We have found no evidence of one or more "lead users" who have been important for the emergence of N&A procedures, but the existence of such lead users cannot be precluded given the current lack of transparency.

Modified diffusion of N&A procedures can be said to occur since it appears that they are to some degree mainstreamed through voluntary soft law instruments and ongoing policy discussions.

Our study foregrounds two observations about evaluating N&A procedures in relation to the model of user generated law. First, technological and market conditions for internet-based business models change rapidly, which blurs the standard concept of "adoption" in user generated law terminology. A possible correction of the autonomy spaces is not likely to establish a final and permanent legal position. Arguably, the legal process might be more aptly characterized as a feedback loop which covers the ongoing interactions between the legal framework (autonomy spaces) established by State-enacted law and the user generated law.

Second, our study of N&A procedures highlights an important (often ignored) issue in user generated law, which is the legitimacy of the regulatory model in question.[78] The primary group of users affected by N&A consists of users of the internet services and this group is not directly involved in the development of the law. The potential lack of legitimacy in this form of user generated law emphasizes the need for statutory control in a field of law that otherwise concerns a balancing of private interests.

---

[78] Cf. Nicolas Suzor and Brian Fitzgerald, 'The Legitimacy of Graduated Response Schemes in Copyright Law' (2011) 34 *University of New South Wales Law Journal* 1, p. 40.

Bibliography

ABA, *Handbook on the Antitrust Aspects of Standards Setting* (American Bar Association, 2004).

Abbott, A., 'The Problem of Excess' (2014) 32 *Sociological Theory* 1.

Abbott, F. M., 'On the Duality of Internet Domain Names: Propertization and its Discontents' (2013) 3 *N.Y.U. Journal of Intellectual Property and Entertainment Law* 1.

Antonelli, C., 'Localized Technological Change and the Evolution of Standards as Economic Institutions' (1994) 6(3) *Information Economics and Policy* 195.

Aoki, R. and Schiff, A., 'Promoting Access to Intellectual Property: Patent Pools, Copyright Collectives and Clearinghouses' (2008) 38 *R&D Management* 198.

Aufderheide, P. and Jaszi, P., *Reclaiming Fair Use: How to put Balance Back in Copyright* (University of Chicago Press, 2011).

Aufderheide, P. and Jaszi, P., 'Fair Use and Best Practices: Surprising Success' (October 2007) *Intellectual Property Today* 26.

Aymé, S., Matthijs, G. and Soini, S., 'Patenting and Licensing in Genetic Testing – Recommendations of the European Society of Human Genetics' (2008) 16 *Eur. J. Hum. Genet.*, Suppl. 1, S3–9.

Bahadur, G. and Morrison, M., 'Patenting Human Pluripotent Cells: Balancing Commercial, Academic and Ethical Interests' (2010) 25 *Human Reproduction* 14.

Baron, J. and Pohlmann, T., 'Who Cooperates in Standards Consortia – Rivals or Complementors?' (2013) 9(4) *Journal of Competition Law and Economics* 905.

Baron, J., Ménière, Y. and Pohlmann, T., 'Joint Innovation in ICT Standards: How Consortia Drive the Volume of Patent Filings' (2012) CERNA Working Paper Series, 12-ME-03, http://www.law.northwestern.edu/research-faculty/searlecenter/innovationeconomics/documents/Standards_consortia_and_innovation_WP_2012.pdf.

Bekkers, R. and Liotard, I., 'European Standards for Mobile Communications: The Tense Relationship Between Standards and Intellectual Property Rights' (1999) *European Intellectual Property Review* 110.

Bekkers, R. and Updegrove, A. S., 'A Study of IPR Policies and Practices of a Representative Group of Standards Setting Organizations Worldwide' (17 September 2012), http://ssrn.com/abstract=2333445.

Benkler, Y., *The Wealth of Networks: How Social Production Transforms Markets and Freedom* (Yale University Press, 2006).

Bergman, K. and Graff, G. D., 'The Global Stem Cell Patent Landscape: Implications for Efficient Technology Transfer and Commercial Development' (2007) 25 *Nat. Biotechnol.* 419.

Bergström, S., 'Program för upphovsrätten', in *Rättsvetenskapliga studier ägnad minnet av Phillips Hult* (Almquist & Wiksell, 1960) 74.

Bergström, S., *Kollektivavtalslagen, studier över dess huvudprinciper* (Almquist & Wiksell, 1948).

Besen, S. and Kirby, S. N., *Compensating Creators of Intellectual Property, Collectives That Collect* (RAND Corporation, 1989).

Bettinger, T. (ed.), *Domain Name Law and Practice* (Oxford University Press, 2005).

Blair, R. and Cotter, T. F., *Intellectual Property. Economic and Legal Dimensions of Rights and Remedies* (Cambridge University Press, 2005).

Bohannan, C. and Hovenkamp, H., *Creation without Restraint: Promoting Liberty and Rivalry in Innovation* (Oxford University Press, 2011).

Bone, R. G., 'Decentralizing the Lawmaking Function: Private Lawmaking Markets and Intellectual Property Rights in Law' (2014) 38 *International Review of Law and Economics* 132.

Brenner, S., 'Optimal Formation Rules for Patent Pools' (2009) 40 *Economic Theory* 373.

Bridy, A., 'Graduated Response American Style. "Six Strikes" Measured Against Five Norms' (2012) 23 *Fordham Intellectual Property, Media & Entertainment Law Journal* 1.

Brooks, R. G. and Geradin, D., 'Taking Contracts Seriously: The Meaning of the Voluntary Commitment to License Essential Patents on "Fair and Reasonable" Terms' (12 March 2010), http://ssrn.com/abstract=1569498.

Burk, D. L., 'Cybermarks' (2010) 91 *Minnesota Law Review* 1375.

Burk, D. L., 'Trademarks along the Infobahn: A First Look at the Emerging Law of Cybermarks' (1995) 1 *Rich. J.L. & Tech.* 1.

Burk, D. L. and Lemley, M. A., *The Patent Crisis and How the Courts Can Solve It* (Chicago University Press, 2009).

Burton, S. J., 'Default Principles, Legitimacy, and the Authority of a Contract' (1993) 3 *S. Cal. Interdisc. L.J.* 115.

Capobianco, A., 'Licencing of Music Rights: Media Convergence, Technological Developments and EC Competition Law' (2004) *E.I.P.R.* 113.

Cargill, C. F., 'Why Standardization Efforts Fail' (2011) 14(1) *The Journal of Electronic Publishing* 31.

Cargill, C. F., *Information Technology Standardization: Theory, Process, and Organizations* (Digital Press, 1989).

Carrier, Michael A., *Innovation for the 21st Century: Harnessing the Power of Intellectual Property and Antitrust Law* (Oxford University Press, 2009).

Carrier, Michael A., 'Why Antitrust Should Defer to the Intellectual Property Rules of Standard-Setting Organizations: A Commentary on Teece and Sherry' (2003) 87 *Minnesota Law Review* 2019.

Caulfield, T., Cook-Deegan, R. M., Kieff, F. S. and Walsh, J. P., 'Evidence and Anecdotes: An Analysis of Human Gene Patenting Controversies' (2006) 24 *Nat. Biotechnol.* 1091.

Chesbrough, H., *Open Business Models: How to Thrive in the New Innovation Landscape* (Harvard Business School Press, 2006).

Chesbrough, H., *Open Innovation: The New Imperative for Creating and Profiting from Technology* (Harvard Business School Press, 2006).

Chesbrough, H., 'The Era of Open Innovation' (2003) 44 *MIT Sloan Man. Rev.* 35.

Chesbrough, H., Vanhaverbeke, W. and West, J., *New Frontiers in Open Innovation* (Oxford University Press, 2014).

Chesbrough, H., Vanhaverbeke, W. and West, J., *Open Innovation: Researching a New Paradigm* (Oxford University Press, 2008).

Christie, A., Waller, S. and Weatherall, K., 'Exporting the DMCA through Free Trade Agreements', in Christopher Heath and Anselm Kamperman Sanders (eds), *Intellectual Property and Free Trade Agreements* (Hart Publishing, 2007) 211.

Clark, J., Piccolo, J., Stanton, B. and Tyson, K., *Patent Pools: A Solution to the Problem of Access in Biotechnology Patents?* (USPTO, 5 December 2000).

Cohen, J. E., 'Copyright as Property in the Post-Industrial Economy: A Research Agenda' (2011) *Wisc. L. Rev.* 141.

Cook-Deegan, R., DeRienzo, C., Carbone, J., Chandrasekharan, S., Heaney, C. and Conover, C., 'Impact of Gene Patents and Licensing Practices on Access to Genetic Testing for Inherited Susceptibility to Cancer: Comparing Breast and Ovarian Cancers with Colon Cancers' (2010) 12 *Genet. Med.*, Suppl. S15.

Cordes, A., 'The Search for a Medieval *Lex Mercatoria*', (2003) *Oxford University Comparative Law Forum* 1.

Cotter, T. F., *Comparative Patent Remedies: A Legal and Economic Analysis* (Oxford University Press, 2013).

Cotter, T. F., 'The Comparative Law and Economics of Standard-Essential Patents and FRAND Royalties' (2013) Minnesota Legal Studies Research Paper, No. 13-40.

Dahin, V., 'The Future of Legal Online Music Services in the European Union: A Review of the EU Commission's Recent Initiatives in Cross-Border Copyright Management' (2010) 32(5) *E.I.P.R.* 223.

David, P. A. and Greenstein, S., 'The Economics of Compatibility Standards: An Introduction to Recent Research' (1990) 1(1–2) *Economics of Innovation and New Technology* 3.

David, P. A. and Monroe, H. K., 'Standards Development Strategies under Incomplete Information: Isn't the "Battle of the Sexes" Really a Revelation Game?' (1994) 2 *Merit Research Memoranda* 39.

De Vries, H. J., *Standardization – A Business Approach to the Role of National Standardization Organizations* (Springer, 1999).

Department of Commerce, Internet Policy Task Force, *Copyright Policy, Creativity, and Innovation in the Digital Economy* (July 2013).

Donaldson, Michael C., 'Fair Use: What a Difference a Decade Makes' (2010) 57 *J. Copyright Soc'y U.S.A.* 331.

Drahozal, C. R., 'Contracting out of National Law: An Empirical Look at the New Law Merchant' (2004–2005) 80 *Notre Dame Law Review* 523.

Drexl, J., 'Abuse of Dominance in Licensing and Refusal to License: A More Economic Approach to Competition by Imitation and to Competition by Substitution', in C. Ehlermann and I. Atanasiu (eds), *European Competition Law Annual 2005: The Interaction Between Competition Law and Intellectual Property Law* (Hart Publishing, 2007) 650.

Drexl, J., 'Competition in the Field of Collective Management: Preferring "Creative Competition" to Allocative Efficiency in European Copyright Law', in P. Torremans (ed.), *Copyright Law, Handbook of Contemporary Research* (Edward Elgar Publishing, 2007) 255.

Drexl, J. et al., 'Comments of the Max Planck Institute for Intellectual Property and Competition Law on the Proposal for a Directive of the European Parliament and of the Council on Collective Management of Copyright and Related Rights and Multi-Territorial Licensing of Rights in Musical Works for Online Uses in the Internal Market COM (2012)372' (2013) *International Review of Intellectual Property and Competition Law* 322.

Dykman, H. T., 'Patent Licensing within The Manufacturer's Aircraft Association (MAA)' (1964) 46 *J. Pat. Off. Soc'y* 646.

Ebersole, T. J., Guthrie, M. C. and Goldstein, J. A., 'Patent Pools and Standard Setting in Diagnostic Genetics' (2005) 23 *Nat. Biotechnol.* 937.

Ellickson, R., 'How Norm Entrepreneurs and Membership Associations Contribute to Private Ordering: A Response to Fagundes' (2012) 90 *Texas Law Review* 247.

Fagundes, D., 'Norms-Based Regulation of Intellectual Property: The Case of Roller Derby Pseudonyms' (2012) 90 *Texas Law Review* 1093.

Fagundes, D., 'The Varieties of Motivation and the Problem of Supply: A Reply to Professor Ellickson' (2012) 90 *Texas Law Review* 311.

Farber, D. and Baran, P., 'The Convergence of Computing and Telecommunications Systems' (1977) 195(4283) *Science* 1166.

Farrand, B., *Networks of Power in Digital Copyright Law and Policy, Political Salience, Expertise and the Legislative Process* (Routledge, 2014).

Farrow, T. C. W., *Civil Justice, Privatization, and Democracy* (University of Toronto Press, 2014).

Fauchart, E. and von Hippel, E., 'Norms-Based Intellectual Property Systems: The Case of French Chefs' MIT Sloan Working Paper 4576-06 (January 2006).

Frischmann, B. M., *Infrastructure: The Social Value of Shared Resources* (Oxford University Press, 2012).

Frischmann, B. M., Madison, M. J. and Strandburg, K. J. (eds), *Governing Knowledge Commons* (Oxford University Press, 2014).

Gabuzda, L. R. et al., *Standard-Essential Patents and Injunctive Relief* (April Jones Day Law Firm Publications, 2013), http://www.jonesday.com/standards-essential_patents/.

Galetovic, A. et al., 'Patent Holdup: Do Patent Holders Holdup Innovation?' IP² Working Paper Series No. 14011, http://hooverip2.org/working-paper/14011/.

Gauch, S. and Blind, K., 'Technological Convergence and the Absorptive Capacity of Standardization' (2015) 91 *Technological Forecasting and Social Change* 236.

Geist, M., 'Fair.com?: An Examination of the Allegations of Systemic Unfairness in the ICANN UDRP' (2001) 27 *Brook. J. Int'l L.* 903.

Geradin, D., 'Standardization and Technological Innovation: Some Reflections on Ex-Ante Licensing, FRAND, and the Proper Means to Reward Innovators' (2006) TILEC Discussion Paper No. 2006-017.

Geradin, D., Layne-Farrar, A. and Padilla, J., 'The Complements Problem within Standard Setting: Assessing the Evidence on Royalty Stacking' (2008) 14(2) *B.U.J. Sci. and Tech. L.* 144.

Gervais, D., *Application of an Extended Collective Licensing Regime in Canada: Principles and Issues Related to Implementation, Study Prepared for the Department of Canadian Heritage 40* (June 2003).

Ghafele, R., 'Europe's Lost Royalty Opportunity: A Comparison of Potential and Existing Digital Music Royalty Markets in Ten Different E.U. Member States' (2015) 11(2) *Review of Economic Research on Copyright Issues* 60.

Giblin, R., 'Evaluating Graduated Response' (2014) 37 *Columbia Journal of Law & the Arts* 147.

Gibson, J., 'Risk Aversion and Rights Accretion in Intellectual Property Law' (2007) 116 *Yale L.J.* 882.

Gilbert, R. J., 'Antitrust for Patent Pools: A Century of Policy Evolution' (2004) *Stan. Tech. L. Rev.* 3.

Gilliéron, P., 'Collecting Societies and the Digital Environment' (2006) *International Review of Intellectual Property and Competition Law* 939.

Graham, I., Spinardi, G., Williams, R. and Ivebster, J., 'The Dynamics of EDI Standards Development' (1995) 7(1) *Technology Analysis and Strategic Management* 3.

Grassler, F. and Capria, M. A., 'Patent Pooling: Uncorking a Technology Transfer Bottleneck and Creating Value in the Biomedical Research Field' (2003) 9 *J. Comm. Biotechnol.* 111.

Greene, H., 'Patent Pooling Behind the Veil of Uncertainty: Antitrust, Competition Policy, and the Vaccine Industry' (2010) 90 *Bost. U. L. Rev.* 1397.

Greenstein, S. and Bresnahan, T. F., 'Technical Progress and Co-Invention in Computing and in the Uses of Computers' (1996) *Brookings Papers on Economic Activity* 7.

Grindley, P., Salant, D. J. and Waverman, L., 'Standards Wars: The Uses of Standard Setting as a Means of Facilitating Cartels: Third Generation Wireless Telecommunications Standard Setting' (Summer 1999) 3 *International Journal of Commercial Law and Policy* 2.

Grøtnes, E., 'IFIP International Federation for Information Processing', in G. León, A. Bernardos, J. Casar, K. Kautz and J. DeGross, *Open IT-Based Innovation: Moving Towards Cooperative IT Transfer and Knowledge Diffusion*, Vol. 287 (Springer, 2008), pp. 343–59.

Guilbault, L., 'The Draft Collective Management Directive', in Irini Stamatoudi and Paul Torremans (eds), *EU Copyright Law: A Commentary* (Edward Elgar Publishing, 2014) Chapter 14.

Guilbault, L. and van Gompel, S., 'Collective Management in the European Union', in Daniel Gervais (ed.), *Collective Management of Copyright and Related Rights* (Kluwer Law International, 2010).

Gyertyánfy, P., 'Collective Management of Music Rights in Europe After the CISAC Decision' (2010) *International Review of Intellectual Property and Competition Law* 59.

Hadfield, G. K., 'Legal Infrastructure and the New Economy' (2012) 8 I/S *A Journal of Law and Policy for the Information Society* 1.

Hadfield, G. K., 'Producing Law for Innovation', in Kauffman Task Force on Law, Innovation and Growth, *Rules for Growth* (2011) 36.

Hadfield, G. K., 'Privatizing Commercial Law' (Spring 2001) *Regulation Magazine* 40.

Hadfield, G. K. and Weingast, B. R., 'What is Law? A Coordination Account of the Characteristics of Legal Order' (2012) 4 *J. Legal Analysis* 471.

Handke, C. and Towse, R., 'Economics of Copyright Collecting Societies' (2007) 38 *International Review of Intellectual Property and Competition Law* 937.

Hansen, G. and Schmidt-Bischoffshausen, A., *Economic Functions of Collecting Societies – Collective Rights Management in the Light of Transaction Cost and Information Economics* (Max Planck Institute for Intellectual Property, Competition and Tax Law, 2007).

Hardin, G., 'The Tragedy of the Commons' (1968) 162(3859) *Science* 1243.

Helfer, L. R., 'International Dispute Settlement at the Trademark-Domain Name Interface' (2001) 29 *Pepperdine Law Review* 87.

Helfer, L. R. and Dinwoodie G. B, 'Designing Non-National Systems: The Case of the Uniform Domain Name Dispute Resolution Policy' (2001) 43 *Wm. & Mary L. Rev.* 141.

Heller, Michael A. and Eisenberg, Rebecca S., 'Can Patents Deter Innovation? The Anticommons in Biomedical Research' (1998) 28 *Science* 698.

Horn, L., 'Case 1. The MPEG LA Licensing Model. What Problem does it solve in Biopharma and Genetics?', in G. Van Overwalle (ed.), *Gene Patents and Collaborative Licensing Models: Patent Pools, Clearinghouses, Open Source Models and Liability Regimes* (Cambridge University Press, 2009) 33.

Horn, L., 'Alternative Approaches to IP Management: One-Stop Technology Platform Licensing' (2003) 9 *Journal of Commercial Biotechnology* 119.

Hovenkamp, H. and Lemley, M. A., *IP and Antitrust: An Analysis of Antitrust Principles Applied to Intellectual Property Law* (Aspen Publishers Online, 2009).

Hugenholtz, P. B., 'Codes of Conduct and Copyright Enforcement in Cyberspace', in Irini Stamatoudi (ed.), *Copyright Enforcement and the Internet* (Wolters Kluwer, 2010) 303.

Huys, I., Berthels, N., Matthij, G. and Van Overwalle, G., 'Legal Uncertainty in the Area of Genetic Diagnostic Testing' (2010) 27 Nat. Biotechnol., 903.

Iversen, E. J., 'Standardization and Intellectual Property Rights: ETSI's Controversial Search for New IPR-Procedures' (2000) *Informatik* IV.

Jakobs, K., *Information Communication Technology Standardization for E-Business Sectors: Integrating Supply and Demand Factors* (IGI Global, 2009).

Jakobs, K., *Standardization Research in Information Technology: New Perspectives* (IGI Global, 2008).

Jaszi, P., 'Getting to Best Practices – A Personal Voyage Around Fair Use' (2010) 57 *J. Copyright Soc'y U.S.A.* 315.

Jehoram, H. C., 'The Future of Copyright Collecting Societies' (2001) 23 *European Intellectual Property Review* 134.

Johnson, J. P., 'Open Source Software', in Martin Peitz and Joel Waldfogel (eds), *The Oxford Handbook of the Digital Economy* (Oxford University Press, 2012) 461.

Kahan, M. and Klausner, M., 'Standardization and Innovation in Corporate Contracting (Or "The Economics of Boilerplate")' (1997) 83 *Virginia L. Rev.* 713.

Kai, J., *Information Communication Technology Standardization for E-Business Sectors: Integrating Supply and Demand Factors* (IGI Global, 2009).

Kai, J. (ed.), *Standardization Research in Information Technology: New Perspectives* (IGI Global, 2008).

Karnell, G., 'Outsiders' Rights: A Dilemma for Collective Administration of Authors' Rights in a Present and Enlarged European Community' (1991) 13 *European Intellectual Property Review* 431.

Karnell, G., 'Avtalslicenskonstruktionen, principiella och praktiska frågor' (1981) 50 *Nordiskt Immateriellt Rättsskydd* 255.

Karnell, G. W. G., 'Protection of Layout Designs (Topographies) of Integrated Circuits – R.I.P.?' (2001) *International Review of Intellectual Property and Competition Law* 648.

Katz, A., 'Open Everything', in Noam Shemtov and Ian Walden (eds), *Free and Open Source Software* (Oxford University Press, 2013) 439.

Katz, A., 'The Potential Demise of Another Natural Monopoly: New Technologies and the Administration of Performance Rights' (2006) 2(2) *Journal of Competition Law and Economics* 245.

Katznelson, R. D. and Howells, J., 'The Myth of the Early Aviation Patent Hold-Up – How a U.S. Government Monopsony Commandeered Pioneer Airplane Patents' (2015) 24 *Industrial and Corporate Change* 1.

KEA European Affairs, *Licensing Music Works and Transaction Costs in Europe*, Final study (September 2012).

Kelty, C. M., 'Conceiving Open Systems' (2009) 30 *Wash. U. J. L. and Pol'y.* 139.

Kelty, C. M., *Two Bits: The Cultural Significance of Free Software* (Duke University Press, 2008).

Kesan, J. P., 'The Fallacy of OSS Discrimination by FRAND Licensing: An Empirical Analysis' (2011) Illinois Public Law Research Paper, No. 10-14, http://ssrn.com/abstract=1767083.

Kesan, J. P. and Gallo, A. A., 'The Market for Private Dispute Resolution Services – An Empirical Re-Assessment of ICANN-UDRP Performance' (2005) Law and Economics Working Papers, Paper 22.

Kieff, S. and Layne-Farrar, A., 'Incentive Effects from Different Approaches to Holdup Mitigation Surrounding Patent Remedies and Standard-Setting Organizations' (2013) 9(2) *Journal of Competition Law and Economics* 1091.

Kindleberger, C. P., 'Standards as Public, Collective and Private Goods' (1983) 36(3) *Kyklos* 377.

Kobayashi, B. H. and Ribstein, L. E., 'Law as Product and Byproduct' (2013) 9 *Journal of Law, Economics and Policy* 521.

Kobayashi, B. H. and Ribstein, L. E., 'Law as a Byproduct: Theories of Private Law Production', Illinois Law, Behavior and Social Science Research Papers Series, Research Paper No. LBSS11-27, 3.

Kobayashi, B. H. and Wright, J. D., *Federalism, Substantive Preemption, and Limits to Antitrust* (Cambridge University Press, 2011).

Krattiger, A. F., 'Financing the Bioindustry and Facilitating Biotechnology Transfer' (2004) *IP Strategy Today*, No. 8-2004.

Kretschmer, M., 'The Failure of Property Rules in Collective Administration: Rethinking Copyright Societies as Regulatory Instruments' (2002) 24 *European Intellectual Property Review* 126.

Kuhn, K., Morton, F. S. and Shelanski, H., 'Standard Setting Organizations Can Help Solve the Standard Essential Patents Licensing Problem' (2013) 5 *CPI Antitrust Chronicle* (Special Issue).

Kur, A., *UDRP: A Study by the Max Planck Institute for Foreign and International Patent, Copyright and Competition Law* (Max Planck Institute, 2002).

Kur, A. and Schovsbo, J., 'Expropriation or Fair Game for All? The Gradual Dismantling of the IP Exclusivity Paradigm', in Max Planck Institute for Intellectual Property, Competition and Tax Law, Research Paper No. 09-14 (2009), http://ssrn.com/abstract=1508330 or http://dx.doi.org/10.2139/ssrn.1508330.

LaFrance, M., 'Graduated Response by Industry Compact: Piercing the Black Box' (2012) 30 *Cardozo Arts & Entertainment Law Journal* 165.

Layne-Farrar, A., 'Moving Past the SEP RAND Obsession: Some Thoughts on the Economic Implications of Unilateral Commitments and the Complexities of Patent Licensing' (2014) 21 *Geo. Mason L. Rev.* 1093.

Layne-Farrar, A., 'Proactive or Reactive? An Empirical Assessment of IPR Policy Revisions in the Wake of Antitrust Actions' (2014) 59(2) *The Antitrust Bulletin* 373.

Layne-Farrar, A., 'The Brothers Grimm Book of Business Models: A Survey of Literature and Developments in Patent Acquisition and Litigation' (2012) 9(1) *J.L. Econ. and Pol'y.* 29.

Layne-Farrar, A., *Viewpoint: What the Rambus Ruling Means for Intellectual Property in Standard Setting* (eSapience Center for Competition Policy, 2007).

Layne-Farrar, A., Llobet, G. and Padilla, J., 'Payments and Participation: The Incentives to Join Cooperative Standard Setting Efforts' (2014) 23(1) *Journal of Economics and Management Strategy*, http://onlinelibrary.wiley.com/doi/10.1111/jems.12046/abstract.

Layne-Farrar, A., Llobet, G. and Padilla, J., 'Preventing Patent Hold Up: An Economic Assessment of Ex Ante Licensing Negotiations in Standard Setting' (5 May 2008), http://ssrn.com/abstract=1129551 or http://dx.doi.org/10.2139/ssrn.1129551.

Lemley, M. A., 'IP in a World Without Scarcity' (2015) 90 *N.Y.U. L. Rev.* 460.

Lemley, M. A., 'Rationalizing Internet Safe Harbors' (2007) 6 *J. on Telecomm. & High Tech. L.* 115.

Lemley, Mark and Shapiro, Carl, 'A Simple Approach to Setting Reasonable Royalties for Standard-Essential Patents' (2013) 28 *Berkeley Technology Law Journal* 1135.

Lerner, J. and Tirole, J., 'A Model of Forum Shopping' (2006) 96 *The American Economic Review* 1091.

Lerner, J. and Tirole, J., 'Efficient Patent Pools' (2004) 94 *The American Economic Review* 691.

Lerner, J., Strojwas, M. and Tirole, J., 'The Design of Patent Pools: The Determinants of Licensing Rules' (2007) 38 *The RAND Journal of Economics* 610.

Lessig, L., *Remix: Making Art and Commerce Thrive in the Hybrid Economy* (Penguin Press, 2008).

Lewis, D. K., *Convention: A Philosophical Study* (Harvard University Press, 1969).

Lindsay, D., *International Domain Name Law – ICANN and the UDRP* (Hart Publishing, 2007).

Loshin, J., 'Secrets Revealed: Protecting Magicians' Intellectual Property without Law', in Christine A. Corcos (ed.), *Law and Magic. A Collection of Essays* (Carolina Academic Press, 2010) 123.

Lüder, T., 'The First Experience with EU-Wide Online Music Licensing' (2007) *GRUR Int.* 649.

Lundqvist, B., 'The Interface between EU Competition Law and Standard Essential Patents – From Orange-Book-Standard to the Huawei Case' (2015) 11 *European Competition Journal* 367.

Lundqvist, B., *Standardization under EU Competition Rules and US Antitrust Laws – The Rise and the Limits of Self-Regulation* (Edward Elgar Publishing, 2014).

Madison, Michael J., 'Commons at the Intersection of Peer Production, Citizen Science, and Big Data: Galaxy Zoo', in B. M. Frischmann, M. J. Madison and K. J. Strandburg, *Governing Knowledge Commons* (Oxford University Press, 2014).

Madison, Michael J., 'Creativity and Craft', in Shubha Ghosh and Robin Paul Malloy (eds), *Creativity, Law, and Entrepreneurship* (Edward Elgar Publishing, 2011).

Madison, Michael J., 'Some Optimism About Fair Use and Copyright Law' (2010) 57 *J. Copyright Soc'y U.S.A* 351.

Madison, Michael J., 'Of Coase and Comics, or, the Comedy of Copyright' (2009) 95 *Va. L. Rev. In Brief* 27.

Madison, Michael J., 'A Pattern-Oriented Approach to Fair Use' (2004) 45 *Wm. and Mary L. Rev.* 1525.

Madison, Michael J., 'Reconstructing the Software License' (2003) 35 *Loy. U. Chi. L.J.* 275.

Madison, Michael J., Frischmann, Brett M. and Strandburg, Katherine J., 'Constructing Commons in the Cultural Environment' (2010) 95 *Cornell L. Rev.* 657.

Mazziotti, G., 'New Licensing Models for Online Music Services in the European Union: From Collective to Customized Management', Columbia (2011) Public Law Research Paper No. 11-269.

McAdams, R. H., 'A Focal Point Theory of Expressive Law' (2000) 86 *Virginia Law Review* 1649.

McCracken, G., *Plenitude 2.0 – Culture By Commotion* (rev. edn, Periph.: Fluide, 1998).

McCracken, G., 'The Politics of Plenitude' (1998) *Reason* (August/September), http://reason.com/archives/1998/08/01/the-politics-of-plenitude.

McDonagh, L., 'Copyright, Contract, and FOSS', in Noam Shemtov and Ian Walden (eds), *Free and Open Source Software* (Oxford University Press, 2013).

McFarlane, G., *Copyright: The Development and Exercise of The Performing Rights* (John Offord, 1980).

McMeekin, A., Tomlinson, M., Green, K. and Walsh, V., *Innovation by Demand: An Interdisciplinary Approach to the Study of Demand and Its Role in Innovation* (Manchester University Press, 2010).

Merges, R. P., 'From Medieval Guilds to Open Source Software: Informal Norms, Appropriability Institutions, and Innovation' (13 November 2004), http://ssrn.com/abstract=661543 or http://dx.doi.org/10.2139/ssrn.661543, p. 19.

Merges, R. P., 'Institutions for Intellectual Property Transactions: The Case of Patent Pools', in Rochelle Dreyfuss, Dianne Zimmerman and Harry First (eds), *Expanding the Boundaries of Intellectual Property:*

Innovation Policy for the Knowledge Society (Oxford University Press, 2001) 123.

Merges, R. P., 'Contracting into Liability Rules: Intellectual Property Rights and Collective Rights Organizations' (1996) 84 *Cal. L. Rev.* 1293.

Michaels, R., 'The Mirage of Non-State Governance' (2010) *Utah Law Review* 31.

Minssen, T., Rutz, B. and van Zimmeren, E., 'Synthetic Biology and Intellectual Property Rights: Six Recommendations – Report from the IP Expert Meeting at the Danish Agency for Science, Technology & Innovation' (2015) 10 *Biotechnol. J.* 236.

Møgelvang-Hansen, P., Riis, T. and Trzaskowski, J., *Markedsførings-retten* (Ex Tuto Publishing, 2nd edn, 2011).

Mossoff, A., 'The Rise and Fall of the First American Patent Thicket: The Sewing Machine War of the 1850s' (2011) 53 *Arizona L. Rev.* 165.

Mueller, M. L., *Networks and States – The Global Politics of Internet Governance* (The MIT Press, 2010).

Müller, F., *Apple's Latest Patent Foe: The World Wide Web Consortium BM Breaks the Taboo and Betrays its Promise to the FOSS Community, FOSS Patents Blog*, http://www.fosspatents.com/2011/07/apples-latest-patent-foe-world-wide-web.html.

Müller, F., *Europe's Friend FRAND, FOSS Patents Blog*, http://www.fosspatents.com/2010/10/europes-friend-frand.html.

Müller, F., *IBM Breaks the Taboo and Betrays its Promise to the FOSS Community, FOSS Patents Blog*, http://www.fosspatents.com/2010/04/ibm-breaks-taboo-and-betrays-its.html.

Mutkoski, S., *Government Procurement Policy, Patent Royalties and the Myth of 'Discrimination' Against Free and Open Source Software Developers* (26 October 2011), http://papers.ssrn.com/sol3/papers.cfm?abstract_id=1949832.

Nagaoka, S., and Nishimura, Y., *An Empirical Assessment of the Effects of Patent Thickets* (SPRU 40th Anniversary Conference, The Future of Science, Technology and Innovation Policy, 11–13 September 2006, University of Sussex, SPRU-Science & Technology Policy Research), http://www.sussex.ac.uk/Units/spru/events/ocs/viewpaper.php?id=32.

Nathenson, I. S., 'Civil Procedures for a World of Shared and User-Generated Content' (2010) 48 *University of Louisville Law Review* 911.

Nguyen, G. D., Dejean, S. and Moreau, F., 'Are Streaming and Other Music Consumption Modes Substitutes or Complements?' (2012), http://ssrn.com/abstract=2025071.

Nicol, D. and Hope, J., 'Cooperative Strategies for Facilitating Use of Patented Inventions in Biotechnology' (2006) 24 *Law in Context* 85.

Noehrenberg, E., 'Implications of Patent Pools on Innovation Regarding Antiretrovirals' (2010) 4 *Open AIDS Journal* 67.

O'Hara, E. A. and Ribstein, L. E., *The Law Market* (Oxford University Press, 2009).

Ogus, A., 'Competition between National Legal Systems. A Contribution for Economic Analysis to Comparative Law' (1999) 48 *The International and Comparative Law Quarterly* 405.

Ogus, A., *Regulation. Legal Form and Economic Theory* (Clarendon Press, 1994).

Oliar, D. and Sprigman, C., 'There's no Free Laugh (Anymore): The Emergence of Intellectual Property Norms in Stand-Up Comedy' (2008) 94 *Virginia Law Review* 1787.

Organisation for Economic Co-operation and Development (OECD), *The Role of Internet Intermediaries in Advancing Public Policy Objectives* (OECD Publishing, 2011).

Organisation for Economic Co-operation and Development (OECD), 'Guidelines for the Licensing of Genetic Inventions' (OECD Publishing, 2006).

Ostrom, E., *Understanding Institutional Diversity* (Princeton University Press, 2005).

Ostrom, E., *Governing the Commons: The Evolution of Institutions for Collective Action* (Cambridge University Press, 1990).

Patry, W., *Moral Panics and the Copyright Wars* (Oxford University Press, 2009).

Perzanowski, A., 'Tattoos and IP Norms' (2013) 98 *Minnesota Law Review* 511.

Perzanowski, A. and Darling, K. (eds), *Creativity Without Law: How Communities and Markets Challenge the Assumptions of Intellectual Property* (NYU Press, forthcoming).

Quintais, J. P., 'Proposal for a Directive on Collective Rights Management and (Some) Multi-Territorial Licensing' (2013) *European Intellectual Property Review* 65.

Raustiala, K. and Sprigman, C., *The Knockoff Economy: How Imitation Sparks Innovation* (Oxford University Press, 2012).

Raustiala, K. and Sprigman, C., 'The Piracy Paradox: Innovation and Intellectual Property in Fashion Design' (2006) 92 *Virginia Law Review* 1687.

Reich, N., 'Competition between Legal Orders: A New Paradigm of EC Law?' (1992) 29 *Common Market Law Review* 861.

Resnik, J., 'The Democracy of Courts: Jeremy Bentham, "Publicity", and the Privatization of Process in the Twenty-First Century' (2013) *NoFo (No Foundations)* 10.

Riccio, G. M. and Codiglione, G., 'Copyright Collecting Societies, Monopolistic Positions and Competition in the EU Single Market' (2014) 7 *Masaryk U.J.L. Tech.* 287.

Riis, T., 'Collecting Societies, Competition, and the Services Directive' (2011) 6(7) *Journal of Intellectual Property Law & Policy* 482.

Riis, T. and Schovsbo, J., 'Extended Collective Licenses in Action' (2012) 43 *International Review of Intellectual Property and Competition Law* 930.

Riis, T. and Schovsbo, J., 'Extended Collective Licenses and the Nordic Experience: It's a Hybrid but Is It a Volvo or a Lemon?' (2010) 33 *Colum. J. L. & Arts* 471.

Rognstad, O., 'Avtalelisens som nordisk løsningsmodell' (2012) 82 *Nordiskt Immateriellt Rättsskydd* 620.

Rognstad, O., 'Avtalelisenser' (2004) 73 *Nordiskt Immateriellt Rättsskydd* 152.

Romer, P. M., 'Process, Responsibility, and Myron's Law', in Olivier J. Blanchard, David Romer, Michael Spence and Joseph E. Stiglitz (eds), *In the Wake of the Crisis: Leading Economists Reassess Economic Policy* (MIT Press, 2012) 112.

Rose, C. M., 'Game Stories' (2010) 22 *Yale Journal of Law and the Humanities* 369.

Rosenthal, J., 'Best Practices' (2010) 57 *J. Copyright Soc'y U.S.A.* 389.

Rothman, J. E., 'Best Intentions: Reconsidering Best Practices Statements in the Context of Fair Use and Copyright Law' (2010) 57 *J. Copyright Soc'y U.S.A.* 371.

Roy, A., 'Reflections on the Uniform Domain Name Dispute Resolution Policy as it Enters its Second Decade' (2012) 1(1) *Int. J. Technology Policy and Law* 20.

Rysman, M. and Simcoe, T., 'Patents and the Performance of Voluntary Standard Setting Organizations' (2008) 54(11) *Management Science* 1920.

Schelling, T. C., *The Strategy of Conflict* (Harvard University Press, 1960).

Schovsbo, J., 'The Necessity to Collectivize Copyright – And Dangers Thereof', in Jan Rosén (ed.), *Individualism and Collectiveness in Intellectual Property Law* (Edward Elgar Publishing, 2012) 166.

Schultz, T., 'Carving up the Internet: Jurisdiction, Legal Orders, and the Private/Public International Law Interface' (2008) 19(4) *The European Journal of International Law* 799.

Schultz, T., 'Private Legal Systems: What Cyberspace Might Teach Legal Theorists' (2007) 10 *Yale Journal of Law and Technology* 151.

Schweik, C. M. and English, R. C., *Internet Success: A Study of Open-Source Software Commons* (MIT Press, 2012).

Schwemer, S. F., 'The Licensing of Online Music Streaming Services in Europe', in Richard Watt (ed.), *Handbook of the Economics of Copyright, A Guide for Students and Teachers* (Edward Elgar Publishing, 2014) 141.

Scott, J. C., *Seeing Like a State: How Certain Schemes to Improve the Human Condition Have Failed* (Yale University Press, 1998).

Seltzer, W., 'Free Speech Unmoored in Copyright's Safe Harbor: Chilling Effects of the DMCA on the First Amendment' (2010) 24(1) *Harvard Journal of Law & Technology* 171.

Seng, D., 'The State of the Discordant Union: An Empirical Analysis of DMCA Takedown Notices' (2014) 18 *Va. J. L. & Tech.* 369.

Seo, D., *Evolution and Standardization of Mobile Communications Technology* (IGI Global, 2013).

Shapiro, C., 'Navigating the Patent Thicket: Cross Licenses, Patent Pools and Standard Setting', in Adam B. Jaffe, J. Lerner and S. Stern (eds), *Innovation Policy and the Economy* (MIT Press, 2001) 119.

Shapiro, C., 'Navigating the Patent Thicket: Cross Licenses, Patent Pools, and Standard Setting' (2001) 1 *Innovation Policy and the Economy* 119.

Sharrock, L. M., 'The Future of Domain Name Dispute Resolution: Crafting Practical International Legal Solutions from Within the UDRP Framework' (2001) 51 *Duke Law Journal* 817.

Sherif, Mostafa H. and Sparrell, Duncan K., 'Standards and Innovation in Telecommunications' (1992) 30(7) *IEEE Communications Magazine* 22.

Siebrasse, N. and Cotter, T. F., 'A New Framework for Determining Reasonable Royalties in Patent Litigation' (2014) Minnesota Legal Studies Research Paper No. 14-45, http://papers.ssrn.com/sol3/papers.cfm?abstract_id=2528616.

Simcoe, T., 'Governing the Anticommons: Institutional Design for Standard-Setting Organizations' (2014) 14(1) *Innovation Policy and the Economy* 99.

Simcoe, T., 'Explaining the Increase in Intellectual Property Disclosure' (1 December 2005), http://ssrn.com/abstract=1396332.

Six, B., van Zimmeren, E., Popa, F. and Frison, C., 'Trust and Social Capital in the Design and Evolution of Institutions for Collective Action' (2015) 9 *International Journal of the Commons* 151, http://www.thecommonsjournal.org/index.php/ijc/article/view/435.

Smits, J. M., 'Private Law 2.0: On the Role of Private Actors in a Post-National Society' (30 November 2010). Hague Institute for the Internationalisation of Law and Eleven International Publishing, 2011; Maastricht Faculty of Law, http://ssrn.com/abstract=1779042.

Solomon, J. M., 'New Governance, Preemptive Self-Regulation, and the Blurring of Boundaries in Regulatory Theory and Practice' (2010) *Wisconsin Law Review* 591.

Solum, L. B., 'Procedural Justice' (2004) 78 *Southern California Law Review* 181.

Spruyt, H., 'The Supply and Demand of Governance in Standard-Setting: Insights from the Past' (2001) 8(3) *Journal of European Public Policy* 371.

Spulber, D. F. and Yoo, C. S., 'Network Regulation: The Many Faces of Access' (2005) 1(4) *Journal of Competition Law and Policy* 648.

Strandburg, K. J., 'Legal But Unacceptable: Pallin v. Singer and Physician Patenting Norms', in R. C. Dreyfuss and J. C. Ginsburg (eds), *Intellectual Property at the Edge: The Contested Contours of IP* (Cambridge University Press, 2014) 321.

Strandburg, K. J., 'Users as Innovators: Implications for Patent Doctrine' (2008) 79 *University of Colorado Law Review* 467.

Sunstein, C. R., 'Social Norms and Social Roles' (1996) 96 *Columbia Law Review* 903.

Suzor, N. and Fitzgerald, B., 'The Legitimacy of Graduated Response Schemes in Copyright Law' (2011) 34(1) *University of New South Wales Law Journal* 1.

Svobodová, I., 'Seeking Injunctions in SEPs' Infringement Proceedings as an Abuse of Dominant Position under Article 102 TFEU', Master's thesis.

Teece, D. J. and Sherry, E., 'Standards Setting and Antitrust' (2003) 87 *Minnesota Law Review* 1911.

Teubner, G., 'Breaking Frames: The Global Interplay of Legal and Social Systems' (1997) 45 *American Journal of Comparative Law* 149.

The Department of Commerce, Internet Policy Task Force, *Copyright Policy, Creativity, and Innovation in the Digital Economy* (July 2013).

Tirole, J. and Rochet, J., 'Platform Competition in Two-Sided Markets' (2003) 1 *Journal of the European Economic Association* 990.

Towse, R., 'Economics of Copyright Collecting Societies and Digital Rights: Is There a Case for a Centralised Digital Copyright Exchange?' (2012) 9(2) *Review of Economic Research in Copyright Issues* 3.

Trakman, L. E., 'From the Medieval Law Merchant to E-Merchant Law' (2003) 53 *University of Toronto Law Journal* 265.

Trumpke, F., 'The Extended Collective License – A Matter of Exclusivity' (2012) 82 *Nordiskt Immateriellt Rättsskydd* 264.

Tsai, C., 'The Trademark/Domain Name Protection War: A Comparative Study of the U.S., UDRP and Taiwanese Law' (2013) 12 *J. Marshall Rev. Intell. Prop. L.* 350.

Turner, F., *From Counterculture to Cyberculture: Stewart Brand, the Whole Earth Network, and the Rise of Digital Utopianism* (University of Chicago Press, 2006).

Tyler, T. R., *Why People Obey the Law* (Princeton University Press, 1990).

Ullman-Margalit, E., *The Emergence of Norms* (Clarendon Press, 1977).

Ullrich, H., 'Patents and Standards – a Comment on the German Federal Supreme Court Decision Orange Book Standard' (2011) 41 *International Review of Intellectual Property and Competition Law* 337.

UNESCO, *Towards Knowledge Societies*, UNESCO World Report (UNESCO Publishing, 2005).

Urban, J. M. and Quilter L., 'Efficient Process or "Chilling Effects"? Takedown Notices under Section 512 of the Digital Millennium Copyright Act' (2005) 22 *Santa Clara High Tech. L.J.* 621.

Van den Bergh, R., 'Towards an Institutional Legal Framework for Regulatory Competition in Europe' (2000) 53 *Kyklos* 435.

Van Overwalle, G., 'Turning Patent Swords into Shares' (2010) 30 *Science* 1630.

Van Overwalle, G., van Zimmeren, E., Verbeure, B. and Matthijs, G., 'Models for Facilitating Access to Patents on Genetic Inventions' (2006) 7 *Nat. Rev. Genet.* 143.

Van Zimmeren, E., 'Towards a New Patent Paradigm for the Biomedical Sector? Facilitating Access, Open Innovation and Social Responsibility in Patent Law in the US, Europe and Japan' (Ph.D. thesis, University of Leuven, 2011).

Van Zimmeren, E., 'Clearinghouse Mechanisms in Genetic Diagnostics: A Conceptual Framework', in Geertrui Van Overwalle (ed.), *Gene Patents and Collaborative Licensing Models: Patent Pools, Clearinghouses, Open Source Models and Liability Regimes* (Cambridge University Press, 2009) 63.

Van Zimmeren, E., Vanneste, S. and Van Overwalle, G., *Patent Licensing in Medical Biotechnology* (Acco, 2011).

Van Zimmeren, E., Vanneste, S., Matthijs, G., Vanhaverbeke, W. and Van Overwalle, G., 'Patent Pools and Clearinghouses in the Life Sciences' (2011) 29 *Trends in Biotechnology* 569.

Van Zimmeren, E., Verbeure, B., Matthijs, G. and van Overwalle, G., 'A Clearing House for Diagnostic Testing: The Solution to Ensure Access to and use of Patented Genetic Inventions?' (2006) 84 *Bulletin of the World Health Organization* 352.

Venit, J., 'Article 82 EC: Exceptional Circumstances – The IP/Antitrust Interface after IMS Health', in Claus-Dieter Ehlermann and Isabela

Atanasiu (eds), *European Competition Law Annual 2005: The Interaction between Competition Law and Intellectual Property Law* (Hart Publishing, 2007) 609.

Verbeure, B., 'Patent Pooling For Gene-Based Diagnostic Testing: Conceptual Framework', in G. Van Overwalle (ed.), *Gene Patents and Collaborative Licensing Models – Patent Pools, Clearinghouses, Open Source Models and Liability Regimes* (Cambridge University Press, 2009) 3.

Verbeure, B. et al., 'Patent Pools and Diagnostic Testing' (2006) 24 *Trends in Biotechnol.* 115–120.

Von Hippel, E., *Democratizing Innovation* (MIT Press, 2005).

Von Hippel, E., *The Sources of Innovation* (Oxford University Press, 1988).

Von Hippel, E., 'Lead Users: A Source of Novel Product Concepts' (1986) 32(7) *Management Science* 791.

Wallis, R., Baden-Fuller, C., Kretschme, M. and Klimis, M. G., 'Contested Collective Administration of Intellectual Property Rights in Music. The Challenges to the Principles of Reciprocity and Solidarity' (1999) 14(1) *Eur. J. Comm.* 5.

Walsh, J. P., Arora, A. and Cohen, W. M., 'Effects of Research Tool Patents and Licensing on Biomedical Innovation', in Wesley M. Cohen and Stephen A. Merrill (eds), *Patents in the Knowledge-Based Economy* (The National Academies Press, 2005) 285.

Weiss, M. and Cargill, C., 'Consortia in the Standards Development Process' (1992) 43(8) *Journal of the American Society for Information Science* 559.

Weiss, Martin B. H. and Toyokuku, Ronald T., 'Free-Ridership in the Standards-Setting Process: The Case of 10BaseT' (1996) 4(4) *StandardView* 205.

West, J. and Dedrick, J., 'Proprietary vs. Open Standards in the Network Era: An Examination of the Linux Phenomenon', in Proceedings of the 34th Annual Hawaii International Conference on System Sciences, 501–1 (2001), http://ieeexplore.ieee.org/xpls/abs_all.jsp?arnumber=926525&tag=1.

Williamson, O., *The Economic Institutions of Capitalism: Firms, Markets, Relational Contracting* (Free Press, 1985).

World Intellectual Property Organization (WIPO), *The Recognition of Rights and the Use of Names in the Internet Domain Name System* (Report of the Second WIPO Internet Domain Name Process, 2001).

Yanagisawa, T. and Guellec, D., 'The Emerging Patent Marketplace' (OECD Science, Technology and Industry Working Papers, 2009/09, OECD Publishing).

Yu, P. K., 'The Graduated Response' (2010) 62 *Florida Law Review* 1373.

Zahle, H., 'Polycentri i retskildelæren', in A. Bratholm, T. Opsahl, M. Aarbakke and Kaare Haukaas (eds), *Samfunn, Rett, Rettferdighet* (Tano, 1986) 752.

Zainol, Z. A., Hussain, W. M. H. W. and Yaakub, N. I., 'WIPO Panels' Interpretation of the Uniform Dispute Resolution Policy (UDRP) Threeprong Test' (2011) 33 *World Patent Information* 275.

Index